# All On One Plate
## Cultural Expectations on
## American Mothers

# All On One Plate
## Cultural Expectations on American Mothers

Solveig Brown, Ph.D.

PARAGON HOUSE
St. Paul, Minnesota

First Edition 2016

Published in the United States by
Paragon House
www.paragonhouse.com

Copyright © 2016 by Paragon House

Cover Design by Greta Anderson

For discussion questions visit the author's website at http://www.solveigbrown.com


**Library of Congress Cataloging-in-Publication Data**

Names: Brown, Solveig, 1964- author.
Title: All on one plate : cultural expectations on American mothers / by
  Solveig Brown, Ph.D.
Description: St. Paul, MN : Paragon House, [2016]
Identifiers: LCCN 2015047800 | ISBN 9781557789211 (pbk. : alk. paper)
Subjects: LCSH: Mothers--United States. | Motherhood--United States. |
  Families--United States. | Sex role--United States. | Group values
  (Sociology)--United States.
Classification: LCC HQ759 .B75945 2016 | DDC 306.874/3073--dc23 LC
  record available at http://lccn.loc.gov/2015047800


The paper used in this publication meets the minimum requirements of American National Standard for Information Sciences—Permanence of Paper for Printed Library Materials, ANSIZ39.48-1984.
Manufactured in the United States of America
10 9 8 7 6 5 4 3 2 1

For current information about all releases from Paragon House,
visit the web site at http://www.ParagonHouse.com

*For my children Zoe and Parker; my mother Anne Mureé;*
*and my late grandmothers, Alphie Larson and Aagot Moen.*

# CONTENTS

# ACKNOWLEDGEMENTS

This book would not have been possible without the help of so many wonderful Minnesota Mothers. I extend my heartfelt appreciation to all of the women who filled out a questionnaire, or participated in an interview or focus group. Your generosity of time and spirit deeply touched me, while your candor, wisdom, and humor about parenting inspired me. Thank you to the Early Childhood and Family Education (ECFE) Centers, daycare centers, and pre-schools, who allowed me to distribute questionnaires on their site, and to the women throughout the Minneapolis and St. Paul metro area who enthusiastically recruited friends, neighbors, co-workers, and acquaintances to take part in this study.

I am extraordinarily grateful to Dr. Gordon Anderson and Paragon House for their commitment to this project. Dr. Anderson and Rosemary Yokoi have been phenomenal to work with in seeing this book through to completion. A special thanks to Greta Anderson for her spectacular cover design, and for coming up with the title, *All On One Plate*.

My sincerest thanks to John Ingham, Kirsten Senturia, and Zoe Brown for taking the time to read a draft of this book and offering their comments and suggestions, which were most helpful. I am fortunate to have had such a fantastic dissertation committee to guide me through the first phase of this project: John Ingham, Karen Ho, David Lipset, and Elaine Tyler May. Thanks to all of you for your teaching and support. I admire Kathleen Barlow's scholarship on mothering and I have benefitted from her belief that focusing on the experiences of mothers is important work. It has been a privilege to know so many wonderful professors and graduate students in the Department of Anthropology at the University of Minnesota. I have especially benefited from all of the interesting and inspiring conversations.

I am so fortunate to have an amazing circle of friends and relatives that have encouraged me throughout the years. Thank-you to: Stephanie Andrews, Kimber Brown, Reatha Brown, Kerry Cahsman, Robin Gudal, Rochelle Hoffman, Mike and Neda Johnson, Ejyo Katigiri, Dianne Larson and Doug Sayles, Joanne Larson, Paige Larson, Carol Lund, Rhonda Mezner, Dwight and Laurence Moe, Rev. Marshall D. Moen, Sam and Mary Moen, Luther and Jane Moen, Peter and Nancy Moen, Jane Nicolai, Sue and Neal Oestreich, Erik and Mie Olson-Kikuchi, Terri and Ken Potter, Deborah Randazza, David and Stacey Schimke, Kirsten and Sam Senturia, Arshebeth Turka and Bill Hrabe, Lisa Turner Horn, Dianne Wegscheid, and Kris Werner. I am also grateful to the members of my Book Club, whose monthly conversations and laughter have buoyed my spirits for twenty years: Kristine Benson, Barbara Buenz, Kristin Cleveland, Cate Fossing, Maiya Grath, Barbara Kappler Mikk, Lisa Meccia, Rebecca Moscatelli, Kristi Pearson, and Amanda Williams.

I have such deep appreciation for my mother, Anne Mureé, and the unconditional love and support she has given me throughout my life. My children Zoe and Parker have inspired me every single day, and have taught me so much about being a mother. They have grown up with me working on this research in some form or fashion, and have always cheered me on. Finally, I am eternally grateful for the love, laughter, and friendship of my husband, Sean Brown, who has worked hard so I could devote the time and energy necessary to complete this book. He has encouraged and uplifted me in countless ways since the day we met.

# Introduction

## Why Is it so Hard to be an American Mom?

What do most mothers want? They want to be good mothers. They want their children to be happy, healthy, and safe; to do well in school; and to have nice friends. They want to spend time with their children having fun, and teaching them skills and life lessons. Mothers also want balance. They want to have time and energy to devote to other things in their lives, such as their careers, relationships, and hobbies. They want to take care of themselves, to exercise, get enough sleep, and to spend time with their spouse or partner, and friends. This all sounds reasonable enough. Then why is it so hard? Why do so many women feel so much pressure in trying to combine their role as a mother with the other facets of their life?

Mothering is difficult in our culture because the expectations for mothers seem to grow exponentially by the day. Instead of feeling balanced, most mothers' minds spin with a perpetual list of what they "should" be doing. They should work harder. They should spend more time with their children. They should breastfeed longer. They should potty train earlier. They should have more date nights with their husband or partner. They should have a cleaner house. They should cook healthier meals. They should try to be more patient with their kids. They should yell less, and listen more. They should monitor their kids' screen time better.

They should feed their kids healthier snacks. They should make sure their kids get enough exercise. They should exercise more themselves. They should sign their kids up for more activities, but maybe they should scale back their activities so their children have more down time. The list is endless. They also "should" have figured this out already.

Scores of books and magazines offer women the promise of being a better mother, partner, or worker. Yet, much of the information is contradictory, which often adds to the pressure mothers feel when they ask themselves, "Am I doing it right?" In *Battle Hymn of the Tiger Mother*, Amy Chua asserts that the Chinese parenting style is superior to the western parenting style because Chinese parents expect their children to work hard to achieve successful outcomes. In *Bringing Up Bébé*, Pamela Druckerman argues that the relaxed French parenting style is superior to the over-involved American parenting style because French mothers supposedly have guilt-free time to themselves, and happy, well-behaved children who have healthy eating habits. Anne Marie Slaughter's article in The Atlantic, "Why Women Still Can't Have It All," suggests that it is indeed difficult for a woman to simultaneously be a top professional, have a happy marriage, and raise children. And, Sheryl Sandberg's *Lean In* encourages women to work hard in their career and expect their partner to equally contribute to housework and childcare.

Some acknowledge that being an American mother is hard. People such as President Obama and Oprah Winfrey often state that being a mom is "the hardest job in the world." However, no one digs deeper to discuss *why* being an American mom is so hard. When asked, "What is the hardest thing about being a mother?" Women responded with practical things such as: 1) "Finding a balance between work, home, children, and relationships while constantly wondering if I'm saying or doing the wrong thing;" 2) "Not having enough hours in the day to get things done;" and 3) "Guilt about not doing everything perfectly." No one mentioned our cultural environment, yet, all of these typical answers clearly relate to broader cultural forces. When mothers routinely feel guilty, stressed out, and overcommitted, it is likely that something in our culture is contributing to this. Yet, many of the mothers I interviewed thought the problem was with them and were convinced that they were doing something wrong, or that it is easier for other mothers.

When I asked women if they ever felt pressure in their role as a mother, stories poured out about the situations that made mothers feel under pressure or stressed out. Lauren, a part-time working mother of three exclaimed, "There's so much pressure it's insane!" Marie, an elementary school teacher, who has two children in middle school, believes that the mothers she interacts with everyday are under enormous pressure because mothers have so many demands and expectations with very little support. Rachel called it the "life load." She elaborated, "It's the laundry, and the lunches, combined with trying to keep your head screwed on and be sharp in meetings. I just try to keep it all held together and keep it all in perspective and hope that I'm not letting something huge slip through the cracks."

Many mothers reported sacrificing their sleep, exercise, or leisure time to manage everything on their plate. This is in line with recent reports that indicate that thirty-five percent of American adults are obese; sleep deprivation has become a public health crisis, putting women at greater risk for depression, diabetes, and heart disease; and women's use of anti-depressants has gone up 30% in the last decade. Currently, a quarter of adult women take anti-depressants; and eleven percent of women take anti-anxiety medication, which is twice the rate of men.[1] We expect that American mothers will individually figure out solutions to manage their workload and stress. However, the fact that millions of American women are having the same *symptoms* of pressure suggests that there is a deeper root cause.

Mothering is a hard job for this generation of women because the United States has experienced significant social changes over the last several decades that have had a major impact on childrearing. We have piled most of the responsibility for managing these changes on mothers' plates. Every mother I interviewed felt that it is more difficult to raise children now than it was a generation ago. Bridget commented, "It's definitely harder now because everything was simpler then and the expectations were different. Now there are expectations that you will perform well at your job, be the room mother, chaperone the field trip, and be home with your kids. Now there is pressure to be able to do everything all the time and not have anything fall, so there are a lot of balls in the air." Women often used the metaphor of "juggling" to describe their daily lives.

Traditional gender roles, which make it seem *natural* for mothers to be primarily responsible for domestic and childcare tasks; and conventional workplace norms, which presume that "ideal" workers will not have childcare responsibilities still influence our expectations for mothers and workers.[2] These beliefs may be outdated, but it is important to acknowledge them because they contribute to: the motherhood wage gap; poor parental leave policies; work-family conflict; the perpetuation of the "Mommy Wars;" conflict over the division of labor; and our lack of public programs to support childrearing. Since a woman's role as a mother has traditionally been important to her identity, many mothers also had high expectations for how they wanted to parent, and felt guilty when they could not do everything as well as they would like.[3]

Criticism of American middle-class mothers suggests that they create their own stress by spending too much time and energy on their role as a mother, which some scholars argue has led to a generation of privileged children, exhausted mothers, and an overall decline in women's status.[4] The image of the over-involved "helicopter parent" has gained a lot of credibility in our culture. The problem with our blanket criticism of middle-class mothering norms is that it assumes that all middle-class mothers parent in the same way, and it overlooks how current middle-class mothering practices are often an adaptive response to social changes.

## THE RESEARCH FOR THIS BOOK

This book reveals the thoughts, feelings, and experiences of self-described middle-class, upper-middle-class, and lower-middle-class mothers in the Minneapolis-St. Paul, Minnesota metropolitan area. Although the majority of participants in this study are white, college-educated, heterosexual, married women; the sample also includes single mothers, mothers of color, lesbian mothers, and mothers in the lower economic rungs of the middle-class.[5] (See Appendix 1 for demographic data and research methodology.) I focus on middle-class mothers because they are the most visible group of mothers in our culture. Middle-class parenting norms set the standard that all mothers are *supposed* to follow, and mass media images typically represent mothers as middle-class women who are beautiful, domestic, and primarily focused on consumption.[6] *All On One Plate* shows the diverse ways that middle-class mothers perceive, incorporate, and resist our cultural expectations for mothers. Fathers have also experienced increased time commitments and pressure in their role as a parent.[7] However, I chose to focus primarily on mothers because there are more than nine million households headed by single mothers, and women experience more pressure, guilt, judgment, and constraints than men do in combining parenting with the other facets of their life.

At the cultural level, my hope is that this book will generate conversations. In order to have meaningful discussions about American mothers, it is crucial to understand the cultural circumstances to which mothers are responding, and it is important to show the diverse ways in which mothers react to the cultural expectations placed upon them. By listening to the collective voices of mothers, we can get a better understanding of what mothers in our society experience, and begin to have productive conversations about what we can do to enact creative cultural solutions to better support parents at the community, state, or national level.

At the individual level, this book is like a conversation with mothers who experience different challenges as they deal with the daily issues that mothers face. I have seen many ways in which women's conversations with other mothers provide support and encouragement. These conversations offer practical advice, a realistic perspective, empathetic understanding, and humor in the face of the daily pressures of mothering. The purpose of this book is to go beyond the idealizations and blame in order to provide a more nuanced understanding of what it is really like to be a middle-class mother in our culture.

## ORGANIZATION OF THIS BOOK

Chapter 1 addresses the question, "What is a good mom?" It contrasts women's perceptions of the cultural ideal of a "good" mother, with their personal ideal of what makes a good mother. The differences are significant. Chapter 2 describes circumstances that make mothers feel stressed out, guilty, judged, or judgmental of other mothers, including the number one reason a woman is likely to judge another mother. This chapter also shows the powerful feelings of love and connection women have for their children. Chapter 3 delves into the transition to parenthood for individuals and couples, which for some was relatively easy, and for others, was one of the most difficult experiences of their life. Chapter 4 reveals the diverse strategies couples use to negotiate the division of labor. There are twenty-three household and child-care tasks that the majority of women report "always" or "usually" doing, which is a sharp contrast to the two tasks the majority reported that their husband, partner, or child's father "always" or "usually" does. This chapter also highlights the responsibilities couples are most likely to share equally, and the three key beliefs and strategies of couples who have created an equitable division of labor. Chapter 5 discusses the factors that influence a woman's decision to work or stay home after a child is born; the positive and negative aspects of being a working or stay-at-home mother; the "Mommy Wars;" and workplace equity.

Chapters six through eleven discuss safety; exercise, nutrition, and body image; managing screen time and social media; raising children in a consumer culture; activities and achievement; and how parents go about raising "good" kids. The best, and perhaps the hardest, thing about being an American parent is that there are no specific rules for childrearing that we all follow. This gives parents a lot of freedom to parent in a way that fits with their personal values. I have spent hundreds of hours reading the scholarly research on these topics, and have summarized the data as best I can so parents can have access to this knowledge as they make their own parenting decisions.

## A FINAL NOTE

We do not have a uniform American "mom culture." In fact, I noticed significant differences between the "mom cultures" of different neighborhood communities in the Minneapolis-St. Paul metro area, where I conducted my research. I suspect there are also regional differences in mothering norms, attitudes, and expectations. The experiences of the Minnesota mothers represented in this book may not perfectly reflect the "mom culture" in your particular community; nonetheless, the topics covered in this book highlight some of the key issues that all American mothers deal with.

Reading about the experiences of other mothers is important because so many of the women I interviewed felt like they were the only ones having a hard time. They wondered if they were doing something wrong, or if was easier for everyone else. The stories in this book show that no mother is immune from feeling challenged, frustrated, or stressed out. Some mothers also face extra challenges because of their race, class, household income, ethnicity, marital status, sexual orientation, age, religious affiliation, health issues, particular needs of a child, and countless other circumstances that mothers deal with on a daily basis.

I have two children, so as a friend, neighbor, co-worker, acquaintance, and relative I have had thousands of conversations with other mothers on issues related to parenting and childrearing. While these conversations have informed my understanding of women's daily mothering experiences, I do not include them in this book. I have given every woman a pseudonym, and in some instances have changed specific characteristics to help ensure my participants' confidentiality.

# Part 1

## The Initiation of Mothers

# Chapter 1

## What Is a Good Mom?

I pulled up in front of a large three-story house located in the heart of a thriving city neighborhood, where sidewalks outlined the block, and neighbors lived in close proximity to one another. I rang the bell, and Tracy warmly greeted me, inviting me to come back to her kitchen while she finished making coffee. We talked as I helped her carry cups, plates, and napkins to the large round table on her deck. She had an open backyard, with a wooden swing set, a sand box filled with various plastic buckets and toys, a garden, and good-sized patch of grass. When the other women arrived for the group interview, we sat around the table on the sunshine-soaked deck, sipping coffee, and eating chocolate "babka" bread from a local bakery. Claire, Fiona, Heidi, and Tracy met when their children attended pre-school together, and had become close friends over the past few years. Heidi was at home full-time with her two children, and had been home since they were born. Fiona and Claire were primarily at home with their children, however they both had periodic part time employment relating to their former jobs. After Tracy's first child was born, she worked full-time for four years, while her husband stayed at home. However, for the last two years, she had been home with their three children, and her husband returned to working full-time.

Early in the interview, Claire talked about how difficult it was to speak honestly about parenting challenges when she first attended her Early Childhood Family Education (ECFE) classes.[1] Without missing a beat, Fiona spoke of her similar experiences.

Claire: When I first started going to ECFE, I felt like you couldn't actually be honest. It seemed like nobody was talking about "how horrible it is, and I can't think straight (laughter)." We weren't complaining because we didn't know each other well. We would mostly talk about expectations, nutrition, and potty training, but there was nobody at the table going, "This sucks. I had no idea!" (Laughter.)

Fiona: In my class, we'd do our check-ins, and we'd go around the circle with our, "Well yes, everything went okay this week." When we got to this one woman, she said, "Oh my God, it was an awful week! My little one swore at Thanksgiving and then she threw a tantrum (laughter)." We would laugh so hard because deep down we're thinking, "Yes it's so true. Oh my God, it's happening to me." Everything opened up from then on, but we had to have that one person say it.

Claire: Or I was crying before I got here (laughter).

Fiona: And I yelled and yelled and I felt so bad (laughter).

Claire: My joy of the week is that I'm sitting over here and my kids are over there (laughter). "I can't handle myself, I can't handle them, I can't handle my husband!" (Laughter.)

Fiona: It always made me feel better if I could find someone who could honestly say that they were having trouble, or that they were having the same thing happening.

Claire: There was some expectation there, and I couldn't articulate it at the time because I thought maybe I'm just weird. Maybe something is wrong with me.

Like Claire and Fiona, many women joke about the challenges of motherhood by telling self-deprecating stories that exaggerate their failures and frustrations. Over the years, I have heard countless "bad" mom jokes, where women implicitly compare themselves to some unspoken cultural ideal of a "good" mom that we all seem to intuitively take for granted. I began to wonder, what is a "good" mom, anyway? The scholarly literature on American mothers implies that a "good" mom is a white, native born, middle-class, heterosexual, married, stay-at-home mother.[2] However, this definition did not describe the spirit of our mythic cultural ideal of a "good" mom that women joked about and unfavorably compared themselves to. Before reading further, I invite you to take a moment to answer the following questions that I posed to women in the surveys and interviews. 1) What do you think is the American cultural ideal of a "good" mother? 2) What do you personally think makes someone a good mother?

I was surprised to find that no two women described their perception of the cultural ideal of a "good" mother in exactly the same way. In fact, every mother had her own projection of our cultural standards for being a "good" mom, which most women described in idealized terms. The women used over 350 different words or phrases in their descriptions, so I combined similar responses in order to generate a "Top Ten" list of traits the women identified as the American cultural ideal of a "good" mother.[3] (See Appendix 2 for a table of the words and phrases women used to describe their perception of the cultural ideal of a "good" mother.)

## THE CULTURAL IDEAL OF A "GOOD" MOTHER

The top ten responses describe the American cultural ideal of a "good" mother as:

> a perfect, self-sacrificing, always patient, never-stressed, happy woman who can 'do it all.' She looks beautiful and

put-together, cooks delicious, well-balanced meals, keeps the house clean, stays at home with her children, while advancing her career and providing financially. She also has perfect, smart, well-behaved children who listen to her without her ever having to raise her voice, and are involved in many extra-curricular activities that she is happy to drive them to in her mini-van.

The women equally identified working mothers and stay-at-home mothers as the cultural ideal.[4] However, seventy percent of the working mothers said the cultural ideal was a stay-at-home mother; seventy percent of the stay-at-home mothers said it was a working mother; and over sixty percent of the part-time working mothers said the ideal was either a full-time working mother or a stay-at-home mother. Remarkably, many women felt that their work choice was not the cultural ideal. Even though our cultural representations idealize both working mothers and stay-at-home mothers, there are also negative judgments of both groups of women. In *The Mommy Myth: The Idealization of Motherhood, and How It Has Undermined All Women*, Susan Douglas and Meredith Michaels contend that media representations of mothers portray working mothers as "neglectful," and stay-at-home mothers as "boring," which means that all mothers "get to be failures."[5] It seems that most women are more aware of the positive representations of women who have made different choices about working than they have, or the negative judgments of women with their respective work status.

For example, Tara, a full-time business executive who loved her job and felt that she was a good role model for her children, stated that she believed the cultural ideal is "still for people to see moms as being much more available for their kids in a physical sense." On the other hand, Christine, who had made a conscious decision to leave a job that she loved to stay home when her first child was born, explained that she felt there was pressure to have it all, to be a strong woman and work outside the home. "You should work and get out there and assert your independence, while at the same time you should be a good mom at home, and be patient and be the typical June Cleaver kind of mother with dinner on the table." As she described this expectation, she realized that her perception of a "good" mother was impossible to fulfill.

## WOMEN'S PERSONAL IDEALS FOR BEING A GOOD MOTHER

A very different portrait of a good mother emerged when women responded to the question, "What do you personally think makes someone a good mother?" The top ten similar responses describe a good mother as someone who:

> loves her children unconditionally, provides her children with rules, limits, discipline, and a safe environment, while teaching them the importance of respect, honesty, kindness, good manners, and healthy habits. She creates balance in her life, choosing what is right for her and her family with regard to working outside the home, while making sure that she spends time with her children and is "there" for them when they need her. Overall, she strives to be patient and to be a positive role model for her children.

(See Appendix 3 for a table of the words and phrases women used to describe their personal ideal for being a good mother.)

The "Top Ten" lists are drqamatically different. While terms relating to perfection, and "doing it all" made the top of the list of the cultural ideal, not one person used any of these terms to describe their personal ideal of a good mother. The second highest number of responses in the overall cultural ideal list was for "selflessness," or "self-sacrificing." While some mothers mentioned, "putting their kids needs first" in their personal ideal, no women used the words selfless or self-sacrificing to describe their personal ideal. Although there were many attributes relating to appearance and keeping a clean house on the overall cultural ideal list of a "good" mother, no one listed appearance or housekeeping as a personal ideal of good mothering. In the cultural ideal list, women identified both working mothers and stay-at-home mothers, however in the personal ideal list the emphasis was on a woman doing what is right for her and her family with regard to work. Perhaps the most interesting discrepancy between the lists is the fact that the top two responses in the personal ideal list, 1) loves child unconditionally, and 2) sets rules, limits, and provides discipline, did not make the top ten responses of the cultural ideal list.

Why does it matter that we have such idealized notions of a "good" mother? Obviously, women are able to differentiate between their perception of cultural ideals and their personal beliefs about what makes a good mother. The detriment of our cultural ideal of a "good" mother is that it has a stealthy way of infiltrating the psyches of mothers. More often than not, women described an ideal "good" mother as having qualities she felt she lacked. For example, women who told me that they had a messy house described the ideal "good" mom as a great housekeeper. Women who did not like to cook often indicated that the ideal was someone who prepared home-cooked meals. Women who were casual in their dress and appearance thought the ideal was someone who "looked good." Women were also more likely to judge themselves against their perception of the cultural ideal. In fact, not one person judged another mother for not living up to idealized standards. There are millions of "Mommy Bloggers" in the United States, and I suspect many of these bloggers have criticized some aspect of the concept of a "good" mother in their posts. Yet, there is still a tendency to believe that the majority of "other" mothers out there are actively trying to be idealized "good" mothers. Meanwhile, there is less recognition that at the individual level, there is a widespread personal rejection of idealized cultural representations of mothers.

## WIDESCALE REJECTION OF CULTURAL IDEALS

Cultural representations of what motherhood *should* be like significantly influenced the expectations of some mothers.[6] Lauren, a mother of three, was shocked by how horrible her birthing and postpartum experience was with her first child because it did not fit her image of what parenting should be like, which she believes was greatly influenced by the media. She remembers crying when she spoke to one of her friends who told her, 'I know, they really make us believe it's just white cotton sheets and sunshine and a breeze blowing through the curtains as we look at our little baby adoringly." Lauren who was simultaneously mocking and angered by media images exclaimed, "That's what the media does! It gives you this idea that it's this idyllic wonderful time, and if you just do these crafts, your children will be so happy. Well God, nothing ever goes like that! They continually project this image. It's just laughable." On the other hand, when Alexis was pregnant with her first child, she noticed "a ton of negativity" about pregnancy, childbirth, and having newborns. "It could be horrible, or it could be great, so I really tried to have open expectations about it."

Christine laughed as she talked about how magazine and commercial images of mothers made her feel like she was not perfect:

> My little getaway is to read *US Weekly* or *People* magazine. They always have the pictures of Angelina Jolie with her six children, and I'm like, "She's not doing that by herself." You flip on the TV and see commercials for anything where there's a mom making dinner and cleaning the house, and she's so happy with a smile on her face. That's why you feel like you're not the perfect mom. You're keeping it all together and then you have one of those days where you feel like you're going a little bit crazy, and you think maybe something's wrong with me. But I feed into it. I buy the magazines.

Celebrity news and gossip magazines fuel our idealization and judgment of mothers in their representations of blissful or "bad" celebrity moms. Christine's remarks show that even though she knows that media representations of mothers are not realistic, she still unfavorably compares herself to idealized celebrity moms, or the happy mothers portrayed in advertisements.

Brooke, a full time working mother of two, who equally shares childcare and domestic responsibilities with her husband, commented that commercials depict mothers as being primarily responsible for domestic work, and pitch cleaning products, organizational products, and anything related to cooking to the moms, despite the fact that women are not the only ones responsible for this arena. She has noticed that ads with working mothers in them have three pictures of a mom: "mom in her work clothes, mom with the kids, and mom cleaning the toilet." Brooke thinks these images "reinforce that you're allowed to get to mommy in her work clothes if you've already mastered domestic mommy, and that's perfectly under control, and parent mommy, and that's under control. Then you can throw in a little career mommy just for kicks." This observation shows how subtly powerful media images are in reinforcing the status quo that it is "natural" for American mothers to be the primary person in charge of domestic and childrearing responsibilities.

In *The Mommy Myth: The Idealization of Motherhood and How it has Undermined Women*, Susan Douglas and Meredith Michaels argue that over the last thirty years, the media has gradually imposed unattainable ideals of motherhood, culminating in the "new momism." The "new momism" dictates that a mother is supposed to be vigilant, fun-loving and easy going, while also putting a child's needs first, understanding a child's point of view, and providing material things to enhance a child's intellectual capacities and self-esteem.[7]

Ashley, a young mother who has worked hard to become the first person in her family to get a college degree, felt like a fraud when the University honored her success as a student at a special recognition ceremony.

I felt like I wasn't worthy of their praise because I am not able to be home after school to have a warm snack for my kids, and I am not able to drive them to basketball or other activities. It seems that no matter how successful a woman is, she is still judged against these idealized standards of being a 'good' mom.

People do judge mothers in our culture, and most mothers are keenly aware of this. I will talk more about this in the next chapter.

Media images wield a powerful *indirect* influence because most people believe that "others are more strongly affected by media portrayals than they themselves are."[8] This "third-person effect" leads people to believe that media representations influence the perspective of other people in one's community or social network. Even though a woman may not personally buy into idealized representations of mothers, she may assume that people within her own community will evaluate her based on these pervasive images.[9]

Mass media representations tend to portray "good" mothers, as having only positive emotions, and "bad" mothers as having only negative traits. The problem is that our cultural portrayals of a "good" mother make it seem that it is unacceptable for a good mother to experience negative emotions. When describing their range of emotions, every mother listed both positive and negative emotions, and many women drew arrows between extreme positive emotions and extreme negative emotions. The top ten responses were joy and happiness; fear, anxiety, and stress; frustration; the full range of emotions; pride; anger; love; guilt; sadness and depression; exhaustion, and fatigue.[10]

Mothering blogs have become sites where women can talk about the emotions and experiences of mothering that we do not deem "positive," especially since our cultural representations of "good" mothers dampen the acceptability that being a parent is going to bring out a full spectrum of emotional reactions. Unfortunately, our cultural ideals of a "good" mother do not offer women guidance or support, but rather are a vehicle for judgment and shame. Anthropologists have shown that in smaller scale societies, cultural values are important for guiding mothering practices, and it would be unlikely that people would differentiate between cultural parenting norms and their personal actions.[11,12]

In *The Cultural Contradictions of Motherhood,* Sharon Hays identifies the dominant parenting ideology of American culture as "intensive mothering." This middle-class parenting model views children as innocent and priceless, and assumes that mothers will be the primary parent responsible for using "child-rearing methods that are child-centered, expert-guided, emotionally absorbing, labor intensive, and financially expensive."[13] Even though most of the women shared these underlying beliefs (with the exception that they did not "always" or "usually" rely on "experts"), there was variability in their parenting practices.[14]

## COMMUNITY NORMS OF MOTHERING

Since our culture does not offer realistic representations of mothers, or universal guidelines for parenting, I observed that neighborhood and community expectations exerted a powerful influence on mothers. Every woman was aware of her community or neighborhood values, and there were notable differences in community and neighborhood norms within the Twin Cities metro area.[15] This suggests that there are also different regional mothering norms as well.

I sat down with Valerie in her modest-sized, urban Minneapolis home. We drank tea at her dining room table while her pre-school son ate his lunch and then worked quietly assembling a new Lego kit she gave him to keep him occupied during the interview. Valerie was a teacher on extended leave from her job, active in her children's school, doing part-time daycare for a friend, and affiliated with several organizations for which she did periodic part-time work. When I asked Valerie about her perception of the broader cultural representations of mothers, she replied, "I feel like there's the typical American mom that we hear about on TV or in newspapers, the work, work, work, daycare kind of thing. Then the other antithesis out there is the stay-at-home mom doing compost with her children in the back yard. Two extremes, and I feel I don't fit into either one of those niches."

Valerie believes that the neighborhood mothers she associates with have the greatest influence on her own mothering style. "I feel like there's a neighborhood mom culture here on our block." She elaborated on her urban neighborhood culture:

> We live on a very open, accepting block and there's a sense that you're there for your kids, and you listen to them. This would be the culture I feel I'm immersed in. It is also a very environmentally conscious neighborhood. If you're caught fertilizing your lawn you want to make sure you got the organic brand, because you feel like there might be a little bit of a look if you got one of those signs that says this lawn has been chemically treated. Our block is like the culture of a family. Everyone is pretty good about teaching their kids manners and kids respecting each other. There's no bullying, and I really trust that the parents are involved in the families my son hangs out with.

In essence, Valerie feels that her neighborhood is like an extended family, where her individual parenting norms, such as teaching children respect and manners, are shared by other members of her community.[16] In Valerie's case, a city block of communicating families is a tangible reference group for parenting norms.

Jessica, a young mother of an infant, had recently moved to a Minneapolis urban middle-class neighborhood from a progressive city on the west coast. She works four ten-hour days, and her husband works double shifts in construction on the weekends in order to have one of them home with their son. She spoke of the differences between the moms in the west coast city she had just left and the urban Minneapolis neighborhood in which she now lives. When talking about her friends from her previous community she observed, "None of them own houses, and they also don't work. Their husbands are working and they're making a conscious decision to have less money and stay home because they feel like it is best to be with your child. Here I don't have any friends that are not putting their child in childcare."[17] Jessica feels an affinity with her former community and remains active in on-line parenting groups from that community.

If we had to vote on a cultural definition for a good mother, based on the two "Top Ten" lists described in this chapter, I suspect the personal ideals definition would easily win. However, it is unlikely that our idealized representations of mothers are going to disappear. Advertising images of mothers feed into the broader cultural mythology of mothering perfection. We will continue to see beautiful, middle-class and upper middle-class, domestically entrenched mothers using products to make their life, and stress, more manageable because these images evoke insecurity and aspiration, a potent combination in creating consumer desire. Advertisements featuring idealized mothers also reinforce the belief that we expect mothers to "do it all," and if being a "perfect supermom" eludes you, then the underlying message is that there is something wrong with you, which many women felt when they were having a bad day.

It will continue to be up to individual mothers to sift through all the cultural images, rhetoric, and data about what it means to be a good mother. Mothers of all races and classes have figured out creative ways to deal with the disconnection between our cultural ideal of being a "good" mom, and the reality of what a good mom really does in her daily life. Some mothers do their best to ignore our idealized images of mothers, or are too busy to think much about them. Other women feel energized by personally taking a stand against our idealistic expectations for motherhood. One can see this attitude when women courageously, and often humorously, speak honestly about their parenting experiences in books, blogs, and amongst their friends and family.

Some women prefer to align themselves with our cultural values. The good news for these women is that in the United States, where we hold freedom and individualism to be of supreme importance, each woman can choose her own cultural ideal of what makes a good mother. In fact, everyone in this study did exactly that. Instead of just defaulting to a projection of a cultural ideal that represents one's shortcomings, mothers can be more proactive in defining an ideal that is aligned with their personal norms and values. When I go back to my original question of what is a good mother, anyway? I realize that even though the "good" mother does not literally exist, the idea of the "good" mother is everywhere in our culture. We are fooled into thinking that the "good" mother in our culture is the mythic "perfect supermom," who can "do it all," when in actuality the good mothers in our culture are our friends, neighbors, colleagues, and ourselves.

# Chapter 2

# Pressure, Guilt, Judgment, and Connection

I sat at a coffee shop with Carla, who met me after dinner one brisk fall evening. Carla's oldest daughter was about to turn five, and she joked that she and her husband were feeling the pressure of being in the "memory making time." "Now we can really ruin her because she's not going to forget if we do something horrible." Lately, Carla has been feeling overwhelmed by "the responsibility of shaping this human being, and wanting her to be a happy, healthy, productive person and wanting her to come into her own. I feel such an enormous responsibility of wanting to do right by both of my kids." Carla's words reminded me of Julie's constant stream of self-judgment running through her mind each day. "Have I done this right? Will it affect my children negatively? Am I spending too much time doing what I want to do, and not enough time with my kids? I don't feel like I got anything done today, is that okay, or should I have gotten the house cleaned?" Similarly I heard Sarah comment, "I'm trying to be the best mother, employee, wife, friend, and homemaker I can when I find it near impossible to do everything as well as I would like."

Three themes emerged when women talked about the challenges of parenting: pressure, guilt, and judgment. Many women felt that daily life was somehow easier for other mothers, which made them reluctant to openly talk about their parenting challenges. "I find it refreshing when somebody actually is vulnerable and doesn't try to act perfect," commented Rachel. "If you open up and say, 'God, we're all just trying to do the best we can,' it is a way to start knocking down that barrier that you have to be perfect." Our culture has high expectations for mothers, women have high standards for themselves, and the stakes of parenting are high, so it is not surprising that mothers feel enormous responsibility and pressure to "do right" by their kids.

## WHY ARE MOTHERS UNDER SO MUCH PRESSURE?

Every woman thought that parenting is harder now than it was a generation ago. The level of pressure individuals experienced, along with the situations that made mothers feel "under pressure" or "stressed out" varied significantly, but common stressors included family responsibilities, workload, balancing competing demands, financial constraints, not having enough time to get everything done, exhaustion, relationship issues, health matters, children's achievement, and a host of things related to raising children. The themes of time and energy came up repeatedly, as women marveled at how being a parent is a 24/7 job, with so much responsibility, and no real days off. Women talked about how much energy it takes to meet everyone's demands, and many said it was difficult to take time for themselves to do things such as exercise, go out with friends, or to spend quality time with their husband or partner.

Women also wanted to get parenting "right," and often questioned whether they were doing or saying the "right" thing. This self-questioning, also referred to as self-reflexivity, is a byproduct of the rise of competitive individualism in our culture, where we expect individuals to be personally responsible for "their success, happiness, and livelihood by making the right choices in an uncertain and changeable environment."[1] As a result, Americans have become more self-reflexive, by consciously questioning what they should do, how they should act, and who they want to be.[2]

This puts American mothers under enormous pressure to be responsible for making good choices for themselves and their children in an era where most middle-class parents no longer believe their children will *naturally* be okay without a lot of parental involvement.[3] On top of this, there are no explicit rules for parenting that we all follow. This gives individuals a lot of freedom in how they parent, which can be liberating; however, it also increases pressure, comparison, and judgment. Jackie tries to remind herself, "There are lots of ways, and there is no right way," but then she thinks, "Oh bullshit, there is a right way!" Sofia commented, "People write parenting books, and then we read the books. We all try really hard to get it right, and right constantly changes." Kendra summed it up well: "There's pressure from other moms, there's pressure from other people within my school community, my friend community, my family community, because everyone has their opinion on what is the right way. I don't think I've ever met a mother that has said, 'everything I do is good enough' and doesn't have any guilt."[4]

Many women felt the pressure of having so much responsibility. "I manage every detail of this family's life, so that puts a lot of pressure on me," explained Lauren.

> I manage our day-to-day finances, our retirement, our kids' college funds, or lack-there-of funds. If something needs to be fixed, I have to figure it out. On top of that, I'm the one wiping the butts, making the meals, disciplining the kids, and trying to teach them manners and rules and bring structure. I also have to wear my worker, wife, and friend hats.

Finding a balance between work and home responsibilities was also challenging for many women. "It can be hard to go home at night and feel okay about leaving your work behind, and feeling okay when you have to go to work and leave your family behind. I'm just trying to do well at both," explained Penny. Ashley exclaimed, "I feel like I'm sucking all the time! I feel like you're always juggling and something falls off the side." Kristina commented that she felt enormous pressure after her divorce "not to be the parent that overcompensates for their circumstances," which, combined with regular parenting pressure was "astronomically challenging." "You try not to beat yourself up, and assume that you're trying to set a good example, and trying to do the right thing for your kids, and balancing all the social pressure. I don't wish that on anyone."

American mothers in the 1950s and 1960s believed that a child's character is "shaped largely by their mothers," which made women worry about "the correctness of their own behavior and that of their children."[5] Today's mothers are equally concerned about how their child's behavior can reflect on them. I heard many stories about those awkward parenting moments when a child was acting out in front of others. A few women felt that our cultural standards have made it more difficult to parent in public. "You can't reprimand your kid anymore without feeling like you're gonna have your child taken away from you or have child services knocking at your door," commented one mother. Jackie worries that if her kids act out in the neighborhood people will think that she can't control her kids.

Mothers also want their children to "fit in" with their peers. Brittany, a young mother of a high-energy three-year-old boy, always felt insecure when she was with an older friend, Martha, whose child was shy and controlled. Martha "dragged" them to "all sorts of museums," where it was stressful for Brittany to manage her son. One day Brittany realized her son was acting like a normal three-year-old boy and that she loved that he was social and energetic, so she quit going to museums with Martha and her son. Valerie talked about the same issue from the other perspective. Parenting her shy son in public has been one of her greatest challenges. "For me it hasn't been having a child who throws a hissy fit in the grocery store aisle, I feel pressure because my son has a shy reserved personality in groups and with his friends."

Women dealt with many different circumstances that made them feel stressed-out. A vivacious stay-at-home mother of three children under the age of five, started to cry as she searched for the words to describe how she felt she had lost her identity to parenting.

> I don't feel like I'm a person. I feel like I'm a ghost. I feel like I don't have the same value, and I can't even explain it. I've gained weight and I keep feeling like this isn't me. My weight is a constant reminder that this isn't where I want to be. I'm not saying that I wish I didn't have kids, but it's definitely a consequence of having kids, and it's frustrating. I need more down time.

Women experiencing personal challenges, such as illness, anxiety, depression, or grief attempted to shield their children from their pain, while also being honest in an age-appropriate way.

## SOCIAL COMPARISONS AND COMPETITION

Several women admitted to having moments where they compared themselves or their children to others. One mother felt there was a lot of "veiled competition" in her community.

> It is taboo to say, "I'm really jealous of that family," and yet, I am (laughter). It feels so childish to admit that, but it's a very real feeling. I've been amazed at how parenthood has brought that much more to the surface than I ever imagined. It's hard not to sometimes feel like, "Wow is everything just going to go right for them in their life? Are there not going to be more challenges that are going to happen to their children (laughter)?"

Social comparison is a universal phenomenon, however, most people do not like to admit that they compare themselves with others. Because social comparison is so "spontaneous, effortless and unintentional" people may not be consciously aware that they are doing it.[6] Psychologists Bram Buunk and Frederick

Gibbons developed a Social Comparison Orientation Measure (SCO) that shows how people vary in the degree to which they compare themselves with others. They found that people who had high SCOs, meaning that they typically compare themselves with others, have several things in common. They tend to be "particularly aware of themselves in the presence of others and tend to engage in reflection upon their own thoughts and feelings."[7] Additionally, these people also have "a strong interest in what others feel, a strong empathy for others, and a general sensitivity to…the moods and criticism of others."[8]

"You're always looking at another mother, and worrying, am I doing it the right way? Why am I not providing that for my children?" commented Nicole. "As moms, we just beat ourselves up, and we're always looking elsewhere to fill the void of what you think that you're missing or what you think your child is missing." Sarah continually looks at other mothers she does not know well and thinks, "Oh my Gosh, she's a really great Mom. They just look so happy, and I think, 'What's her secret?' I know it's stupid to think that way." Some women tried to counteract their own comparisons when they came up. "There are other kids you hold up and think, oh if my kid were more like this," said Sofia, "but if you really step back there are probably things that go on in their life that I have no idea about." In twenty years of conversations with hundreds of mothers and fathers, I have never met a parent who has not experienced challenges in parenting an individual child.

With the rise of social media, social comparison has become much easier. A recent *Psychology Today* article notes that women use Facebook for "social surveillance" and making comparisons. "Everyone is posting what they're doing, and I'm like shoot, I'm not there. I'm not doing that," observed Ellen. Even though most women knew that others only posted the best things in their day, many said it was hard to remember that the idyllic images on Facebook or Instagram did not reflect reality. Some women, like Lynette, were critical of social media posts. "I can look right through those pictures and think, 'Oh my God, the mother is in the corner crying, and the dad is yelling at the kids.'" Other mothers felt there was constant pressure to post updates and pictures, which just added to their overall "to do" list. Some women intentionally chose not to participate in social media. "I can't surround myself with that because it brings me down," commented one mother. 'It's really great to see all of their achievements, but it's sucking so much out of me to hear this, and it makes me feel that my kid doesn't know how to do all that, so he must not be keeping up, or there must be something wrong with him." It is also easier for people to compare themselves or their children with a much wider group of people. "We used to be able to compare ourselves to others without the level of guilt," observed Jordan. "Now it's not the person down the street that I compare myself to, or the kid down the block, it's the kid on the east coast who got into eight Ivy League schools." I will come back to the pressure of children's achievement in chapter 10.

Some felt there was more pressure on mothers to be "perfect." When Kendra hosted a going away party for her kids, she wrote a disclaimer on the invitation: "This is not a Pinterest themed party. No bags are being given out, and there are no activities being planned." Kristen McHenry and Denise Schultz argue that "competing to be the perfect mother, the best dressed, host the coolest birthday parties for our children, pack the healthiest lunches, and be the skinniest mom at the park has become the norm."[9] They contend that women must "prove" and "demonstrate" that they are good mothers by maternal "performances" and "competitive communication" which demonstrate that they are constantly meeting their children's needs, and lavishing "enormous amounts of time and energy on their children."[10] Other researchers assert that mothers perpetuate "perfectionist understandings of motherhood," more than the media.[11] The women who described their local "mom culture" as being highly competitive were more likely to live in wealthier suburbs, although mothers across the socioeconomic spectrum felt pressure, and many women from both wealthy and middle-class neighbor-hoods, felt fortunate to be part of a supportive community of mothers who were not competitive.

The competitive aspects of motherhood revolve around traits (i.e. being a "perfect supermom") that people described as the cultural ideal of a "good" mother. Even though women personally rejected idealized notions of mothering, some women may strive to be "perfect," if they perceive it to be their community standard of being a good mother. Many women lived in neighborhoods where there was no competition to be a "perfect" mother. "I see a lot of wrong ways to parent in my neighborhood," commented one mother from a low-income city neighborhood, "so if some-one's trying and putting in effort, and the kid's got clean clothes, and food in their belly, hats off to you. You're doing great today!" Another woman's daily interaction with challenged parents has given her a different reference point. "I think, 'Well I haven't hit anyone today,' and I am constantly reminded of how fortunate my kids are just by the lottery of birth." In other words, it is much easier to feel that you are doing a good job of parenting if you do not compare yourself to an unrealistically high bar. British pediatrician and psychoanalyst D.W. Winnicott coined the term the "good enough mother" in 1953 to defend mothers against the intrusion of experts and idealized images of mothering. He notes that a "good enough mother" trusts her own instincts, physically cares for her child, provides warmth and love; and will fail her children in tolerable ways so children learn to deal with life's frustrations.[12]

## GUILT

Mothers felt guilty for many reasons. Some felt guilty for not being as patient as they thought they should be, or for yelling, grabbing, or hitting a child in anger. "I am very hard on myself for the stuff that comes out of my mouth when I lose my tem-per," confided one mother. Some women felt guilty about not volunteering more at school. Others felt guilty for not being able to provide their children with more material goods, enrichment opportunities, or vacations. Some felt guilty for having a messy house or not feeding their children better food. Some stay-at-home mothers felt guilty for giving up their career or not contributing financially, whereas some women felt guilty because they worked.

One of the biggest triggers of guilt related to the amount of time a mother spent with her child. Gloria, who is always aware of "how little time you experience together" explained, "I may want to sit down and check email, but I remind myself the clock is ticking, so I go do something with my kids." For many women, it was difficult to strike a balance between their personal needs and responsibilities outside of parenting, and spending time with their children. "I am constantly negotiating the balance of how much quality time to spend with them, how much to be involved in activities, and whether or not I'm doing the right thing," explained Brittany, who always feels that she is not able to give "enough" anywhere. "Because I only have my kids 50% of the time," commented Danielle, "I feel pressure to really spend quality time with them. I only date when they're with their dad. I've left once or twice when they were in my house in the last 6 years." Some women felt guilty over things that took them away from their child, such as exercise, going out with friends, and work; or when striving to better their own circumstances meant their children did not have as many opportunities. Kendra explained, "I worked full time, got my college degree on weekends and nights, and we had to live on a lower income so I could finish school. I had to sacrifice what my kids ate, where we shopped, and what they could do."

The same circumstance could make one woman feel guilty, whereas another woman would not feel guilty. This suggests that how a person thinks about a situation can affect whether or not she chooses to feel guilty about it. Sheila, who intentionally tries not to feel guilty, frames the activities that take her away from her children as a positive thing. She believes that exercise is the best thing she can do to keep herself mentally and physically healthy; spending time with her friends gives her an invaluable support network and energizes her; and she thinks it is important to role model having interests and hobbies outside of one's children. In other words, she prioritizes doing things that will fill her up and make her feel happy. In her *Ask the Children* survey, Ellen Galansky asked 600 parents what they thought their children would wish for in their interactions with their parents. Over half the parents responded that their kids would wish to spend more time with them, whereas children were more likely to wish that their parents were less tired or stressed-out.[13]

## JUDGING MOTHERS

American mothers feel a great deal of pressure and guilt because we are a culture that routinely judges mothers. We have blamed mothers of all ages, sizes, classes, ethnic and racial backgrounds, marital statuses, sexual orientations, religious beliefs, and levels of economic production for various wrongs with our society's children.[14] There are seventy-two psychological disorders, such as autism, schizophrenia, anorexia, and ADHD, which have at one time or another, been blamed on mothers.[15,16] Several mothers joked that they are already setting aside money for their children to seek counseling when they are older.

Women worried to varying degrees about others in their local community judging their parenting. On one end of the spectrum, some women appear never to worry about what others think of them, and at the other end of the spectrum, some mothers worried considerably that others were judging their parenting. Some women had experienced overt judgment, and others *felt* like people were judging them. Most mothers probably fall somewhere in the middle of this continuum, and are at times self-conscious about their parenting, especially when they are in a stressful situation.

Most women tended to be their own worst critic, judging their mothering performance against the cultural ideal of a "good" mother, which is often a projection of the specific things that make an individual feel vulnerable. Women were also more likely to be insecure about others potentially judging them than to express judgment about other mothers. Several women stated they were so busy that they did not have time to scrutinize another mother's actions, and many women made a conscious effort not to be judgmental of other mothers. Alex exclaimed, "You are not walking in another parent's shoes, so let them parent their child in the way they choose as long as they're not beating their child or doing anything illegal. It's not your child!" Claire commented:

> Parenting is so hard. You work so hard at it. You think so hard about it. You develop expectations for yourself, your kids, your family, and your house, and you work so hard at that, that you can't help but have judgments about the way other people do their thing, but in the last couple of years, I have made a conscientious effort to value what other parents are doing and how they're doing it.

Maria offered a blanket apology for her judgmental thoughts. "I have had to apologize to all of my friends who were mothers before me for any judgmental statements I have made or thought before I became a parent myself (laughter). I've learned how much kids are hard-wired to be a certain way, and you realize how little parents really can control a kid's personality and energy."

Most women who expressed judgment about another mother also commented that she felt badly about being judgmental, or immediately offered a counter example to show that her judgment was not always accurate. Very specific circumstances would cause some women to be judgmental of another mother, such as when they felt the safety or overall social or psychological well-being of another child was at stake. Overall, the most frequent judgment women expressed related to the amount of "quality" time a mother spent with a child (which is also the main reason that mothers felt guilty). This played out in several ways. It was more common for women to express judgment about mothers whom they did not feel spent enough "quality" time with their children if it appeared that the parents were pursuing excessive material gain, or trying to compensate for their absence with material goods, especially if they thought that the child was suffering in some way as a result.

One mother talked about a wealthy family where both parents worked intense jobs, and went out most nights, leaving their kids with nannies and babysitters. She felt that the children had "behavioral problems" because "they did not get enough attention from their parents." Another mother who worked in an affluent school district noticed that many of the kids on her caseload who had emotional or behavioral disorders "were at school for eleven hours a day. There wasn't obviously a lot of time to be more relaxed at home and just reconnecting with mom and dad." This mother felt it was "such a faux pas to give an honest opinion" on this issue, and quickly noted that, "long hours in daycare has worked blissfully for many families." Another mother, who works part time, made the point that staying home does not necessarily mean a person is a better parent. "I know a lot of moms that stay home and put their kid in front of the TV all day and feed them fast food. They don't do any quality time with their kids when they get to spend all day with them." This woman quickly added, "There are some super great parents that do amazing things with their kids."

Women were overwhelmingly sympathetic toward working single mothers, whom no one criticized for not spending time with a child because they were working to support their family. One mother marveled at the workload of working single mothers, and commented, "I wish there was something more we could do for them." The underlying belief many women held was that spending "quality" time with a child is a good thing, if there are enough economic resources to meet the family's basic needs, but if a family is financially struggling, then work should take priority over spending time with children. This fits with our culture's negative portrayal of welfare mothers, who do not have the same status as stay-at-home mothers because they do not have adequate economic resources.[17] A study of Welfare-to-Work program managers in Ohio found that they define a good mother as a woman who works to support her family.[18]

Every mother noted that she spends more time intentionally listening, connecting, and playing with her children than her own mother did. Psychologist Madeline Levine, author of *The Price of Privilege*, states that a warm, caring mother who has an emotionally close relationship with a child, "is as close as we get to a silver bullet against psychological impairment."[19] Most mothers seemed to be intuitively aware that they are "the silver bullet" for their kids and were mindful of making it a priority to spend "quality" time with their child. The majority of mothers also made an effort to volunteer at school, or to help with extra curricular activities their child was involved in. In fact, spending time with a child, and being emotionally present while interacting with a child, were two of the top ten responses of women's personal ideals of being a good mother. Psychiatrist and behavioral economist George Ainslie argues that time and attention have become our scarcest resources, and "the failure to meet this need will prove the most serious and enduring mental health problem of the future."[20]

Some anthropologists have noted that across cultures a mother's job is to provide her children with scarce resources. It appears that for American middle-class parents who are economically secure, the scarce resources we expect good parents to provide for their children are "quality" time and attention. People may judge middle-class mothers for not providing enough of these scarce resources to their children, but on the other hand, some women were judgmental of helicopter parents. This suggests that providing a child with too much of a scarce resource is also a bad thing. I will come back to helicopter parenting in Part Two.

## NEGATIVE CULTURAL STEREOTYPES

I also found that women encountered judgment if they were part of a group of mothers that has a negative stereotype. Negative cultural stereotypes profoundly affect the lives of individual mothers who mother outside of dominant cultural norms (i.e. single mothers; teen mothers; mothers of color; mothers living in poverty; welfare mothers; lower class mothers; immigrant mothers; lesbian mothers; non-custodial mothers; and incarcerated mothers.)[21] The detriment of negative cultural stereotypes is not only that they create an atmosphere where people are more likely to judge a group of mothers, but they also make individual mothers *feel* like others are judging them, even when they do not experience overt judgment. Every mother who had just one attribute outside of the dominant white, middle-class, heterosexual, married cultural "norm," had experienced judgment in some form or another.

Catherine, a white, middle-class, lesbian mother of two, talked about how she feels pressure because she believes that people judge her mothering more than they judge other mothers. Catherine feels she has to work harder than other mothers do "because I'm under the spotlight, as to how I'm raising my kids." She consistently worries that "someone is going to give us trouble because we're a two-mom family. When my kids were little, I was so afraid they weren't going to be invited to a birthday party because they had two moms, or that people wouldn't let their kids come over to our house." In Catherine's case, there have been comments and exclusions that she feels were because she is lesbian, however she also assumes that people in her suburban community setting are more likely to believe negative stereotypes about gay parents. Catherine knows she is like every other parent. "All I want to do is live my life and give my kids the best that I can give them, just like any parent."

Ashley, an American born and raised non-white mother, married a man who grew up in Central America. When their infant son spiked a dangerously high fever, they brought him to the emergency room closest to their home. Ashley felt confident that the doctors would be able to treat her son, but after two days, when he showed no signs of recovering, her husband spent hours on conference calls with his family in Central America. The matriarch of her husband's family diagnosed that "El ojo de venado" (which literally translated means "eye of the deer") was responsible for their son's illness. In order to protect their son from malevolent entities, Ashley's husband placed a red band around his arm. While many of the hospital staff "were great," Ashley felt that some hospital workers viewed her with "disdain" and assumed she and her husband were irresponsible parents. In the end, doctors diagnosed her son with meningitis, and he recovered after "nineteen horrendous days" in the hospital.

Ashley felt blamed from so many different perspectives. She blamed herself for not protecting her son from microorganisms. Her husband's family blamed her for not knowing enough to protect her child from something as common as "*El Ojo*," which she had never even heard of. Some of the hospital staff blamed her for being a "non-compliant" parent, and the insurance company blamed her for going out of network. She contrasts all the blame she felt with the fact that "my husband was never blamed for failing to protect our son even though he knew about '*El Ojo*;' the doctors were never blamed for their multiple misdiagnosis; and the insurance company was never blamed for forcing a family into a network that was impossible to access." In retrospect, she feels that the underlying beliefs some of the medical professionals held about her as a mother could potentially "impair their ability to treat my child effectively."

## THE BEST THING ABOUT BEING A MOTHER

When asked, "What is the best thing about being a mother?" There was an amazing uniformity of responses such as: experiencing unconditional love and connection; watching children learn and grow; the hugs and kisses; the laughter and joy;

spending time with children, teaching them, and being needed. While the stories related to pressure, guilt, and judgment, tended to highlight the harder things about being a mother; women also told many stories about the joy, love, happiness, pride, satisfaction, fun, and connection of being a parent.

Sociologist Anthony Giddens notes that people in market-driven cultures often lack a feeling that they are part of a "succession of generations going back into the past and stretching forwards into the future." Furthermore, he notes that, "personal meaningless—the feeling that life has nothing worthwhile to offer—becomes a fundamental psychic problem in circumstances of late modernity."[22] That may be, but it seems that for many women, the relationship they have with their children helps them resist feelings of alienation and meaninglessness. Tara's father passed away when her children were very young. During this difficult time, Tara felt that it was so reassuring to be able to look at her kids and say to herself, "This is what it's all about. In the end, it's love and passing on lessons, and continuity, and life, and the circle of life, and all of those things." There will be many examples throughout the rest of this book that show how pressure, guilt, comparison, and judgment, along with profound feelings of love, connection, and responsibility affect the thoughts, feelings, and actions of mothers.

# Chapter 3

# The Rite of Passage for New Mothers

Most women laughed as they reminisced about the "freedom" and "fun" of their "life before children." Lauren's whole demeanor changed as she sat on the edge of her chair, smiled broadly, and exclaimed, "Before I had kids, life was great!" Although she was quick to reassure me that, "Life is great now." Like many women, Lauren worked, went to the club, and hung out with her husband and friends in the evenings. "It was easy, and the whole focus is on your career and yourself. You can do whatever you want." Carla said she and her husband joke that, "Life before children was that you could just at a moment's notice, stand up, walk out of the house, lock the door and leave (laughter)." Most women spoke of this time-period as a carefree phase that ended when their life as a mother began. This suggests that the birth or adoption of a middle-class woman's first child is a transformational life event that signifies the end of a relatively carefree era of her life.

Many cultures recognize that becoming a mother is an important Rite of Passage, and perform social rituals during pregnancy, childbirth, and postpartum to support a woman in making the physical, emotional, and mental adjustments necessary for her new role as a mother.[1,2] The United States has few cultural rituals to recognize the Rite of Passage of new mothers, other than perhaps a baby shower and a hospital birth.[3] We are also the only industrialized country that does not mandate paid maternity leave, nor offer extended job protection for unpaid maternity leave.[4] A generation ago, women routinely stayed in the hospital for up to a week after the birth of a baby. Nurses took care of new mothers and made sure they got their rest. Now, women who have a normal hospital delivery can expect to stay in the hospital for twenty-four to forty-eight hours, depending on their insurance coverage, and many first-time mothers leave the hospital feeling exhausted and overwhelmed.

The majority of women did not have clear expectations about the range of experiences she and her partner would encounter as their daily activities shifted in response to their parenting roles. In lieu of realistic expectations, some women had romanticized notions of parenthood; a few anticipated it would be terrible; and many focused on the external preparations like a decorating a nursery, getting a crib, bedding, and outfits, without thinking about how a baby would change their life.[5] Many people assume that women *naturally* become mothers, but the stories in this chapter illustrate that women *learn* to mother, usually through intense immersion.

## First Days and Weeks Postpartum

Most women laughed as they talked about how weepy and anxious they felt after their first child was born. Postpartum blues, often referred to as "baby blues," generally occur between day three and day twelve postpartum. It is estimated that fifty to eighty percent of women across cultures experience this transient mood fluctuation, and it appears to have little or no relation to psycho-social factors.[6,7] A common symptom of postpartum blues is crying, however the bouts of tearfulness can be a response to a variety of feelings, and women may also feel elated during this time-period.[8,9]

Women described a broad range of postpartum experiences. Some had an emotional letdown when they returned home from the hospital. Others felt it was chaotic as they learned how to do basic things like changing a diaper. The physical changes, such as breast heaviness with milk letdown, or the length of time they bled, were surprising to some. Those who had colicky infants felt overwhelmed by the constant screaming. One woman found it depressing to leave her premature twins in the Neonatal Intensive Care Unit.

Women who had adopted infants told emotionally-charged stories about meeting their child for the first time. Marie cried as she said, "I think that is something people don't understand that somehow these children are not just as much a part of us as a child would be who is a birth child." For some mothers the transition to motherhood was relatively easy, especially if their baby slept a lot or had a "good temperament." One mother felt "it was more stressful having a puppy than having a baby." Bringing a baby home can be exciting, stressful, chaotic, boring, or anticlimactic, and it is totally normal to feel tearful, sad, emotionally reactive, anxious, unprepared, bored, or overwhelmed in the days and weeks following the arrival of a baby.

## POSTPARTUM DEPRESSION

Some women talked about feeling sad or depressed for several weeks after their first child had been born. Postpartum depression affects anywhere from twelve to twenty-two percent of new mothers in the United States.[10] There are so many things going on in a woman's life during the postpartum period that it is often difficult for women to recognize that they have symptoms of postpartum depression. The DSM-IV defines postpartum depression as a reduced ability to function socially or professionally, combined with a "depressed mood," or "diminished pleasure or interest in activities." Additionally, women must experience at least four of the following symptoms for two weeks in a row: "sleep disturbance (insomnia or hypersomnia); weight loss or gain; psychomotor agitation or retardation; loss of energy; feelings of worthlessness or inappropriate guilt; diminished concentration or indecisiveness; and frequent thoughts of death or suicide."[11]

About ten percent of the women I interviewed mentioned their feelings of depression following the birth of their first baby. None of the women who believed in retrospect that they had postpartum depression received medical acknowledgement or treatment for their condition, and all of the women stated that it eventually passed on its own.[12] Usually when women spoke of their first days of mothering, they laughed as they told me how unprepared and overwhelmed they felt at the time. However, the women who experienced postpartum depression spoke with a serious tone as they recollected a very difficult time.

Erica began feeling apprehensive in the hospital. She felt inadequate and inexperienced and thought, "These nurses here are crazy because they're going to let me take this baby home with me and I have no idea what I'm doing." Erica realized in retrospect that she had a "pretty severe" short-term case of post-partum depression that lasted three to four weeks after the birth of her first child. "Those first few weeks were just horrible," she recalled. "I'd plaster a grin on my face, and I'd take him for a walk down by the lake and I'd think, 'My life is over.' 'Who thought this was a good idea?'" Erica's depression got better, when she realized, "My life is not over, my life is different. I started adding back the things that were most important to me. I can hardly even remember because the transition was so complete I think this is my life now. But it was pretty rough those first few weeks."[13]

Several biological and psychosocial factors can potentially trigger post-partum depression.[14] Women must also deal with the loss of their former identity.[15] Carla was at work when her water broke a month before her daughter was due. Her daughter was healthy and able to go home right away, however for the first month Carla felt like she was depressed but did not realize it. "I cried and cried and cried. It took me awhile until I would feel like my new normal." None of the women felt comfortable talking about their condition when they were in the midst of the depression. This indicates that the atmosphere of our culture, which promotes idealized images of motherhood, along with a belief that becoming a mother is *natural*, makes it difficult for women to talk about their experiences that may feel "wrong" in comparison to the cultural ideal.

## SOCIAL SUPPORT

Some anthropologists have argued that postpartum support helps a woman make the transition to her new role as a mother and even has the potential to deter postpartum depression.[16] Overall, women appreciated support from people they felt comfortable with who were helpful without taking over. A woman who had a homebirth felt the frequent postpartum home visits from her midwives were a great source of support. She adhered to the Chinese recovery process where she was in bed for five days, around the bed for five days, and then had an additional five days where her family members continued to take care of her. Some women had no family in town and did not receive any help after they came home with the baby, leaving some to feel isolated and lonely, whereas others liked having the time on their own with their infant and partner.

Women were generally appreciative of the support they received from friends. Fiona vividly remembers the "best help" she got from a friend who came over and told her to lie down and not to talk to her. "My friend did my laundry, made me a sandwich, and left, and I didn't talk to her once." Christine felt overwhelmed when her husband returned to work, and she was alone with the baby for the first time. "I looked at her in her bouncy seat and I'm like, 'I have no idea what to do with you' (laughter). I started crying and my girlfriend called and she said, 'Okay, you're totally normal this is totally fine.' She talked to me for an hour, and it was the best phone call I've ever had." Every woman who had three or more children commented that when their younger children were born they received little support from extended family at a time when they felt they could have used it the most. One mother joked, "When my first child was born, my mother-in-law came and dusted my blinds. It made me uncomfortable because I felt she did not think I was a good housekeeper. When my third child was born, I would have been thrilled to have my mother-in-law come over and dust my blinds."

## THE BABY FOG

Many women described the post-partum period as being in a "fog," or in the "dark," or a "blur." Lack of sleep is probably a common reason for feeling like one is in a fog. William Dement and Christopher Vaughn, pioneers in sleep research, argue that chronic sleep loss, or accumulated sleep debt "degrades nearly every aspect of human performance: vigilance (ability to receive information), alertness (ability to act on information), and attention span. In simple terms, a large sleep debt 'makes you stupid.'"[17] Studies show that both new mothers and fathers experience sleep disruption and fatigue during the postpartum period, especially after their first baby.[18]

## ATTACHMENT AND BONDING

To clarify these frequently interchanged terms, attachment is an infant or child's emotional connection to a caregiver, and bonding refers to a parent or caregiver's feelings toward the child for whom they are caring. Women had different perceptions of what attachment and bonding "should" be like, different levels of worry about their capabilities to bond with a child, and different experiences of what they considered bonding and attachment. Parents who adopted children were especially mindful of issues of bonding and attachment. The adoption agency told us, "You really, really, really need to work at having that child attach because that's one of the biggest issues in adoption," commented Catherine.

Not every mother assumed that she would initially bond with her child. Tara felt scared about "whether or not I'd have the maternal thing." Shortly after her baby was born, "I was so overwhelmed with love for her and it was such a huge relief." Carla had watched several episodes of *A Baby Story* while she was pregnant and was surprised and "thrown off" when, "I didn't have the sobbing emotional kind of feeling when I first saw her and held her." Ultimately Carla felt like, "It took awhile for me to fall in love with her and really like her. I loved her and I took care of her because I knew that was what I needed to do."

It took Amy a long time to feel bonded to her baby, and for her baby to attach to her. Her daughter had some neurological issues, "cried twenty hours out of everyday for the first year," and "was stiff as a board" when you touched her. "There was none of that bonding stuff." Amy had quit her job to stay home because she believed that it would be wonderful to be a stay-at-home mom of two children. However, the first year was horrible, and she felt tense all the time. When she brought the baby in for her check-ups, she asked the doctor, "When am I going to love this baby?" The doctor replied, "You have to learn to live with her how she is verses trying to make her be what you want her to be." After a year, she felt that she and her husband had figured out their daughter, and things got much better.

## POSTPARTUM RELATIONSHIP SATISFACTION

Relationships also go through a transition after the birth or adoption of a child. The postpartum period can be challenging because both partners are adjusting to their new role, and are most likely suffering from sleep deprivation. Postpartum marital dissatisfaction correlates with an incongruity between what one expects the relationship will be like with the reality of daily interactions.[19] Women are more likely to have higher expectations about postpartum relational happiness than men, and therefore usually feel more dissatisfied than men.[20] Some women felt their relationship did not change after having children, and several loved seeing their partner as a parent, and thought that having kids was a "fun project to do together."

Considering that prior to having a child, most couples are free to go out as much as they want, several women thought their biggest change was that it was difficult to find the time and energy to schedule a babysitter to have regular dates. Lauren and her husband had a "really rough time" after their third child was born. In retrospect, she realizes they probably weren't getting enough sleep, and her husband was in a job that he hated at the time. They went to a counselor where they came up with a plan that Lauren's husband would do more housework and childcare, and they would start having a regular date night. The combination of her husband's increased household participation, their date night, her husband finding a new job, and Lauren going back to work part-time made a positive impact on the quality of their family life.

Other couples found it challenging to get personal time. Katie recalls that one of the main tensions between she and her husband, Steve, was who was going to get time alone on the weekends. Every weekend she and Steve competed for that time, which was "really hard and challenging" because we both felt that "if one person gets it then the other person is not going to get enough." Eventually they figured out that Steve was okay if he had "two or three hours away," whereas Katie needed five or six hours to really come home and feel like, "Oh good. I got filled up." She explained that it was not that she did not want to be home with their daughter, she just needed to "be away for awhile."

Carla, who stays home full time, feels that she and her husband have not quite figured out how to incorporate their relationship with their parental roles. "We seem to function really well as a family of three, either me and the children, or my husband and the children, but we don't know how to function as a family of four, which is pretty sad." Carla gets frustrated because she feels that she and her husband cannot have a conversation at dinner. They have a couple of hours together after the kids go to bed, which is nice because it is just the two of them, but interacting as a family unit continues to be challenging. Christine feels that one reason their relationship changed so much is that "it wasn't all about us anymore, which is fine, but sometimes he calls me Mom. 'Go see Mom. Where's Mom?' I'm like, I used to be your wife (laughter) now I'm the Mom, it's so weird."

Other women also talked about how having children changed the focus of their relationship. Amy's "honeymoon baby" had a profound affect on her first marriage. "It was different in that you didn't have the one-on-one relationship time. I think that is probably what dissolved the marriage. Once our son was born, the focus was on him. There was a lack of money, and so many worries and pressures that we grew apart." Kendra felt the tremendous workload of both parents affected their relationship. "There's a point where there's so much going on in your life and you're in survival mode for too long, and when you finally get the chance to get a breather, you look at each other and realize we're two different people at this point. We didn't make it with the raising of the kids. We did the best we could."

Vanessa observed that even though having children initially made her and her husband closer, there was also "a lot of competitiveness on our parts because we were both so madly in love with the baby. I always would win out because I was the nursing mother and she always needed her Mama. Now that we're divorced, I see that as the beginning of some resentment." As Sabrina spoke about the conflict she and her husband experienced, her voice fell to a whisper as she said, "Maybe it's also that I feel (pause) more devoted to my child than my husband." Sabrina did not want to belabor this point, and quickly focused her attention on her son who had accompanied her to the interview. Her comment raises an interesting issue about how sometimes the affection a parent feels for a child takes precedence over the affection they feel for their spouse or partner.

Jessica talked about how she was deeply affected by an episode of *Oprah* she saw before she was even married, where Ayelet Waldman said, "I love my husband more than my kids."[21] Several women who were part of a small group panel discussion were bitingly critical of Waldman, and as Jessica watched, she thought, "That will never be me." It made her consciously decide not to lose touch with her husband. After their baby was born, she and her husband began to have relationship difficulties. At that time, a part of her felt that she and her baby were "buddies," while at the same time she "couldn't even deal" with her husband. She is thankful their financial situation is such that they both have to be the caregivers, remarking, "I could see how you could get so into your kid that you ignore your spouse, especially if your spouse is being a pain."

Ayelet Waldman believes that women's decreased sex lives after having children has to do with women refocusing their attention to their children. While I did not specifically ask women about their sex life, a few women did bring it up in their interview. One woman said she is so busy and so tired that when she crawls into bed at night she just wants to go to sleep. Another woman said she needed a break from intimacy from her husband because her children were "hanging on my body all day." I have been in groups where individual women have jokingly said they would trade sex for their husbands increased participation in childcare or cleaning. Another woman joked that she tells her husband she thinks it is "really sexy" when he empties the dishwasher. All of the factors that create conflict after children, combined with the increased workload of the couple, their new roles as parents, and lack of sleep most likely to contribute to a decline in sexual activity many couples experience after a child is born or adopted.

Several women felt it was imperative to focus on their marital relationship after they had children. Bridget explained that she thinks being a good spouse is an important element of being a good parent. "There's a school of thought that you can't be a good parent unless you're a good spouse, so you should focus on your marriage first, and make sure you take time out to nurture it and continue to connect with your spouse, even if it means going out on dates and leaving your children with a babysitter." Jan's parents divorced after their kids left home. Jan never saw them fight, but she believes they just grew apart. She and her husband make an effort to take time for each other so that when their children leave home, they will have other interests they share besides their kids. She thinks it is important for her children to see that she and her husband do not focus all of their attention solely on them, but are role modeling how to have a happy relationship and be good parents. Realistic information about the challenges, opportunities, and likely sleep deprivation new parents may encounter can help close the gap between romanticized expectations and reality, while also helping couples intentionally create rituals and habits to stay connected with each other during their Rite of Passage to parenthood. The next chapter covers one of the most challenging issues for many couples: the division of labor.

# Chapter 4

## "It's your turn to put the kids to bed."

### HOW BECOMING A PARENT AFFECTS THE HOUSEHOLD DIVISION OF LABOR

Ashley was taking 19 university credits, working three jobs, doing an independent research project, and taking care of four children. She would fall asleep studying every night around midnight, and wake up between 4 and 5 a.m. to throw in two loads of laundry, pack lunches, and make breakfast for the kids. Ashley was perpetually exhausted and felt her husband should do more around the house. "I don't know why when you do the dishes, it's helping me," she explained to her husband. "I don't know why if you sweep the floor it's helping me. It's not my job." The final straw happened when her husband "got pissed" because he had to take their son to the doctor by himself. "I lost my shit," Ashley exclaimed. "I told him I needed a divorce because he was not a supportive husband." Her husband did not want a divorce, and Ashley feels lucky that he loved her enough to totally change his ways. "Now we actually have a partnership, and it's really nice. Our kids have learned a lot from that experience because they went from seeing me do everything all the time, to seeing their dad do his share around the house."

The division of labor is not a trivial matter. A woman's perception of the fairness of the division of labor is a major predictor of marital satisfaction, and relationship experts consistently rank the division of labor as one of the top things couples fight about, right up there with money and sex.[1] A 2011 TIME cover proclaimed, "Chore Wars." "Let it go. Make peace. Men and women, it turns out, work the same amount."[2] Based on my interviews, surveys, and informal conversations with hundreds of mothers, it is premature to call a truce to the "chore wars."

While many couples have negotiated a peaceful resolution to the division of labor, many couples have not. Figuring out the division of labor is messy, and there is no one-size-fits-all solution. Communication styles can range from no discussion to daily discussions and from calm conversations to arguments. Couples that divide the workload in a way that suits both partners have done so in countless ways. Some have detailed chore lists, others have each person do what they like best, some switch up responsibilities daily, and others have jobs they always do.

In 1989, *The Second Shift* revealed that most working mothers also did the majority of household labor. I was curious whether this was still the case, and so I asked eighty working mothers and stay-at-home mothers to fill out a detailed survey on who does thirty-two common household and childcare tasks, and who works more hours outside the home. Over half of the women indicated that they do a majority of the household and childcare labor, which is consistent with other studies.[3] The specific tasks women "always" or "usually" reported doing are as follows:

1. Buys clothes for children (97%)
2. Schedules play dates (91%)
3. Keeps the family calendar (89%)
4. Chooses classes/activities (86%)
5. Buys presents for birthday parties (85%)
6. Buys presents for children (82%)
7. Makes lunch for children (82%)
8. Buys presents for extended family (78%)
9. Gets dinner ready for family (77%)
10. Schedules a babysitter (77%)

11. Does the grocery shopping (75%)
12. Does the laundry (73%)
13. Makes daycare/pre-school arrangements (73%)
14. Cleans the bathroom (70%)
15. Takes care of child if they are sick (70%)
16. Picks up stuff around the house (66%)
17. Vacuums (65%)
18. Gets up with child in night (64%)
19. Drives child to activities (63%)
20. Prepares breakfast for children (62%)
21. Picks up child from daycare/preschool (55%)
22. Brings child to daycare/preschool (52%)
23. Changes diapers/used to change diapers (52%)

The women's list seems quite long in comparison to the two tasks over half of the women reported that their husband or partner "always" or "usually" does, which were: mow the lawn (82%); and take out the garbage (52%). In addition, 75% of the women said their husband "always" or "usually" worked more hours outside the home. The four tasks that more than half of the women reported sharing equally with their husband were: disciplines a child (82%); puts child to bed (63%); plays with child (61%); and decides who does what job around the house (52%). Managing the household finances was also equitable, in that 33% of fathers and 39% of mothers "always" or "usually" do this task, and 28% report sharing the task equally. Twenty-three percent of the men "always" or "usually" do dishes after dinner, and approximately 11% of male partners "always" or "usually" prepares breakfast for a child, puts a child to bed, vacuums, and cleans the bathroom.[4] Ten percent of the respondents had a cleaning person.

Work status made little difference in the number of tasks more than half of the women reported "always" or "usually" doing, or the number of tasks they shared equally with their partner.[5] The biggest difference between women based on their work status was that a quarter of full-time working mothers reported sharing 22 tasks equally with their husband or partner; whereas a quarter of part-time working mothers reported sharing 9 tasks equally, and a quarter of stay-at-home mothers reported sharing 11 tasks equally with their spouse. This suggests a fair number of dual-income, heterosexual couples in this sample have figured out strategies to have egalitarian housework and childcare responsibilities.

## How Couples Negotiate the Division of Labor

Just over half the women reported that they regularly discuss childcare and domestic responsibilities with their husband or partner, but several noted that their discussion often began with an argument or disagreement. The rest of the women said they did not discuss the division of labor with their spouse or partner, or only occasionally discussed it. Couples with similar gender attitudes, whether traditional, egalitarian, or somewhere in between, were less likely to have conflict about the division of labor.

Some couples discussed each task, switching up their responsibilities daily or weekly; others relied on chore charts, or weekly schedules; some had a set routine of who does what task, but checked in with each other periodically, especially about scheduling. "We seem to do what we are best at or like the most and split the rest," explained a part-time working mother. A full-time working mother replied that she and her husband "have our own preferences as far as which chores to do and which are important to us. I can't stand a dirty kitchen, and he hates a messy living room, so we clean what we want." Several women stated that they were for the most part satisfied, although some said they would appreciate more help or acknowledgement.

Sometimes it took couples a while before they came up with a plan that worked for both partners. A part-time working mother said that she and her husband used to split tasks down the middle, however they were both unhappy until they began to do the tasks that they each enjoyed. Jan and her husband wanted a 50/50 split, but they felt it was hard to achieve because it is based on "your own perception," so they both decided to "try to give sixty percent and only expect forty percent from the other person." Jan believes that "if both of you are doing that, then you're probably going to end up closer to a 50/50 shared relationship." One woman who was dissatisfied with the division of labor while she was married, is now very satisfied because their divorce agreement mandates their specific responsibilities.

Not all women who talked about household and child-care responsibilities with their spouse were satisfied with their division of labor. "We've discussed it many times, but we have different opinions about workloads," explained Kelly. "I feel I do 90% of the housework, but he feels we're evenly split. Given that I am working from the moment I wake to the moment I go to bed, I can't understand how he can make that claim when he watches two-plus hours of TV per day." Kelly works longer hours and makes more money than her husband, however she finds it "strange" that her husband does not see all the things one needs to do to keep up a house and take care of a child. "I can see what needs to be done around the house without anyone having to tell me, or point out, or encourage me." Women who make more money than their husband does, usually do as much or more household labor, even if their husband is unemployed. Men who make more money than their wives do, contribute significantly less to household labor.[6]

Kelly feels that their household work has become more and more gender divided. "I hate the stereotypical nature of it and I hate to complain about it because I don't want to be that person, which also seems stereotypical. So I just keep doing it, and I get stuck with it." Many married, heterosexual couples move toward conventional gender roles after the birth or adoption of a baby.[7] After venting about her husband, Kelly quietly said, "It's a major disappointment because I always believed we could get past that."[8]

Many women were resentful about the inequality of their division of labor. When Robin quit work to stay home with their first child, she began doing "everything" around the house. "I was the one who got up in the middle of the night, and I did all of the laundry, the dishes, the cleaning, and the vacuuming. Everything! I did all the childcare, even when he was home." Robin began to feel like a "servant" and became increasingly resentful of her husband. "We fought about the division of labor for a good long time," Robin confided. She felt the bigger issue was the message her husband was sending to their children. "I had to be the bad guy and he could be one of the kids. They could get up and leave their mess, and go on to the next thing, and then I would come yell at all of them to clean it up. Then if he didn't listen, and they watched him not listen, what does that say to my kids, and where does that put me?" Counseling helped them create a more equitable division of labor and figure out how to be a unified team in front of their children. Robin is much happier because she feels her husband will "do his share."

Some women talked about the challenge of both partners working demanding jobs. "My husband is the love of my life," Celeste exclaimed, but when they both had corporate jobs that required long hours and frequent travel, "our quality of family life just exploded." During a particularly stressful time, Celeste's husband said, "Something's got to give. If you don't quit, I have to. We just can't keep this up." Celeste decided to quit her job for a few years, and their family life became much more manageable. I consistently found that women were more likely to scale back work commitments when there was work-family conflict.

Several women talked about the invisibility of the domestic and childcare work they do. Kim, who works part-time, and her husband, who is employed full-time, reside in an affluent neighborhood where most people can afford to hire people to do housework, yard work, and childcare. Their neighbors, Kathy and Bill, have full-time demanding jobs and hire a nanny, a cleaning person, and a lawn service. Kathy told Kim, "Now that my kids are all in school I don't need a nanny as much as I need a house manager." When Kim told her husband about Kathy's comment, he replied, "We need one of those." Kim exclaimed to her husband, "You have one of those (laughter)! Who do you think is doing all of that?" Kim's voice got louder and higher pitched as she went on to say that she is always trying to juggle the cleaning, the lawn mowing, the grocery shopping, doing the Target runs, filling out the forms for school, and going on the field trips. One mother exclaimed, "I don't know of a husband who has ever found daycare for the summer. I don't know of a husband who signs their kids up for activities."

Jackie, a stay-at-home mother, likes having a traditional division of labor.

> I'm inside, and he's outside. If it happens in the house, I'm in charge. He doesn't grocery shop. He doesn't do the laundry. He doesn't clean. He is a pigpen. He always has been. I'm the cleaner and the organizer. I'm the social calendar, doctor's appointments, I'm the everything. He does the gutters and fixes the house, but I do the lawn now.

They have little stress because her husband "is so laid back. He does not give a rip if there's dinner, or if there's clothes, so, it's up to me." He will do things Jackie puts on a list "beautifully, but if it's not on a list, it doesn't exist for him. So I write a list, and he crosses things off, and it works for us." She likes it that he is an involved father and will periodically take the kids camping for a weekend to give her a break.

When Maria transitioned from part-time work to staying home full time, she felt frustrated because her husband "assumed" she would be in charge of childcare, even when they were both home. She feels that one of the negative aspects of being home full time is "that both partners feel like that's your job." Maria explains, "I need to ask if I can leave, or let him know if I'm leaving, but he would never think to ask if it's alright to leave when we're both in the house." She is happy with her husband's contribution to housework because he will "pick up and do laundry." Patty who works full time while her husband stays home with the kids feels he has a much harder job, however she is still responsible for signing them up for pre-school, making sure they've got food in the house, and cleaning. Patty exclaimed, "Why do I still have to do everything because I am the woman?"

Several former long-term stay-at-home mothers felt it was difficult to change their household dynamic when they returned to work because their spouse and children were used to them doing more cooking and cleaning. Some got a cleaning person to fill in the gap, others worked to change family habits, and some were exhausted from trying to keep up the pace of working and being primarily responsible for household chores. "I come home from work at 9 o'clock and nobody has brought out the garbage or the recycling," commented Jill. "We've had our garbage collected on Friday for fifteen years, and I have the recycling marked on the calendar every other week, and my husband isn't capable of remembering to take out the garbage, yet he can manage to do his work." Jill sighed as she remarked, "We were equal when we first got married, and things got unequal when we had our kids. My husband got spoiled."

## SECRETS OF COUPLES WHO HAVE AN EGALITARIAN DIVISION OF LABOR

There were three things that egalitarian heterosexual couples had in common. 1) Both partners were committed to mindfully organizing their domestic responsibilities in a non-gendered way. 2) The male partner was primarily responsible for childcare at some point. 3) Women expressed their conscious decision to let their partner parent in his own way.

I sat with Tara at a conference table in her spacious corner office. Framed pictures of her children lined her desk, and their artwork hung on a bulletin board behind the conference table. Tara, who exuded an energetic confidence, works closely with her husband Rob, whom she met at work. After their first child was born, Tara took a six-month maternity leave, which Rob followed with a six-week paternity leave. Tara and Rob are committed to "trying not to have traditional gender stereotypes." Over the years, she and Rob have defined equal in different way than before they were actually doing it. "It isn't half and half, it is doing different things and being equally engaged in our kids' lives." Tara feels they have been successful at giving their children two active, engaged parents, and is proud of the fact that "when either child wakes up in the middle of the night, it is completely random who they call for."

Rob's ability to take a six-week paternity leave, six months after their child was born, without it affecting his job, or negatively impacting their household income is rare. American companies do not have standard policies that support the expectation that both mothers and fathers will be responsible for caring for an infant. Few companies offer paid paternity leave, and when they do, it is usually just a week or two.[9] Many middle-class fathers combine sick leave and vacation days to take time off after a child is born, however their wife or partner is usually also off at the same time so they are not exclusively in charge of caring for the infant. Some studies indicate that when men request family leave, they suffer a "femininity stigma," and a "poor worker stigma." They are viewed as being "weak and uncertain," and are penalized in the workplace as a result.[10]

Men in Norway, Sweden, and Canada were reluctant to take paternity leave for decades, however once these countries offered well-paid, nontransferable leave for fathers, over eighty percent of men took advantage of these policies. The rationale for these provisions was to "disrupt a deeply rooted pattern and social norm of women as primary care-giving experts and men as main breadwinners."[11] The fact that we live in a country where extended paternity leave is rare and stigmatized can have a negative impact on the day-to-day division of labor for couples, especially when their children are young.

I met Jessica late one fall afternoon at a coffee shop in a busy urban neighborhood. Jessica stopped at home after work to pick up her infant son to bring to the interview. Jessica grew up in a household where her parents had a traditional division of labor, and she did not want to have that kind of relationship with her husband. After their son was born, Jessica spent the first several months at home with the baby, and then her husband Steve, who was unemployed at the time, stayed home when she returned to work. Now she works full time in four days while Steve cares for the baby, and Steve works double shift construction jobs over three-day weekends while she takes care of their son.

When Jessica returned to work, she had to be "really sensitive" about commenting on what Steve got done throughout the day. On the days Jessica works, Steve cooks dinner and does the dishes while she gives their son a bath and gets him ready for bed. Jessica admires some of the things Steve has been able to do, like get their child in a napping routine. She has also learned to "let the little things go," like the fact that Steve often leaves their son in his pajamas all day. "I put this on him last night after his bath" (pointing to her son's pajamas) "and he's still wearing them (laughter). You know as a mom, I would never do that. I would put him in clothes." Even though she and Steve both feel that their workload is never-ending, Jessica is happy that her husband "loves staying home with the baby" and that they both share the feeling that having a baby is adventurous.

Brooke grew up in a household where her mother worked full time to support the family while also doing everything on the home front because Brooke's dad was not very reliable. Her mom was "a total feminist who hates to cook" so she was not the kind of mom "to be baking a warm something and have a flawless house." Brooke feels that her husband Tom is "a complete 50% parent," but she has noticed that if she complains about her husband not doing certain things to friends who do most of the domestic work themselves, they are not sympathetic at all. She gets frustrated because she feels they think she should not expect more from him because he is "already being so nice by pitching in." She exclaimed, "Why is it 'pitching in' to co-parent your own kids?"

Brooke stayed home for the first three months with their firstborn, and Tom stayed home for the fourth month when she returned to work. Brooke believes that having time alone with their first child helped Tom become an expert. "With your first, the mom has the boobs, so she becomes the expert," elaborated Brooke. "She's the one that's been home for three or four months, and even when she goes back to work she's the one that knows the routine, and she's the one who knows how to comfort the baby." When their baby was nine months old, they went on a vacation with another couple whose baby was the same age as theirs. She and her friend decided to spend a few hours walking around the town, so when they left, she told Tom, "We'll be back around 3." Her friend gave her husband a list of things he needed to do, like change and feed the baby.

Brooke noticed that even though her friend was working full time, the dynamic was that the mom was the main parent, and the dad was just stepping in, because they had "conceded to the idea that she was the expert, and she had taken over all control, while the husband had given up all control." Brooke believes that the secret to equal parenting is being able to "let go," and decide that "he's going to know what to do and be able to be a good parent."

## WANTING CONTROL AND HAVING HIGHER STANDARDS MEANS MORE WORK

Many women felt that letting go of control was a major factor in transitioning to a more equitable division of labor. "I'm not OCD about the cleaning shit anymore," commented Ashley from the opening story. "My husband does all the laundry now. When I was in charge of laundry, the towels had to be just so in my linen closet, and there was a hand space between every hanger in my closet. I let all that go, and now I don't care how the towels are stacked." When Alex's husband was unexpectedly laid off, their roles quickly reversed when she got a job and he had to "take over the cooking and the cleaning and all the stuff that

I used to get done. I was always the one in charge and had the control. Because I was the one who took care of it, I didn't ask for his input," explained Alex. "Now suddenly he's the one in charge and he's not asking for my input, and it bothered me greatly in the beginning because he was stepping on my turf. I wanted the control. I finally had to concede that his decisions may not be the same as mine, but they are not necessarily wrong."

Rachel distinctly remembers a point when they had two children in diapers and she and her husband were both working full time. After compiling a list of all the tasks she was doing, Rachel sat down with her husband to "vent" about everything on her plate. She calmly told her husband, "This is everything I'm doing and you've got to help me." After looking at the list with her husband, she said, "All I could find that he was capable of doing was emptying the diaper pail!" She realized that it was her problem because she did not want her husband to do things if he was not going to do them to her standards. She believes the feeling that "nobody else can do it quite as good as we can" runs deep in many women.

Individuals who had strong opinions of how they wanted things done, tended to do more household or childcare work. Janet's husband "definitely does more of the cleaning" because Janet has "never been into cleaning, and if he wants it clean, he has to deal with that." Amy does "everything" around the house and works part-time in order to accommodate her household and childcare responsibilities. Amy recognizes that she is "kind of a control freak" and likes things "a certain way (laughter)," admitting that her husband "would never be able to do it right anyway (laughter)." Amy frames her ability to "balance" household and childcare responsibilities better than her husband does, as being a product of innate gender differences. "I think maybe guys are not wired to juggle all that stuff." She worries how her husband would manage if something happened to her because she believes "moms are so important and they teach their kids so much about the ways of the world." Mothers who believe that women are "naturally" better at parenting tend to do more domestic and childcare work, usually because of "maternal gate-keeping."[12] Claire does more parenting on weekends than her husband does because she believes their kids get better care from her. When her husband is in charge, he will take them to Dairy Queen, or put on a movie so they will sit quietly while he works. She does not think that the kids should spend the weekend eating ice-cream and watching movies, so "I naturally step in to do it."

## CONSUMERISM, THE WORK OF KINSHIP, AND MATERNAL POWER

There are couples fully committed to equal parenting, both in principle and in action, so it is interesting to look at the tasks that heterosexual couples are least likely to share equally. These are: 1) buy clothes for the children (97%); 2) schedule play dates for the children (91%); 3) keep the family calendar (89%); 4) choose activities for child to participate (86%); and 5) buy presents for children to bring to birthday parties (85%). There could be several reasons why women usually do these tasks. Perhaps they are so deeply engrained as "feminine" tasks that it is difficult for even the most egalitarian-minded couples to share them equally. They might also be tasks that women are reluctant to give up because they enjoy doing them, or because they facilitate maternal power or control. It is likely that a combination of these factors may come into play.

Anthropologist Michaela di Leonardo's observes that in addition to housework, childcare, and market work, women also consciously engage in kin work. She defines "the work of kinship" as follows:

> the conception, maintenance, and ritual celebration of cross-household kin ties, including visits, letters, telephone calls, presents, and cards to kin; the organization of holiday gatherings; the creation and maintenance of

quasi-kin relations; decisions to neglect or to intensify particular ties; the mental work of reflection about all these activities and the creation and communication of images of family and kin.[13]

She further argues that kin work is "crucial" for the functioning and maintenance of kinship systems; is a potential source of "women's autonomous power" and "emotional fulfillment;" and can also be a vehicle "for actual survival and/or political resistance."[14] In the five tasks that women are most likely to do, three of them, scheduling play dates, keeping the family calendar, and buying presents for children to bring to birthday parties, could be classified as kin work, which suggests that the "work of kinship" is still predominantly a female activity.

The top four activities most likely to be carried out by mothers—buying clothes, scheduling play dates, keeping the family calendar, and choosing extra activities or classes—are activities that are deeply influential in socializing children by shaping their individual preferences, fostering potential abilities, influencing friendships, promoting reciprocal relationships, and overseeing their daily activities. Additionally, the person in charge of the family calendar exerts a fair amount of control over the activities of all household members. The maternal domestic power that women have traditionally wielded in their influence over childrearing methods, child socialization, local education, allocating of family resources for domestic goods and services, kinship ties, and community ties has been chronically undervalued in the our culture because we over-value the public sector.[15] It appears that at a personal level, women are deeply aware of maternal power and influence.

# Chapter 5

## The "Life Load"

### NAVIGATING THE CONFLICT BETWEEN FAMILY AND MARKET WORK

I met Rachel at a local coffee shop at 9:30 in the morning. The morning of the interview, Rachel rose at 5 a.m. so she could run five miles before getting ready for work. Then she woke her three children, fed them breakfast, made their lunches while solving a Brownie Troop crisis on the phone with her troop co-leader, and got her kids off to the bus stop before beginning her paid workday with an 8 a.m. conference call. Rachel is mindful of all of the things she does, to balance what she calls, "the 'life load.' It's the laundry and the lunches, combined with trying to keep your head screwed on and be sharp in meetings, and be on top of your work. I just try to keep it all held together, and keep it all in perspective, and hope that I'm not letting something huge slip through the cracks." Before having kids, Rachel worked a sixty-hour a week job with 50% travel, however as her family has grown, she has made different career choices, ranging getting a full-time job that "felt like it had more balance to it," to working part-time, to going back to full-time.

American women make the "choice" to work or stay home with children, within a vortex of powerful cultural forces. 1) We have a cultural assumption that mothers should be the parent primarily responsible for managing childcare.[1] 2) We believe that managing childcare is an individual responsibility.[2] 3) Full-time American employees put in long hours, have relatively little vacation time, and do not have job protected parental leave of more than 12 weeks.[3] 4) Most families need two incomes to make ends meet. 5) High quality daycare is expensive. 6) We have unrealistic and idealized representations of a "good" mother, which sets the expectation that mothers should "do it all" with minimal help from their partner, employer, or the government. 7) We expect that being a mother should take top priority in a woman's identity, and therefore we judge mothers more than we judge fathers in our culture.[4]

These beliefs and practices may seem obvious, but it is important to acknowledge them because they contribute to the daily pressure many mothers experience as they balance their work and family commitments. The good news is that some of these cultural beliefs and practices are slowly changing. Many parents equally share responsibility for childrearing. Some organizations offer generous parental leave and have an environment that is conducive to work/life balance. Women do their best to ignore idealized representations of mothers, and many make an effort not to judge themselves or others. Nevertheless, American mothers are still subject to these competing expectations as they navigate the conflict between market work and family work. The majority of women in this study, even if they continued to work full-time, made career sacrifices to accommodate the increase in their "life load" after having children.

## CULTURAL CONFLICT OVER THE LIMITS OF COMBINING WORK AND MOTHERHOOD

Even though it is old news, the media reaction to Sarah Palin's nomination as John McCain's U.S. Presidential running mate in 2008 is worth mentioning because it is a perfect example of our deeply rooted cultural conflict over the limits of combining paid labor with mothering responsibilities. Within days of the announcement, Sally Quinn of *The Washington Post* questioned, "Is she prepared for the all-consuming nature of the job? … When the phone rings at three in the morning and one of

her children is really sick, what choice will she make?"[5] Hilary
Rosen was quick to respond that no one ever questioned Barack
Obama's ability to manage potential presidential duties with his
role as a father of two young girls.[6] Joe Scarborough of *Morning
Joe* articulated the angst of his co-anchor Mika Brzezinski in an
interview with *Washington Post* correspondent Ruth Marcus, one
of the journalists critical of Palin's choice to accept the offer.

JS:   You know Mika has been very upset …with pro-
      gressive women who have said, 'She can't do this.
      She's got five children. She needs to put the children
      first.' Mika takes that as a personal insult because of
      course, anybody that works with her knows, her life
      is crazy. She's juggling a husband, and two children.
      …She calls kids during the commercials. She's set-
      ting up nannies. She's setting up tennis. She's setting
      up vacations. It makes us all exhausted. But she's
      very offended because when people say Sarah Palin
      shouldn't be able to do this, she feels like people are
      saying she's [referring to Mika] a bad mother because
      she's trying to have it all.

RM:   Mika, if you're watching, you're a good mother!
      We're all trying to be good mothers. …We all juggle
      in these crazy ways, and I really don't want to judge
      anyone being a good mother or a bad mother. We're
      all trying to do our best.

The reaction to this story shows how our cultural assumptions
make it seem impossible that a "good" mother, who we expect to
be the intensive primary parent responsible for managing childcare, is able to commit to a demanding job, where the expectation
is that the job will always come first. It also shows that even the
most accomplished women feel vulnerable to being judged as a
mother.

## FACTORS THAT INFLUENCE A WOMAN'S CHOICE ABOUT COMBINING MARKET AND FAMILY LABOR

For some women, deciding whether to work or stay home was a complex and emotionally wrought decision, while for others it was relatively straightforward.[7] Many women reported that their mother's work status influenced how they envisioned combining market labor and family labor. Several women did the same thing their mother did. Abby and her husband both came from a family where their mother stayed home with them when they were young. When it came time to have children, she and her husband were in "complete agreement" that she would stay home "because that's what felt right to us." Brooke's decision about working was in alignment with her mother who worked full time. "I've got friends whose parents guilt them into staying home but my mom would freak if I blew everything I've worked for by not working," observed Brooke.

On the other hand, some women made a deliberate decision to do things differently than their own mother. Bridget's mother stayed home full time while her father worked extremely long hours. Bridget did not like that her parents had such unequal childrearing and financial responsibilities and wanted to organize her household differently. "I never made a conscious decision of yes, you have to stop working, or yes, you will keep working. My career was important to me. I liked what I did. I got a lot of fulfillment out of it and I thought that I could balance both and still be a good mom." Most of the women agreed with their spouse or partner over both partners' work status, however, some couples had fundamental disagreements, which created ongoing conflict. Several women felt they did not have a choice to stay home because they were the primary breadwinner, or because their family relied on two incomes, although there was considerable variation in what constituted enough money to live on. For example, a primary breadwinner earning $50,000 may be sufficient for one two parent family, whereas, another family may not consider this income adequate to support a family.

## DAYCARE AND WORKPLACE ENVIRONMENTS

Daycare and workplace environments were also important factors in women's decision to work or stay home. Some women who stayed home full time with their first child tended to have anxiety about putting their child in daycare. When Jackie found out she was pregnant, "my biggest fear was, 'Oh my God, I'm going to have to send my kid to daycare,' and that terrified me." She and her husband have made financial sacrifices so she could be home with the kids. A few women planned to resume work, but were not able to do it when the time came. Midway through Robin's eight-week maternity leave she became anxious about leaving her baby at daycare. She decided to quit because "I didn't want someone else to raise my kids. I wanted to do it. I just couldn't drop them off at daycare five days a week."

The women who worked full time were generally happy with their daycare arrangements. "With your firstborn, you feel like they are the most precious thing in the whole world and nobody else knows how to take care of them," observed Brooke. "Even you don't know how to take care of them! We were kind of nervous about putting him in daycare, but the baby room was wonderful, and we loved it." Kelly likes that her daughter goes to daycare "because she's exposed to a diverse set of people teaching her different parenting styles, and she interacts with different kinds of kids, and she's very social as a result."

High quality childcare is "associated with enhanced social skills, reduced behavior problems, increased cooperation, and improved language in children," with "no detrimental effects of infants' attachment relations with their mothers as long as mothers provide adequate attention to infants at home."[8] The monthly cost of accredited childcare for one infant and one preschooler is extremely expensive in Minnesota, therefore several women I interviewed quit work when their second child was born because they would either lose money or break even after they paid for daycare.[9] Most women calculated daycare costs against their salary, which reveals the assumption that women should either care for their children or be responsible for paying for it. Studies have shown that costly daycare significantly impedes the employment of married mothers.[10]

## WORKPLACE CONSTRAINTS

Several women who had full-time demanding jobs, and whose partner was also working a high pressure job, either found another full-time job at a more "family friendly" company, cut back their hours to part-time, or quit to stay home full time. None of the women who quit their job due to excessive workforce demands, expressed anger at the institution, nor expected that their workplace had any obligation to accommodate them in any way.

Kelly worked at least sixty hours a week before her child was born and knew she could not continue working this pace after the baby was born, so she negotiated with the company to reduce her position to four days a week. Kelly said it took her almost a year to realize that:

> the four-day work schedule was probably harder than five days because I was pressured to try to put everything in those four days. On the fifth day, when I was supposed to be off with my daughter, which meant I had her and I didn't have alternate care, I was on the phone all the time with clients and my team anyway.

She feels that working four days, and therefore being paid eighty percent of her full-time salary, was an "expensive experiment" because she ended up doing a full-time workload without full compensation. Kelly got a position with another firm that she thought was more "family-friendly" because a full-time position would not require her to put in sixty hours a week.

Many women felt that pumping breast milk in the workplace was one of the more difficult aspects of returning to work. "I would pump twice a day at work," commented Brooke. "I just hated pumping. I had my own office, but the firm was run by old white men, who were prepared to be supportive of the idea, but it also totally freaked them out. Whenever my door was closed, they would give me a 15-foot berth, because you know, her boobs might be out (laughter)." Pumping during extended travel was very difficult for Kelly. She found someone to cover her longer trips while she was nursing, however, she still was required to travel for one or two day trips. "I found it really draining and hard. I was trying to pump on the road, when I'm meeting with clients, and in airports with no facilities. I just kind of suffered through it." When she left her job, she suggested that giving women an extra couple of months with no travel after a maternity leave would make it a lot easier.

Celeste was responsible for generating millions of dollars in revenue each quarter for a Fortune 500 company. After she had her first child, "my bosses and the executive staff were waiting to see, was this a mommy who would be willing to go all the way and sacrifice her family to get to the top?" After her second child was born, she transferred to a job within the company that was supposed to have limited travel requirements. However, Celeste's business travel kept increasing, and because the nature of her job was "all consuming," it began to take a toll on her.

> I hit the wall, and I just couldn't keep it up. I was losing weight and drinking coffee. I put the kids to bed at eight, trying to keep up on this high-powered thing. I was up at midnight doing emails every night. I wasn't sleeping, I was doing work. I worked so many hours I can't even tell you, but not in the hours between five and eight when my kids were around. It was so hard.

During this stressful time her husband said, "Something has got to give. If you don't quit, I have to. We just can't keep this up." When Celeste found out that her travel requirements were going to increase even more, she decided to quit, which may appear that she was "opting out" of the workforce, but her job demands kept escalating beyond the scope of the original job expectations.

## POSITIVE AND NEGATIVE ASPECTS OF STAYING HOME WITH CHILDREN

Overall, stay-at-home mothers expressed appreciation that they were able to spend time with their children, although sometimes this time could seem "boring" or "unending." Haley remarked, "I complain a lot about being a mom, but the good definitely outnumbers the bad experiences." Women also liked that they did not have the pressure of getting their young children out the door in the morning, and many enjoyed connecting with other parents who were also home with children. "It's like having your own business," commented Erica. "Yes, you're working 24 hours a day, but you're the one that's calling the shots, and that's what I like about it the most. I run my own small business."[11]

Everyone commented that the work of full-time mothering is time-consuming, and felt annoyed when people assumed they had ample amounts of free time to do other things. Many stay-at-home mothers felt that society does not value what they do as work, and some felt patronized by people who assumed that stay-at-home mothers had few interests outside of their children. I heard many variations of stories where women's interactions with strangers at a social event were abruptly cut short when the person found out they were a stay-at-home mother. "I keep up with the news, and I am well-read," remarked one stay-at-home mother, "but people assume I can only talk about my kids."

Women who were out of the workforce for a significant amount of time found it difficult to find a job when they were ready to return to work. Oftentimes going back to their old career was not an option because they had lost so much ground. Even though some women had done amazing volunteer work, they felt that potential employers did not value their skill set because it was not paid labor. Several women took jobs well below their educational level to have flexibility or because they felt it was the only path to re-entering the workforce. Some women had to do some "soul-searching" to figure out a life plan once they were not fully immersed in caring for children. "It took me a while just to figure out again who I was not in relation to being a mom," commented Mary. "I didn't keep up with the other dimensions of my life very well." Many stay-at-home mothers wished there were more options for part-time work that would coordinate with their children's school schedule.

## POSITIVE AND NEGATIVE ASPECTS OF WORKING FULL TIME

Full-time working mothers expressed joy about working and parenting, but found the workload challenging at times. Some felt that balancing everything was easier because they had an equal partnership with their spouse or partner, whereas others still did the bulk of childcare and housework. Some working single mothers had great support networks, whereas others did not. Most women liked that their children could see them in a role outside of being a mother. Tara believes that working full time in a job that she loves is "a huge gift to give my kids, especially my daughter." Even though Tara is "100% clear" that there is no negative impact to her children being in daycare, there are good days and bad days. "Some days I ask myself, 'Am I missing out on things, and spending time with them', and some days the answer is yes and some days no. In a perfect world, I'd be able to have more time with them and still do this."

Bridget also finds her job rewarding, and believes it is good for her kids to see that she believes in what she is doing. However, the hardest thing about balancing full-time work and mothering is all of the expectations. "There are expectations that you will perform well at your job, that you will be the room mother, that you'll be on the field trip." Bridget finds that it can be a challenge for her and her husband to meet their responsibilities and "continue to be responsive to the kids' needs, and to coach, and fulfill other specific responsibilities besides just working and raising our kids." Bridget and her husband routinely have to negotiate who gets to stay late at work.

Katie enjoys working full time and felt that it was important to communicate to her daughter, "I like my work and I could even be the primary breadwinner." Her husband has taken on many of the childcare responsibilities, however, one of the conflicts Katie felt was, "As much as I wanted to work and wanted him to pick up some of those pieces, I still wanted to be doing those pieces. It wasn't like, 'Oh good, now that's taken care of.' In my heart, I still wanted to be the one who was driving her, picking her up, and doing homework with her."

Kelly does not think of herself as a "working mom," instead she makes the distinction that "I enjoy being a mom and I enjoy working." She feels she would not "function very well not having something to focus on outside of home and family." Her current job is immensely rewarding as is spending time with her daughter. "I love the workplace. I love doing well at what I do. I appreciate that I'm successful, and I make good money and I have an exciting job. I love all those things. Whereas I also love being a parent and spending time with my daughter. I think I'm a better parent because I have other things to think about other than my child."[12]

## POSITIVE AND NEGATIVE ASPECTS OF BEING A PART-TIME WORKING MOTHER

Many mothers settled on working part-time, often after working full-time, or being home full-time. Most part-time working mothers felt that working part-time gave them a better work/life balance. Some felt that working part time helped them avoid being judged by both the negative stereotypes of full-time working mothers and stay-at-home mothers.

While most felt they had the "best of both worlds," some women felt they were not fully part of either world. "There's this perception that you're not committed when you only work 30 hours a week," commented Gloria. She is grateful that she has had the flexibility to work three days a week, but she feels, "You're not included in certain things even though you have to work just as hard as anybody who's doing full time just to keep up. I feel like you're punished. I think that career wise I would be in a completely different place if I didn't work part-time, and I'm trying not to have regrets about that and remember all the reasons I chose to do this."

Caroline made a "tortured" decision to quit her job and stay home full-time after her first child was born. However, being home full-time "drove me insane because I was home 24/7." When her second child was born, she knew she had to do something to get out of the house, so she found a part-time job where the pay was horrible, but the hours were flexible. She told her husband, "I know by the time I pay the babysitter and pay for parking, it's going to be a wash, but it's cheaper than therapy." What Caroline loved the most about the re-entry into the work force was having someone say, "Nice job." "You don't get that as a stay-at-home mom. Nobody says, 'Wow, you're working really hard.'"

Alexis had no idea what her workplace maternity leave policy was until she became pregnant. When she read the policy, she was "floored" by how bad it was, and "made a big stink about it." The new president of the company was a woman who was not aware of the policy, and quickly moved to change it. What surprised Alexis was that there were other women in her office who were also pregnant, and none of them had said anything about the terrible policy. When aspects of the workplace created work-family conflict, most women did not say anything, switched jobs within the company, or left the organization. In addition to changing the maternity leave policy, Alexis's company accommodated her request to job share after her maternity leave ended, which has made her "incredibly loyal" to her organization.

## THE "MOMMY WARS"

We often assume that working mothers and stay-at-home mothers are homogenous groups of women, when in fact they are not. I observed that not all stay-at-home mothers stay home for the same reasons, nor do all working mothers work for the same reasons.[13] The concept of the "Mommy Wars" did not resonate with most mothers. A few women reported isolated incidents of conflict with another mother based on her work status, however most of the women in my sample were supportive of the work choices of their friends, relatives, and neighbors. Women were also sympathetic to the workload of mothers with a different work status, often because they have the perspective of experiencing different work-home trajectories themselves. Rachel expressed appreciation for stay-at-home mothers and "what they've committed to, because there are many times as it relates to school things, they're picking up the slack on stuff that I can't do." Most women went out of their way to be respectful of mothers with a different work status.

Haley, who is at home full time, has many friends with children who are working outside the home full time. "We're just trying to support each other. We're going through the same thing with our kids whether we go through it 12 hours out of the day if we're staying home with them, or the 4-5 hours we get with them at night." Haley feels that most of her friends who work feel pressure that they should be staying home, whereas she feels pressure to work because people do not see staying home with children as a job. Erica believes there is "a big misunderstanding between each camp as to how much time the other one has." Both stay-at-home mothers and working mothers consistently felt they did not have enough time to get everything done

Claire has noticed that when she meets a working mother and states that she is a stay-at-home mother, "there's this little silence, and we don't know what to talk about, because I don't know how they feel about what I do, and they might have an impression about what I think about them working." Women tended to have more friends who have the same work circumstances. Some felt this was primarily because they had similar schedules, while others, like Holly, believed that, "Women align ourselves with friends in our same situation because it helps you feel supported, especially when the grass is always greener on the other side." I also heard several stories of stay-at-home mothers and working mothers supporting each other.

Brooke observes that the judgment she "feels" from other people is probably self-imposed. Brooke thinks her perception of the "Mommy Wars" comes from the fact that she projects her own insecurities onto what other people—in particular stay-at-home moms—may be thinking about her. She compares herself to her sister-in-law who is currently home full time. "Literally every aspect of her domestic life is a vision of perfection, and my domestic life is just a big fat joke." Brooke sometimes assumes her sister-in-law is being judgmental about her life even when her sister-in-law has never said anything. Brooke is starting to realize "I'm judging myself through this impossible standard and bouncing it off stay-at-home moms."

Lily used to think that it was okay for women to choose whether they wanted to stay at home or continue working.

> Seeing so many acquaintances get divorced and then not having their own income to fall back on, or a career to support themselves and their children, has made me believe that all women should seriously consider continuing to work after they have children so that they are always able to support themselves.

This is another twist on the time verses financial resources judgment in that Lily believes a woman should never jeopardize her ability to support herself or her children by not working outside the home.

Women overwhelmingly expressed their admiration and compassion for single mothers. Some also recognized the classism in our portrayal and opinions of stay-at-home mothers and working mothers. One urban mother remarked, "There is more value in the mother at home, but only if you're middle-class, or wealthy, but if you don't have a lot of money, and you decide to stay home, then there is judgment that you should be working." Laurel West argues that the "Mommy Wars" sets up a competition between the "Soccer Moms" (i.e. stay-at-home mothers) and the "Super Moms" (i.e. career-oriented mothers) in a battle for the "ideal construction of motherhood;" while the "Welfare Queen" (i.e. single mother on welfare) and the "Waitress Mom" (i.e. poor, working mother) are not even candidates for the cultural ideal.[14]

## WORKPLACE EQUITY FOR PARENTS

Sheila feels fortunate to be working in an office where people work well together, and there is "no looking down on each other." She believes the "environment of fairness" at her workplace is because her company offers flextime, so no one feels that people who have children get more time off than people who do not have kids. However, many women had stories of workplace tension between people with children and people who do not have children. Bridget believes that the people without children in her workplace perceive that the people with children get advantages. "They are very resentful of the fact that people with kids have hard cut-offs when they have to leave on specific days." When Kelly was responsible for assigning people to accounts and making promotion decisions, she often heard complaints from younger people who did not have children about people who did have children. Most of the conversations were, "Why does so and so get to leave at 5?" She would advise the complainers to focus on their own work because by the time someone has kids, they are usually more established in their careers and are "either more efficient in their jobs, or have put in a good deal of time over the years."

Tara manages a large group of people where some have children, and some do not. She knows "there's a tension with parents being out more than other people," and thinks there is some resentment toward people with children. She tries to be fair in scheduling time off requests, and feels that all employees need to be accountable regardless of whether they have children. Rachel, who has also managed employees, thinks that it is important for working parents to have contingency plans. "You've got to know who is your back up if your kid is sick, because you can't just call in every time." Rachel clarified that she is thinking about it in the context of white collar privilege. "I'm not thinking through the lens of the single mom who's working two jobs just to pay rent. But in my demographic, if you choose to work, you need to deal with it."

There is a motherhood wage penalty for women throughout the world. In the United States, the gap in earnings between women with children, and women who do not have children is greater than the gap between women and men. Studies indicate that reduction in hours alone is not enough to account for the wage differential. A recent experiment revealed that mothers in the workforce are subject to "status-based discrimination" where "evaluators rated mothers as less competent and committed to paid work than non-mothers and consequently discriminated against mothers when making hiring and salary decisions."[15] In contrast, fathers were seen as "more committed to paid work" and received higher salaries than men without children. This same study also found that "real employers discriminate against mothers" in that mothers are less likely to get job interviews than women who are not mothers.[16] This shows how negative stereotypes about mothers have real life consequences.

In *Lean In: Women, Work, and the Will to Lead*, Sheryl Sandberg notes that the revolution to create equality has stalled. "A truly equal world would be one where women ran half our countries and companies and men ran half our homes."[17] Sandberg argues that we need to take down institutional barriers that prevent more women from assuming leadership positions, that women need to get rid of their internal barriers to gaining power, and that men need to be more supportive of women in the workplace and in the home. Part of the individual and institutional work to create greater equality for women and men lies in dismantling our negative stereotypes about all mothers. Being a mother does not make a person boring, or less capable, or less likely to be committed to doing a good job in the workforce, nor does working make a mother less capable of caring for children. These are ridiculous stereotypes, yet they contribute to the systemic status-based discrimination and negative judgments of all mothers in our culture.

# Part 2

# The Work of Mothers

Most mothers in this country work hard to do the best they can for their children on a daily basis, within the constraints of their time, energy, financial resources, community expectations, and perceptions about what their children need. Yet, American parents are often subject to criticism. Journalist Pamela Druckerman spells it out in the introduction to *Bringing Up Bébé*: "I'm hardly the first to point out that middle-class America has a parenting problem. In hundreds of books and articles this problem has been painstakingly diagnosed, critiqued, and named: overparenting, hyperparenting, [and] helicopter-parenting."[1] There are indeed many books and articles claiming that Americans are "helicopter"[2] or "snowplow" parents,[3] raising children, who are spoiled,[4] entitled,[5] materialistic,[6] narcissistic,[7] and lazy.[8]

Are parents of this generation more involved in raising their children than parents of the previous generation? It appears that they are. Yet, we seldom ask the next logical question: Why are parents more involved than they were a generation ago? One reason is that parents feel enormous individual responsibility for ensuring the physical, emotional, mental, financial, and spiritual wellbeing of their children, in an environment where many middle-class parents have lost faith that their children will "naturally" be okay without a significant amount of parental investment.

Another reason is that factors in our current cultural environment have affected the wellbeing of American children who are experiencing higher rates of anxiety, depression, eating disorders, attention-deficit disorder (ADD), attention-deficit-hyperactivity disorder (ADHD), autism, learning disabilities, asthma, food allergies, and obesity. Many mothers spend a great deal of time and energy dealing with the ramifications of physical, emotional, or mental distress in their children. The second half of this book shows how social changes have affected childrearing, which in turn has significantly increased the workload, expectations, and pressure for today's parents.

# Chapter 6

## Keeping Kids Safe

I attended a baby shower where the mother-to-be opened a present that contained, among other things, a small plastic cylinder. She held up the cylinder, looking perplexed, until the woman who gave her the gift explained that the cylinder measured things that were potential choking hazards. The logic being that if something could fit into the cylinder it could fit into a baby or toddler's mouth. One of the women in the older generation broke into laughter when she heard the explanation, exclaiming, "It's a wonder any of you survived! We didn't strap you into car seats, there were no bike helmets, and we didn't even think about choking hazards!" The other mothers of the older generation laughed along, interjecting their own examples of practices that by current standards seemed ridiculously unsafe.

The issue of safety, or perhaps more accurately, a mother's anxiety about a child's wellbeing, came up repeatedly in my interviews and focus groups. Every mother echoed the sentiment that the world feels so much less safe for children of this generation than it did when they were growing up. The word "freedom" came up countless times as women nostalgically recalled their childhood days where they rode their bike around their neighborhood or town, and spent hours playing outdoors with neighborhood kids. Most women felt that the freedom they experienced was one of the best things about their childhood and they genuinely felt sad that their children do not have the same level of freedom that they did growing up. However, when they compared the stories of their childhood experiences with today's standards, most thought it was unimaginable to give their children the same level of autonomy that they enjoyed. As Emily explained:

> When I was a kid, I rode my bike downtown everyday in the summer, which was a mile or two away, and I don't remember setting a certain time when I would be back. Now, if my kids are getting together with friends it's a pre-arranged play date, and I know exactly where they are going to be all the time.

In fact, ninety-nine percent of the mothers I surveyed with a child under age ten, always or usually knew where their child was at all times.

Sheila commented that her husband's parents sent him to visit his grandparents on a Greyhound bus when he was five years old. "The bus driver knew that he was by himself, and he would look out for him, but can you imagine putting your kid on a bus by himself at five?" She believes that even though statistically the incidence of bad things happening to children is lower than it has ever been, "our perception of it is so heightened, from stranger danger, to getting hit by cars, and dying of accidents and illnesses. Kids' safety is at an all time high, and yet we think of it as at an all time low, and that's a curious cultural shift that I can't account for." Sheila raises an important question. Why do we have such a heightened perception of childhood danger?

## LIVING IN A RISK SOCIETY

Every mother felt that she worried about her children's safety much more than her parents ever did. "There wasn't the mentality of being so afraid," commented Andrea. Women worried about things such as: whether their child would "fit in" at school; the quality of education; the safety of schools; the environment; abduction; molestation; physical safety; illness; mental illness; eating disorders; drinking; drugs; sex; and many other things.

Anthropological studies of 1960s American mothers who lived in "Orchard Town," a New England community, found that mothers were most worried about "busy thoroughfares."[1] The concepts of child abduction, sexual predators, eating disorders, and a host of other things mothers are currently worried about were not part of the Orchard Town mothers' consciousness of potential physical and social dangers.[2] This does not mean that bad things did not happen to children in the 1950s and 1960s, or that parents did not worry about their children.[3] The difference is that parents of the 50s, 60s, and 70s, were not in the habit of envisioning and preventing every possible risk their child could potentially be exposed to, and most people had faith that their children were safe walking to school, or playing outside by themselves in their yard and neighborhood.

When did this shift in our awareness of safety and risk occur? German sociologist Ulrich Beck and British sociologist Anthony Giddens coined the term "risk society" to describe the phenomenon that began in the late 1970s in the United States and other market-driven countries where people began to develop a heightened awareness of risk. Risk does not simply refer to new forms of danger, but rather is a way of thinking where people are aware that their present actions will affect future outcomes. In this scenario, our ability to envision potential danger means that we must either be individually responsible for using precautions to prevent future misfortune from occurring, or endure the social responsibility for the consequences of our decisions if they lead to a bad outcome. Our awareness of risk has infiltrated how we think about everything, and has transformed how we perceive the world.

We have become skilled at anticipating future catastrophes, or even little things that could potentially go wrong, and media outlets frequently try to predict potential future outcomes of any event.[4] In other words, we tend to split our attention between the present moment, and the future. For example, we put on sunscreen not only to prevent sunburn in the present, but also to prevent wrinkles and skin cancer in the future. Our awareness of risk may not seem like that big of a deal since it is so common-place in our society, but it has exponentially increased pressure for today's parents because we expect that mothers in particular, should be able to anticipate and prevent every possible thing that could be detrimental to their child's wellbeing today and in the future. Parent education classes, magazines, and books routinely offer parents safety tips about common household dangers.[5] For the most part, parents are always willing to take precautions to create a safe environment for their children. Our laws, warning labels on products, and educational campaigns that have raised our collective awareness about childhood safety have no doubt prevented many childhood injuries and deaths.

Every mother I spoke with had to come to terms with what she was going to worry about, and what she could reasonably control. When Sylvia's children were young, she made a con-scious decision to try to control the controllable.

> I decided seatbelts, helmets, and sunscreen were the three things that I was going to be worked up about because those are three things that are totally in my control, and they are three things that have a huge impact on my kids' health, safety, and wellbeing. I decided I can't worry about everything all the time.

Oftentimes mothers worried the most about events outside of their control, and worried less about the mundane risks that they felt they had control over. In *The World Until Yesterday: What We Can Learn from Traditional Societies*, Pulitzer prize winning author Jared Diamond compares our cultural obsession with low risk dangers we have little control over with traditional soci-ety's attention to low-risk actions that a person can control.[6] Americans "obsess about the wrong things, and we fail to watch for real dangers," Diamond writes as he describes our tendency to "exaggerate the risks of events that are beyond our control," while underestimating the risks of mundane events within our control.[7]

Some women were able to deliberately choose what to worry about and what to let go, whereas others felt they had no control over the issues that piqued their anxiety. In *The Science of Fear: Why We Fear the Things We Shouldn't—and Put Ourselves in Greater Danger*, Dan Gardner notes, "We are the healthiest, wealthiest, and longest-living people in history. And we are increasingly afraid. This is one of the greatest paradoxes of our time."[8] Gardner's book on how the brain processes fear sheds light on why our collective anxiety level is so high. Gardner explains that our brain has two systems it uses to make judgments and draw conclusions: feeling and reason. Our reasoning brain works slowly and deliberately to analyze evidence, and consider all sides of a problem. It makes calculations at the conscious level so when a person makes a decision based on reason, it is usually easy to explain how she came to her conclusions. In contrast, our feeling brain processes information at lightening speed, often at the subconscious level, and it is responsible for our snap judgments, intuition, and hunches. When an individual makes a decision based on the feeling part of her brain, it is hard to articulate her reasons for the decision.

The two systems frequently work together, with the feeling part of one's brain making routine snap judgments, often based on little evidence, which is then passed into the conscious mind where the reasoning part of one's brain makes adjustments to the conclusions. Fear is the product of one's feeling mind. The feeling brain uses three rules when getting its information. First, the feeling brain uses the "anchoring rule," which means that when we have to make a guess or a decision about a number that we are not sure about, our feeling brain grabs hold of the most recent number it was exposed to as a starting point. Then the thinking brain adjusts the value, but the final guess or decision tends to lean toward the initial anchor number. Advertisers, news and entertainment producers, and politicians understand this tendency of the brain and use it to manipulate public opinion.

"The rule of typical things" is the second rule, so if a person is able to *quickly* come up with an example of something, then their feeling brain judges that situation as common, and more probable. The third rule is the "example rule," which is the process where your feeling brain looks for examples to make its judgments. Gardner notes that it is not the examples themselves that are important, but rather how easily your brain can come up with an example.[9]

Humans learn and remember their own experiences along with the experiences of others, and people are more likely to remember things that evoke a sense of fear. The unconscious part of our brain does not discern between reality and fiction, so it stores all of the images we see in the news, television shows, and movies, as examples of events that have happened. Since our feeling brain has access to all of our unconscious images, we think that being able to quickly come up with an example, or vividly imagine a scenario, indicates that it is a common situation, which is likely to happen. This triggers our intuition, which makes something feel plausible.

Many other factors influence our perception. We tend to remember unusual, vivid, emotional, traumatic, and negative images and events, more than mundane things. Once we have a belief in place, our tendency toward "confirmation bias" means that we screen the information we see and hear in such a way to support our beliefs. The people we associate with influence us because the more people we know who share our beliefs, the more certain we become that these beliefs are correct. Our culture also guides our attention, beliefs, and actions.

The snap judgment mechanisms our feeling brain uses were very important for the survival of early humans. The problem for us today is that the information our brain draws on to make snap judgments is skewed by the images and reports we see and hear in the media.[10] At the same time as our society's awareness of risk was increasing, there was a rise in broadcast media. In 1980, CNN became the first twenty-four hour news channel, which ushered in a new era of around the clock news coverage. Parents used to primarily be exposed to local incidents, however this era of 24/7 media saturation makes national news feel local, filling people's "feeling brains" with vivid examples of danger, and heightening people's perception that unlikely scenarios could happen to their children.[11] Gardener suggests that we need to rationally correct "our mistakes of intuition" by having greater awareness of the scientific process behind our decision making.

Our cultural perception that the world is less safe is not just a "natural" reaction to the changing times. In fact, market forces contribute to the wide-scale dissemination of stories that deliberately promote fear in our culture. As media outlets compete for people's attention, they have figured out that fear is an excellent way to get people to notice something. Politicians use fear to rally their base, the news and infotainment media use fear to bolster their viewership, and advertisers use fear to market and sell products. Caryl Rivers argues that it is profitable to "sell anxiety to women the way that advertising sells insecurity about their faces, body, and sex appeal."[12] With the increased segmentation of our media market, there are countless news, entertainment, and shopping outlets vying for our attention, who use misleading, dramatic, frightening, sensational, and emotionally charged headlines and images in hopes that it will make us pause for just a second to view their content. This fills people's minds with unrealistic images of danger that our feeling brain then uses as a catalogue of "typical things" and "examples." The misleading statistics we often hear gives our brain an unrealistic "anchor" from which to draw conclusions and make judgments.

## THE RISE OF STRANGER DANGER

More than three decades of news stories that simultaneously emphasize childhood dangers, and the importance of safety, have created deeply engrained worries and fears in the psyches of many mothers.[13] In particular, mothers' fear of stranger-abduction and sexual predators has led to a dramatic increase in this generation's vigilance over their children's activities out-side of the home. According to the Crimes Against Children Research Center, there are four myths about missing children that are commonly believed to be true. The first myth is that most children have been abducted by strangers. Stranger abduction accounts for only 1/100th of 1 percent of missing children, which means that statistically a child has a 1 in 1.5 million chance of being abducted by a stranger, and never being returned. The second myth is that more children are going missing. Missing person reports of people of all ages, including children, are down by about 31 percent. The third myth is that the internet has made kidnapping easier. Internet predators are not randomly looking for children online, but are more likely to target children who are communicating online with strangers, going to sexually oriented sites, or appearing online as sexualized personas. The fourth myth is that prevention of childhood abduction and abuse lies in teaching children to avoid strangers. The reality is that in 93% of reported sexual abuse cases, the child knows the offender, and in half of the cases, the perpetrator is a close or extended family member.[14] Since kids are more likely to be abducted or molested by people they know, it is better to teach children how to tell if someone is acting inappropriately.

The U.S. Department of Justice issued a report on the National Incidence Studies of Missing, Abducted, Runaway, and Thrown Away Children (NISMART). The report notes that out of 70 million American children and teenagers, there are approximately fifty kids each year abducted by a stranger and murdered, or never returned. We probably hear about every American child abducted by a stranger who has been missing for more than a day, and each time our hearts go out to the parents as we hope and pray for the safe return of their child. Technically, the risk is of this happening to any one child is considered "de minimis," which means that statistically "it is so small that it is beyond concern, or equivalent to no risk at all."[15] However, because our mind can quickly come up with examples of abducted children, and because we can vividly imagine the terror, grief, and guilt, we would feel if it happened to us, many parents are incredibly fearful of child abduction. Parents who have lost their child in a store or crowded area for even a minute have felt panic rise in them when they worry that someone has taken their child. Parents who live in a geographic area where a child has been abducted experience heightened anxiety because the unthinkable happened to someone in their community.

Stranger danger was vivid in the minds of several mothers, often raising their anxiety level every single day as they tried to manage their child's environment to prevent bad things from happening. Amy feels so "stressed-out" about abduction and watches her daughter carefully whenever she is outdoors.

> If my daughter wants to walk two houses down to visit a friend, I stand on the sidewalk and watch her ring the doorbell, and I wait until she goes into the house and the mother waves at me. I make her call me before she leaves. If she's in the back yard I sit outside, or am constantly looking out the window. I am totally stressed out when she's in our fenced in back yard. The world is wacky. I just don't understand if there's more wacky people or if it's the internet that's just making it where we hear more about it now.

Even though mothers understood that media sources try to scare them, many still felt afraid

Kim's biggest fear is sexual abuse because her parents, who were both social workers within the penal system, witnessed many "alarming situations." Kim also works in a field where she is in contact with people who are in and out of the criminal justice system. She knows there are "dangerous folks" in the community who are not always supervised or supported.

> My biggest concern is sexual predators. When they're in school, do I really know who their teacher is? My son was just at a birthday party at The Children's Theater and

I told him, "You can't go to the bathroom while you're there. You can't ever be alone." I don't know how to explain that to him without really scaring him.

While Kim was genuinely fearful of sexual predators, she also joked about her own level of anxiety. Like many mothers, she struggles with finding a balance between teaching her child to be aware of potential dangerous situations without scaring him.

## SOCIAL PRESSURE TO BE VIGILANT AND THE THINGS MOTHERS WORRY ABOUT

Mothers talked about the social pressure they feel to be vigilant of their child's neighborhood activities. Maria gives her children a fair amount of freedom on their city block; however, she realizes that not everyone is comfortable with her kids being alone outside. "I've had people kind of give me looks." She feels that there is a widespread belief that "if anything happens to a child, someone must have done something wrong for it to happen because you should always be able to prevent any possibility instead of letting them take the risks." Maria's comments get to the heart of what it is like to live in a risk society.

Several women talked about the Silver Springs, Maryland family who in 2015 were investigated by the Montgomery County Child Protection Services (CPS) for letting their ten- and six-year-old children play alone at a neighborhood park, and later allowing them to walk home by themselves along a busy street. CPS found the children's parents to be responsible for "unsubstantiated" child neglect. "Where did the idea come from that a child by themselves at a park is in danger?" asked Josie. "We have people in our neighborhood who called the police because kids were playing at the park by themselves. It makes you feel like, oh my God, if I'm not there, they're going to call the cops." Josie realizes that sometimes she over-parents, "but you feel judged if you're letting your child do things without adult supervision." This creates another source of stress in the lives of mothers who may fear that letting their children play alone at a neighborhood park will create a legal crisis.

Rachel's kids are home by themselves during the summer, and she worries that some of the stay-at-home mothers in the neighborhood are thinking, "'Oh God, her damn kid is always at my house.' Am I the working mom in my neighborhood where everyone is sick of my kid? I tell the parents I know well, 'If you get sick of my son, just send him home.' I worry that I'm getting judged as being the mom that's not watching her kids." These stories indicate that there are three social forces women worry about when they give their children freedom in their neighborhood: fear of "stranger danger;" worry that an unaccompanied child will create a legal crisis; and awareness that others may judge them for letting their kids be on their own.

Carla feels that having children has made her feel so much more "vulnerable to the world" than she did before she had children. On the other hand, Brooke observed that she used to have a lot of "ambient anxiety" before she had children. "I would lie in bed and worry about work things or global things. I was stressed out a lot, but when I had kids that went away." She attributes this to the fact that "I no longer had the luxury of distant worry. I had so many real things to worry about and get done (laughter)."

Most mothers tried to find a balance between promoting safety, not making their child afraid, and allowing their children some freedom. Emily feels that there is a fine line between protecting her children and giving them the freedom to explore so they "do not grow up in fear." Abby worries about the long-term affects of children and teens not having any freedom. As Rachel's kids get older, she is more anxious because of the "severity of some of the decisions your kid can make now." She wants to give her high school daughter freedom, but she also wants to guide her enough so she doesn't go "off the rails." "I'm sure I'm over-worried, but the stakes are just so much higher. You hear about so many kids that go down the eating disorder path, or the drug path. I don't want to fret over nothing but I don't want to be naïve either."

Most mothers of teenagers were aware of the serious issues many American teens face such as eating disorders, drinking, drug use, depression, anxiety, and inflicting self-harm. Women had additional worries about girls, and many mothers had cautioned their teenage daughters to be careful on dates, to never leave their drink unattended at a party, and to follow their gut if they ever felt unsafe. "I think we've ruined our daughter going to college because she's so afraid of a lot of things," observed Josie. "We have to be careful of making girls fearful all the time. Damn, I hate that. We still live in a world where what we have to teach our daughters instills fears. Protect yourself. Watch out for this." Celeste was comfortable giving her two boys a fair amount of freedom in their city neighborhood, however she feels it is harder now that she has a ten-year-old daughter "who wants all this freedom." This suggests that parents tend to be more protective of girls.

When I give presentations about the changes in our cultural perception of safety, parents often ask me, "What can I do so I don't feel so afraid all the time?" In *Free Range Kids: Giving Our Children Freedom We Had Without Going Nuts with Worry*, Lenore Skenazy offers advice to parents on how to feel less afraid in this fear-based society. She suggests that parents reduce their level of news exposure. People who watch more media content that induces fear tend to be more fearful, however, it is impossible to say whether watching anxiety-provoking content leads to being more fearful, or whether someone who is more fearful is likely to read or watch fear-provoking stories.[16] She also states that when you feel yourself worrying about something in relation to your child, get very specific about what you are actually worrying about, instead of just thinking that "something terrible" could happen. If you think about a specific scenario, then think about whether or not your child would be able to handle that situation. She also encourages parents to trust themselves as a parent, trust their child's judgment, and to remember that the odds are against something terrible happening to a child. It is also helpful to rationally correct "our mistakes of intuition" as Dan Gardener suggests.[17] Breathing evenly and deeply also helps people when they are feeling stressed.

There has been a fair amount of criticism of American parents for being "helicopter" parents. The discussion of over-involved parents, which is usually about a mother's level of involvement, has been divorced from the cultural shifts to which mothers are responding.[18] We live in a country where we have a keen awareness of risk; with access to unprecedented levels of news, media, and information; where there is market pressure to promote fear; judgment of mothers; and social pressure to be vigilant of our children. These cultural changes have affected the behavior of parents. The impact of these cultural shifts means that middle-class mothers no longer assume that their children will "naturally" be okay, and the ripple effects of this belief have dramatically increased the workload and stress level of individual mothers. The fact that many American children do not roam their neighborhoods freely means that children spend less time outdoors, and do not "naturally" get enough exercise anymore.[19] This means that parents now must manage two things children used to do on their own, namely, get exercise and play with friends. I found that mothers, were the parent most often responsible for making sure their kids get exercise, arranging play dates, and finding activities for their children to participate where they can ideally get exercise and be with friends. In the chapters that follow, I show how today's parenting norms are all related to significant changes in our culture.

# Chapter 7

# Raising Healthy Kids

## NUTRITION, EXERCISE, AND BODY IMAGE

Jess worries because her son is a "big boy." "He's a 66 pound 5-year-old boy, and I put every morsel of food in him—organic eggs, and soy milk, and pineapple, and an occasional donut. I worry about his weight already. He's off the charts and he doesn't stop. He came out big. He's active and athletic and strong, but I worry about somebody teasing him because he's big." It bothers Jess that his brother and other neighborhood kids have called him fat although she realizes that the strong emotional reaction she has to her son's weight stems in part from the fact that she has worried about her own size since she was in kindergarten. For Holly, getting her children to eat is one of her biggest challenges. "My kids never say, 'Mom, I'm hungry.' They don't seem to like eating that much and it's hard because I don't think I'm giving them enough balanced nutrition. I feel like other people are judgmental about my kids and think they are brats because they don't eat." Tanya, whose relationship with food is "fraught," is learning what nutritional value means verses eating what you like. "It's probably the place around my parenting where I most feel like I have not done what I would love to do with my kids because I worry about what I am teaching them about good choices." Missy is almost certain that her teenage daughter is trying to keep her weight down in an unhealthy way.

Today's mothers face significant challenges raising healthy kids in a culture that has so many mixed messages around food and body image. The United States idealizes thin bodies, while at the same time the food and beverage industry spends $25 billion per year promoting unhealthy food and beverages.[1] The number of Americans who are overweight has significantly increased since the 1970s, when obesity rates for adults hovered around 11%, and less than 5% of children were obese.[2] Surveys conducted in 2011-12 indicate that 66% of American adults, 22% of 2- to 5-year-olds, and 34% of 6- to 19-year-olds, are overweight or obese.[3] Medical experts warn that the "obesity epidemic" is a serious public crisis, and that children and teenagers who are obese are at greater risk for developing high blood pressure, high cholesterol, pre-diabetes, Type 2 diabetes, bone and joint problems, and sleep apnea. They also have a higher chance of being overweight or obese as adults. Overweight youth are also more likely to be stigmatized, or have low self-esteem, both of which can contribute to psychological or social problems.[4]

In *Fat Shame: Stigma and the Fat Body in American Culture*, Professor Amy Erdman Farrell cautions that metaphors such as "epidemic," with its connotations of "disease, contagion, proliferation," and "war," create a "moral panic" about the "guilt" of one who "causes" such a catastrophe.[5] She argues that the two issues related to fat in our culture—our discussion of fat as a health crisis, and our feelings about fat as an appearance issue worthy of shame—are "deeply intertwined."[6] Fat shaming is common, and being fat in our culture carries with it both a *physical* stigma, and a *character* stigma."[7] The promise of diets to free people from "the social stigma of fatness" often "coincides with or even takes priority over issues of health," Farrell writes, because fatness in our culture is a "discrediting attribute for which people will go to extraordinary lengths to eliminate."[8] Over 50% of adolescent girls, and nearly 33% of adolescent boys use weight control measures such as fasting, skipping meals, smoking, purging, and taking laxatives.[9] Every day mothers are in the forefront of dealing with these issues.

## CULTURAL CHANGES IN FOOD AND EXERCISE HABITS OVER THE LAST GENERATION

At least ten changes in our culture have potentially contributed to the increased likelihood that children of this generation will be overweight. 1) Children spend less time "naturally" getting exercise by playing outdoors, or walking or biking to school (in part because of our concern over safety).[10] Federal guidelines recommend that children get sixty minutes of vigorous activity on most days, however, 58% of 6- to 11-year-olds, and 92% of 12- to 19-year-olds, do not meet these recommendations.[11] 2) Children engage in significantly more screen time than they did a generation ago. 3) There has been a dramatic rise in food advertising targeted to children.[12] Each year, the average American child sees around 4,000 ads for foods high in sugar, fat, or sodium, which influence their food preferences, requests, beliefs, behaviors, and their consumption of unhealthy food.[13] Commercials frequently make associations between the food or beverage being advertised, and athletic ability, fun, good times, being cool, and being happy.[14]

4) Our national consumption of fast food has significantly increased over the past 30 years.[15] Approximately one-third of American adults eat at one of 240,000 fast-food restaurants in the country on any given day, and children consume over a billion kids' meals per year.[16,17] 5) Our national consumption of sugared beverages has also increased.[18] 6) Our diets are higher in fructose, due to the food industry's shift to sweetening products with high fructose corn syrup (HFCS) instead of sugar, and our greater consumption of food and beverages that contain HFCS.[19] 7) Seventy percent of America's calorie intake comes from processed foods, which are often higher in sugar, fat, and salt than home-prepared foods.[20] 8) On average, Americans eat 530 more calories a day than they did in 1970, with the top three categories of extra calories coming from refined grains, added fats and oils, and sugar.[21] 9) The overall glycemic load of the typical American diet is higher than in the past.[22] 10) There has

been a significant rise in American children's food allergies and asthma, which correlate with rising obesity rates in children.[23]

## FOOD AND EXERCISE

Every mother was aware of cultural expectations that children should eat a well-balanced diet and get plenty of exercise. Most women felt it was relatively easy to keep their toddlers active, and mothers of elementary school-age children often signed their kids up for activities and sports to supplement their daily exercise. One mother, who doesn't live "in the greatest area," and who doesn't have the time or money to sign her kids up for activities, thought it was difficult for her 9-year-old son to get adequate exercise because there were no safe places for him to be outside in their neighborhood. American children who live in unsafe neighborhoods are 20% to 60% more likely to be overweight or obese than children who live in safe neighborhoods.[24] Mothers of pre-teens and teenagers who played sports, took active classes or had daily gym classes, felt their children got enough exercise. Women who had pre-teens and teenagers who were not involved in sports felt it was difficult to get their children to exercise.

Many women were conscientious about the food they served their children, consistently striving to provide fresh fruits and vegetables, and a variety of healthy home-cooked food. Getting their children to eat the food they served was challenging for some mothers. Some mothers were "not proud" of what their kids ate, and others frequently dealt with constraints such as lack of time or interest to home cook meals, their busy family schedule, having picky eaters, needing to have kids prepare their own or family meals, or the expense of food. One mother explained, "You get so tired, and you want convenience, you want everything quick, so I've struggled with that."

Some mothers were strict about making their children eat what they served for dinner, whereas others fixed "kid-friendly" meals. Tory grew up eating the healthy foods her mother served. "I thought it was a no-brainer, you just eat what's out there, and I have a husband and children who are very picky. Getting my kids to eat healthy has been one of the hardest challenges of being a mom." Eva feels she ruined her daughter's diet from the get go. "I always make something that she likes, therefore it's my fault she doesn't really eat vegetables." Other parents cooked special foods if their child wanted to be a vegetarian, or if they were vegetarian and their child wanted to eat meat.

Many women felt their pre-teen and teenage daughters did not eat enough, and others thought their teens ate more junk food and fast food when they were able to get it on their own.[25] One mother was concerned when she found "hoards of wrappers" in her teenage daughter's room, and several women commented that they had to get rid of all the junk food in their house because it was so hard to resist. In *Salt, Sugar, Fat: How the Food Giants Hooked Us,* Pulitzer Prize winning author, Michael Moss contends that scientists working for food manufacturers, also known as "Big Food," have intentionally designed products to be addictive by increasing the sugar, salt, or fat content of processed foods and beverages as they compete for customers' "stomach share."

One mother worried that her pre-teen daughter was suffering from mild depression, which she felt could be related to hormonal changes, or stress related to some issues their family was going through. "She lays down on the couch or on the bed, and she snacks while she's watching TV when she wants to check out." Watching a lot of TV may increase the risk of obesity because it can displace exercise, lower a child's metabolic rate, and food advertisements also encourage snacking because they prime "automatic eating behaviors" and trigger "automatic snacking of available food" in both adults and children.[26]

## SUGAR

Sugar was the main thing many mothers intentionally tried to limit in their children's diet. There are no federal nutrition guidelines for the maximum amount of added sugar a person should

consume on a daily basis. The American Heart Association recommends that children should consume less than 24 grams, or
6 teaspoons of added sugar daily.[27] American children typically
consume anywhere from 48 grams (12 teaspoons) to 136 grams
(34 teaspoons) of added sugar daily.[28] Sugar-sweetened soft
drinks, which include all soft drinks such as soda, fruit punch,
lemonade, energy and sports drinks, are the number one source of
added sugar in the American diet, accounting for about one-third
of sugar calories.[29] Scientists have found that liquid sugar calories
do not stimulate the natural regulation systems of the body to cut
back on total calorie intake to compensate for the liquid sugar
calories, and sweetened drinks can make a person hungrier.[30]

Sugar is a powerful food additive because our bodies are
hard-wired to like sugar. Sugar is eight times more addictive than
cocaine and every one of our ten thousand taste buds have sugar
receptors, which ultimately trigger the reward center, or pleasure
zone, in our brain. Food manufacturers employ scientists to figure
out the "bliss point" of sugar. In other words, what is the exact
level of sweetness something needs to be to trigger the brain's
pleasure center. Children in every culture studied innately like
sugar, and tend to have a higher bliss point for sugar than adults
do, which is why cereals targeted at children are sweeter than
adult cereals. Early childhood experiences shape our food preferences, which means that the average American child, who has a
diet high in sugar, is learning that foods should taste sweet.[31]

Some women who were strict about the amount of sugar
their children ate felt they got pushback from others. Lucy
recently spent a weekend at a cabin with her extended family
where relatives brought Lucky Charms and donut holes for their
kids to eat for breakfast, and said things like, "Lucy's kids don't
get sugar," which Lucy said is absolutely not true. She just wants
her kids to be mindful that they need to make conscious treat
choices. Another mother of an infant had serious health issues
before getting pregnant, and eliminated sugar from her diet,
which dramatically improved her health. As a result, she feels

strongly that she does not want her child to eat sugar and already worries about how to help her child navigate in a world that is not set up to support healthy nutrition, while also not being so restrictive that her child will rebel and binge on sugar, or be seen as a "weirdo." She feels that people do not understand that for her; nutrition is not a vague notion of health, but is "absolutely core to every facet of wellbeing."

A mother of an asthmatic teenage daughter reduced the sugar in her children's diet and eliminated dyes and processed foods, and makes sure her children drink enough water and get enough sleep. Her teenagers play sports, have steady energy levels, and consistently good moods, which she attributes to their nutrition, exercise, and sleep habits. Closely monitoring her children's nutrition and sleep patterns is not "fun or easy," and her kids see her as "naggy," but she feels strongly that it is her job. Others commented that it was challenging to limit sugar when there are "three times a Saturday where it could be a special occasion." One mother felt social pressure to loosen her healthy eating standards because she did not want to be "the curmudgeon mom who didn't give treats at play dates." Another woman is doing an experiment to see how much sugar and junk food her family is actually consuming by tracking their groceries for a year.

## A MOTHER'S BODY IMAGE

Regardless of their size, the majority of women felt that they had their own issues with body image. Studies indicate that 80% of American women are dissatisfied with their appearance.[32] Many women tried to intentionally change how they felt about their body, or at least how they talked about their body, after they had children. When Lindsay's daughter was an infant, she read that girls emulate their mother, which influences the development of their self-esteem and feelings about their appearance. She noticed that both her mother and mother-in-law frequently talked negatively about their appearance, so she called them together and said, "Alright ladies, here's the plan, we are talking about ourselves with love." Even though Lindsay does not say anything negative about her body in front of her daughter, she still feels badly about her body and worries "what subliminal messages will I give my daughter just because I feel it." She is happy that her 6th grade daughter seems very comfortable with her body.

Tanya, who described herself as morbidly obese, found it challenging to convey to her children that she is trying to lose weight and still talk about herself in a positive way. Instead of saying, "I hate myself," I tell them "I feel that my body doesn't properly reflect how awesome I am, so I'm working on paying attention to the food I eat and make different choices, so we're going to have less stuff in the house." She also wants to make sure that her children know that being overweight has nothing to do with her character. Her husband always tells their children that they are lucky because "they have the most beautiful mom on the planet." She believes that losing weight will not make her "more beautiful, but differently beautiful."

Other mothers worked to change family patterns of body shaming. Cindy commented that she comes from a "long line of string beans." Her mother would always look at her when she was young and say, "You're too skinny," and as she got older, her mother would make negative comments about her flat chest. When Cindy had a daughter she made a choice that she did not want to pass on the internalized message that your body is wrong if you are skinny, "so I made a concerted effort to give the message that your body is okay, whatever it is." Cindy is thrilled that her daughter, who is thin and small breasted, feels great about her body, and she exclaimed, "I totally broke that pattern!"

Nicole said that growing up she never felt her butt was big enough because she did not have the "round bubble." She always tells her daughter that she is beautiful and wants her daughter to love herself "no matter what way she came out." She feels that in the black community people might say, "Your skin's not fair enough, or you're too dark, or you have good hair, or your hair is too kinky." When her daughter was young, she decided not to allow people "to make comments about her hair or skin. If someone is about to say, 'She has good hair,' I cut them off and say, we don't use that term."

Other women felt that judging or commenting on their own body was so deeply engrained that it was a difficult habit to notice. Lynette, who was thin until she put on weight after having five children, did not even realize that when her kids were growing up she always said, "I've got to lose weight." When one of her daughters pointed it out to her, Lynette was stunned because she did not want to be "that kind of mom." "I never said anything to my kids because I knew enough not to do that, but I did it to myself and I was modeling terrible behavior. All I can do now is apologize and say I am growing to love my body."

## DAUGHTERS' AND SONS' BODY IMAGE

Women were delighted when their daughters had a positive body image and felt strong and confident in their own skin. Yet, many mothers had daughters who were self-conscious or dissatisfied with their body. Bridget feels angry about the messages her daughter gets from clothes advertisements about the ideal body type. "When an 8-year-old looks in the mirror and says, 'Mommy, I look fat,' that's crazy! Kids should not be thinking that way." One mother feels stressed out on a daily basis because her eleven-year-old daughter, who is physically active and has a healthy body, continually thinks she is fat and "looks like crap in everything." Alex's 5th grade daughter, who is the tallest girl in her class, recently had a health unit about puberty, which made her start unfavorably comparing her body to her smaller classmates. Sofia feels that both of her daughters "judge their bodies every day of the week." She thinks her oldest daughter emulates the bodies she sees in the Victoria Secret ads, and is trying to look like that by not eating.

There are several factors that influence youth eating habits, size, and body image observes Diane Neumark-Sztainer, principal investigator for Project EAT (Eating Among Teens). These influences include: "individual characteristics" (i.e. genetics, personality and eating behavior); "family factors" (i.e. family meal patterns and weight talk); "peer influence" (i.e. playing sports and dieting norms); "school environment" (i.e. lunch options and "weight teasing policies"); "community factors" (i.e. safe neighborhoods and opportunities for kids to be active); and "societal factors" (i.e. media representations and gender expectations).[33] She also notes that girls have more media, parental, and peer pressure to alter their weight.[34]

Most women who had sons did not hear them verbalize any body image issues. However, one mother of three teenage boys, who were all involved in sports, observed that her sons feel pressure to be lifting weights.

> They're constantly talking about how buff they are, or how flabby they are, and they are normal. I'm surprised at what I'm seeing in my boys. My oldest was trying to convince me to buy him protein powder so he could bulk up faster. It's like they're all supposed to look like Popeye, they're supposed to be skinny, but have all this muscle.

Adolescent girls are more likely to think they should lose weight, whereas adolescent boys want to increase muscle tone.[35]

Mothers were mindful of how they talked to their children about their weight and size. Adolescents of any size whose mother or father have "weight-related" conversations with them are more likely to diet, binge eat, and "use unhealthy weight-control behaviors."[36] Children whose parents encourage them to diet, or tease them about their weight, are more likely to have negative eating behaviors, low self-esteem, and depression. Parents who engage their children in "healthful eating conversations" without focusing on weight, or who have no conversations about eating or weight, are less likely to have adolescents that diet, binge eat, or use unhealthy weight control behaviors.[37]

## OVERWEIGHT CHILDREN

Women with overweight children were mostly concerned about the stigma of being fat in our culture. A mother of a "healthy, but chubby" daughter feels that people are looking at her and thinking, "What are you feeding that kid?" Another mother constantly worried about her daughter's weight when she was growing up, and feels the messages she projected to her daughter negatively affected her daughter's body image. "I feel like I always saw her as fat. When I look back at pictures of her I realize now there was nothing wrong with that kid, and it makes me so sad. She was always a little project for me." She is glad that her daughter "got away" from her in college because she feels that she has a healthier body image as a result. What kept going through this mother's head was that her daughter's size would affect her life chances. "I just know that in life prettier, thinner people are perceived as more successful."

A mother of two teenage sons who are overweight feels it is her responsibility to point out that they are not eating well and exercising enough, especially because she can see that they are not comfortable in their bodies. She never says, "You're fat, go out and exercise," but she tells them they need to be healthy because they are setting themselves up for problems later on. She thinks the health talk is a bunch of BS because her kids know what it is really about. "They know they're overweight, and every time I bring it up they don't hear that they need to be healthy, they hear that they're fat." She feels that she has brought it up too much and it is affecting their self-esteem, so she is now taking her husband's approach, which is to say nothing because he believes they will figure it out on their own.

Another mother, whose son is at the top of the weight charts, involved in sports and physically active every day, eats healthy food, and has a positive body image was "floored" when her husband signed their son up for a food program that teaches kids about healthy eating. "I took it as a personal insult because

I'm the one who's responsible for the meals, and my son already knows about good nutrition." She found the process fascinating because the doctor asked her son questions about how he feels about his weight "because he's supposed to admit that he feels badly, and to the best of my knowledge, he doesn't feel bad about it." The judgment of fat people in our culture frustrates this mother deeply. "If you're thin you can be a total butt head to people and it's okay. It's like being thin in our culture makes you a better person. You can be a skinny rail and eat crap because you fit the image." These mothers are all aware that discrimination or bias against overweight people, also known as "weightism," is prevalent in our society.

## CULTURAL RESPONSES TO REDUCING OBESITY

Michelle Obama took up the issue of childhood obesity and in February of 2010 launched the *Let's Move* campaign to get parents and children to make lifestyle changes that promote healthy eating and exercise. This campaign creates a sense of shared responsibility at the community, state, and national level for implementing policies, building infrastructure, creating physical activity opportunities for all children, and changing current exercise and nutrition habits. Several national groups have taken on the cause of encouraging exercise and good nutrition for children.[38,39] The FDA will require new Nutrition Fact labels on all foods that make it easier to see calories, the number of servings per container, and the number of calories for the entire bag. The food labeling will also include added sugar separate from naturally occurring sugar.[40]

In response to external pressure, many of the largest food and beverage companies pledged to follow the Children's Food and Beverage Advertising Initiative (CFBAI) beginning in 2006, to "shift the mix of foods advertised to children under 12 to encourage healthier dietary choices and healthy lifestyles."[41,42] At a 2013 White House Meeting, the CFBAI reported that its members have committed to advertise healthy products based on

CFBAI nutrition criteria, or to not specifically target children in advertisements in media where the audience share of children aged 12 and under is greater than 35%. Additionally, the CFBAI states that the recipes of hundreds of processed food items have improved to meet stricter nutrition standards, by reducing the levels of sugar, salt, and fat.[43] However, some studies note that there are significant loopholes in the CFBAI self-regulation policies.[44]

Thomas Friedan, director of the CDC, has outlined several interventions the United States could make to offset the rise in obesity rates. 1) Banning advertising of unhealthy foods to children such as Norway, Sweden, and the United Kingdom have done could potentially reduce American children's obesity levels by one-third.[45] 2) Implementing counter-advertisements that show the detriment of poor quality nutritional food, without stigmatizing individuals, could be effective in the same way anti-tobacco ad campaigns reduced tobacco use.[46] 3) Enacting legislation to create "buffer zones" around schools and recreation areas would reduce the availability of unhealthy food options for minors.[47] 4) Adding a "1 cent an ounce" tax on sugar-sweetened beverages would most likely "be the single most effective measure to reverse the obesity epidemic."[48] The food and beverage industry is opposed to government regulations that would restrict or ban advertising to children, and in 2010 alone, spent more than $41 million to lobby against congressional action that would negatively affect their interests.[49]

In *Sick Societies: Challenging the Myth of Primitive Harmony*, UCLA Professor Emeritus Robert Edgerton, argues that not all cultural beliefs and practices are adaptive. Instead, he suggests that "people are not always wise, and the societies and cultures they create are not ideal, adaptive mechanisms, perfectly designed to provide for human needs."[50] This even happens in large, complex societies such as ours, where often times the well-being of powerful people, and the institutions they control is favored.[51] The cultural changes we have experienced, which have contributed to a greater likelihood that American children will be overweight, have benefited "Big Food," advertising, the pharmaceutical industry, diet and exercise franchises, and many other institutions.

Mothers have the lion's share of offsetting these cultural changes, which can be daunting. Managing a child's exercise and nutrition requires daily planning, awareness of healthy nutrition information, access to healthy food, time and resources to buy and cook healthy food, resources and infrastructure to promote physical activity, going against current cultural norms for eating, and above all, the time and energy to supervise these things every single day.

# Chapter 8

## Buffer Mothers

### MANAGING SCREEN TIME, CELL PHONES, AND SOCIAL MEDIA

Jill has two high school kids who are good students, and involved in sports, music, church, and other activities year round. When her children were toddlers, she would regard herself as having a "successful day" if they did not watch TV. Fast-forward to high school, and Jill is surprised by how "uninterested they are in television," however, during the summer she finds it "impossible" to set limits on her kids' screen time. Her son loves to play video games, and when her daughter has free time, she is on her iPad, which concerns Jill because she does not know what websites she is going to, or what movies she is watching. "My husband is not as worried about any of this as I am. Apparently guys aren't. I'm worried about all of it: the sexting, the inappropriate photos, the bullying, the websites." She sighed as she said, "I'm happy they are almost grown and I can let go of that because I feel powerless."

Our cultural expectation is that good parents will monitor their kids' screen time, buffer their children from media exposure that may be inappropriate, while also making sure their children have the skills and equipment necessary to access media and technology which may be beneficial to them. Like Jill, most women found that monitoring screen time was much harder as kids got older, and when kids had more free time. The American Pediatric Association recommends that children over age 2 should not have more than two hours of daily screen time, however most American kids exceed these suggested limits. The average pre-schooler has more than four hours of daily screen time, and children and teenagers from 8 to 18 use screen media more than seven hours per day, not including the time they spend using computers to do their homework, talking on the phone, and texting.[1] Every day mothers deal with the inconsistency between our cultural ideal that children should have limits on their screen time, with the reality that most kids like to spend their free time watching TV, playing video games, or being on the internet.

Researchers disagree on the effects of screen media for children. Some conclude that excessive technology and media exposure is a negative force that displaces in-person social contact, ultimately making people feel more lonely, isolated, and vulnerable to health issues.[2] Others argue that media exposure can potentially have an impact on "virtually every health concern that practitioners and parents have about young people" such as developmental concerns, violence, aggression, bullying, obesity, eating disorders, early or risky sexual behavior, substance abuse, and school performance.[3] Some observe that the problems we associate with media consumption and technology use are not specific to growing up in a digital environment, but rather are extensions of "youth development and social problems."[4] Many researchers contend that media technology is a positive force in children's lives, citing its ability to educate, entertain, and connect people with others.[5] Mothers could see both positive and negative aspects of watching television and movies, playing video games, participating in social media, and using cell phones, depending on their child's personality and peer group interactions.

## TELEVISION AND COMPUTER SCREEN TIME

Most mothers were mindful of their toddlers or pre-schoolers' screen time. Some women did not let their young children watch TV or use the computer, others used it sparingly, and many did not have specific daily rules, however they did monitor what their young kids were watching, and tried to keep their viewing time reasonable. Studies show that the content of programs young children watch is important. Exposing children younger than three years of age to violent and non-educational media is associated with attention deficit symptoms later in childhood.[6] There is no association between children who watch educational television and later attention problems, and studies indicate that watching educational shows can have positive benefits for young children.[7] Women who had "intense" children were glad that watching TV could give them and their child some downtime, although some mothers thought certain shows could make their kids hyper. Other women talked about their ideal verses reality. "The day wears on, they're tired, you have to cook dinner, they're fighting, and you're like go ahead and turn on the TV," commented one mother.

As children got older, monitoring screen time became more challenging for many parents. Amber was "very structured" about screen time when her kids were little, however, now that they are in elementary school, and enjoy being on the computer or playing video games, it has gotten more complicated, especially in the summer. "Right now there are no rules because every time we set a rule you're sick of trying to keep track of it, and you're exhausted and you find yourself saying things like, 'Go watch TV, it's time to get off the computer.'" A few women had a child who liked screen time to the extreme. "Unless you tell him otherwise," exclaimed Ashley, "my son will wake up and immediately go onto a screen and he won't stop until he goes to bed. This is a kid that would pee himself before he would walk away to go to the bathroom."

Leah found it difficult being the gatekeeper because "electronics are like candy for my little kids and there's the pressure of having candy available all the time." Sofia "slacked off" monitoring her children's TV and computer time because "I'm always the cop. It's exhausting when you're the one who is always saying 'Turn it off,' or 'time's up.' I would ask my husband to deal with it when he was home, but he never wants to be the bad guy." Another mother has rules, but is lax about enforcing them, "so it becomes this pendulum, it swings too far one way or too far the other." Some women had conflict with their husband over screen time. "My husband travels a lot, so on the weekend, he would tell our son he needed to do such and such or there would be no TV next week," exclaimed Sylvia. "I asked my husband, 'Am I supposed to take a shower next week?' He finally got that it was not his punishment to dole out."

Other couples had differences of opinion about what shows their kids should be able to watch. "*Family Guy* was on way too early for the younger one," Erin commented, "and probably too early for the older one, but their dad is sitting there watching it with them." Several mothers were concerned with the sexualized images prevalent in commercials and shows.[8] "The commercials that are shown during sports games are totally inappropriate for the people watching them, which would be my son," commented Bridget. While mothers of young girls felt frustrated that girls' fashion trends emulate sexy adult women's clothes represented in shows and commercials. "Try to find a dress for confirmation that doesn't look like they're going to go hang out on a corner and work," exclaimed Sofia.

Several families used television or computer time as a reward once their child completed other tasks, and most parents had stricter rules for limiting television and computer time on school nights. Some had a "no TV" rule, and others felt that their kids' busy schedules limited their screen time. "They have their homework, their activities, and their chores," commented Penny, "and they know they have to get that done, and then screen time is a reward." Children and adolescents who are "heavy" media users are twice as likely to report getting fair or poor grades compared to "light" media users, who get less than three hours of media content on a daily basis. These differences held up, even when controlled with other possible contributing factors to school performance, including race, gender, parental education, single or dual parent household, and a child's personal contentedness.[9]

Several parents reflected on their own screen time. "We all know that Facebook can be a time suck," remarked Celeste. "I think about how easily I can spend 20 minutes looking at crap and I feel like I'm a pretty disciplined person and I get sucked in. If I was a kid and I didn't have decades of not having that, I think it would be hard to control." The average American adult spends the equivalent of 12 hours per day using and consuming media when you factor in the fact that they often media multi-task.[10]

Mothers would get frustrated when they thought their child was doing homework on the computer, and instead they noticed they were watching YouTube videos. "You either have to literally sit over their shoulder and watch every single thing and make them justify it, or you don't have any control," exclaimed Sheila. Tory, who traditionally had a no television policy during the week because her kids would get "glazed eyes when they saw a screen," found it challenging when one of her kids got an iPad for school. "All of a sudden, they could have screens during the week, and it got really hard." Many parents thought tablets and smartphones made controlling screen time much more difficult, and several women found their kids watching shows on their tablet or smartphone on a school night after they were supposed to be in bed. Most experts recommend that children should not have access to a television, computer, gaming device, or their phone when they are going to bed, mainly because they reduce a child's sleep time.

Parents appreciated the educational information to which their children had access, and I heard many stories about the amazing things children learned, and the creative iMovies and other projects kids did with technology. Many women felt their children were well-rounded kids and did not have much concern about their screen time. "Maybe I'm just being Pollyanna about it," commented Lindsay, "but we don't have any regulations, and she loves to read and she does her homework first." Danielle is not concerned that her children's lives are "going to crumble because of screen time. But if I felt like all they were doing was screen time, and their grades were terrible, and they weren't participating in sports, and they weren't outside in the summer, or if there were one strange thing they were doing, I would renegotiate screen time." Mothers often relied on external indicators such as grades, peer relationships, and participation in activities to assess whether or not their child's screen time was reasonable.

Several mothers worried about the things their children had access to online. "My relationship with my daughter and the computer has been one of real suspicion," commented Beth. "I'm anxious about it all the time. I march into her bedroom at 11 o'clock and take her computer and phone away, or she would have it by her all night." Chloe was concerned when her 10-year-old daughter's friend taught her daughter how to delete her search history. "That scares me a bit," remarked Chloe. The daughter and her friend had looked at "some sexual stuff" online, which upset the daughter enough that she told her mother about it. "That friend has a really protective mother," Chloe observed, "and I think it's actually working against her because the girl is rebelling and is going to be trouble." Some mothers of teenage sons felt it was too easy for kids to access pornography on their various devices, and several mothers felt there were no good guidelines for talking to their children about pornography. Even though Leslie's kids are good students and athletes, with nice friends, she finds "the things they're faced with without any emotional ability to decipher it mind-blowing. Damage control is 90% of what we do now deprogramming them every day from what they hear at school and what they see."

## COMPUTER AND VIDEO GAMES

Some kids rarely played video games, and others wanted to play them all the time.[11] Parents of children who loved playing video games found it challenging to set time limits. "My son, Zack would spend 24/7 playing video games if he could," Tara commented. She has come to appreciate the cognitive benefits of video games because for Zack, who has autism, gaming is a way into relationships. Holly observed that her son loves the technical and graphic aspects of gaming, and is constantly drawing his own games on paper. "I feel like that is a good thing, but my husband thinks he plays too many video games. I know we need to have a limit, but it's just hard. We can't totally cut him off because he'll pick the friends whose parents just let them play unlimited video games, and then he'll go over to their house." Lynette's daughter is really into playing SIMS, and plays it all day on weekends. After Lynette met a computer engineer who told her that she did hours of computer games as a kid, Lynette is trying to "find a good to it because it's really obnoxious."

Video games are addictive for some because they can stimulate the brain's neural reward system, causing a release of dopamine, which positively reinforces the video game behavior.[12] Several studies indicate that children who play video games that require spatial skills enhance their spatial reasoning skills; while other studies show that playing video games can improve visual attention, attention capacity, attention deployment, problem solving, and reaction time.[13] In *Don't Bother Me Mom, I'm Learning!* Mark Prensky, argues that video games provide children with "unforced learning opportunities" by teaching them how to think, multi-task, experiment through trial and error, and figure out what is essential to concentrate on within the gaming environment where there is a lot of stimuli.[14] Complex games stimulate a "flow" state by giving the player an opportunity to improve their skills by providing the perfect zone where the game is neither too hard, nor too easy.[15]

Many parents of older children were concerned about their child's exposure to violence in video games. "If I wouldn't allow them to do it in real life, why would I allow them to do it in a video game?" Alex exclaimed. "Their minds can't necessarily distinguish reality from a video game." Sheila is reluctant to get video game devices for her sons in part because there is so much violent conflict in video games.

> I feel like I'm constantly having to be vigilant against that, and nobody else seems to really care. We spend so much time in our schools working on bully-free zones, and how to handle conflict, and how to use your words, and then most people, still think its okay for them to play video games that involve all kinds of putting on the hurt.

Amber commented that her 8-year-old son is "very attracted to violence and guns. He asked me yesterday, 'How many different kinds of guns can you name?'" Right now her son likes to play games on an open source gaming website, so she and her husband are having a lot of conversations about how to monitor the games he's playing and limit his exposure to violence. "If it is cartoon violence is it okay? If there is no blood is it okay?" Amber's husband feels their son is more "aggressive and defiant," after playing certain computer games because he will walk up to his sister and push her. Amber would explain his behavior in other ways, but she is not sure. "It is one of the hardest things we're trying to figure out right now." Tara has also noticed a change in her son's personality after he's been playing video games. "He does not like violence so he doesn't play those games, but I still see a difference in him when he re-engages with the world. He's shorter, and he's usually a caring, sensitive kid, and I lose some of that."

Jill finds it almost impossible to limit her 17-year-old son's gaming time in the summer.

> For him it's all about the games, and they're violent. They're first person shooter, and he's always doing it with

other people. They're interactive and they're fast moving. I've kind of given up. I like the idea of limiting it to 6 hours, but it just doesn't work. He's almost grown, and I can't fight it. I just have to conclude that this is what he loves to do, and he is a well-rounded kid, and he is involved in activities, and is getting good grades, and he's engaged with other people.

Several women commented that the social aspect of online gaming was fun for their children. "I've noticed that on a Friday night, my son will get together with all of his friends online," said Ellen, "and they'll all be in their separate houses, and they're playing a game, and they're laughing and talking and strategizing. They play for several hours." In *It's Complicated: The Social Lives of Networked Teens*, author Danah Boyd contends that teens do have less physical freedom than they did in previous generations, and have less free time because of homework, sports, jobs, and other extra curricular activities. Connecting with friends online is a way for teenagers to be social and get some downtime without having to physically get together.

In response to growing concerns about youth violence, a multi-disciplinary task force reviewed the significant body of research on children's exposure to media violence and its relationship to children's aggressive behavior. They briefed congress that: "viewing entertainment violence can lead to increases in aggressive attitudes, values, and behavior, particularly in children."[16] In *Violent Video Games Effects on Children and Adolescents: Theory, Research, and Public Policy*, Iowa State psychology professor Craig Anderson and his colleagues conclude that high levels of exposure to video game violence: 1) is related to moderate and violent verbal and physical aggression; 2) is positively associated with anger, hostility, and incorrectly perceiving hostile or violent intent in the actions of others; 3) created a "longitudinal change in physical aggression;" and 4) had a negative effect on pro-social behavior.[17] Their review of the studies found that television and video game violence accounts for about 10 percent of the variance in children's levels of aggression. Critics of Anderson's work note that the statistical effect is relatively small.

A U.S. Department of Health and Human Services longitudinal study indicates that exposure to television violence is a greater risk factor for a youth acting violently than substance abuse, abusive parents, poverty, a broken home, low IQ, and anti social parents. Viewing television violence is just slightly less of a risk factor than physical violence, being male, and having poor parent-child relations. Gang membership is the largest risk factor for youth violence. There is no longitudinal data about video game violence as a risk factor for youth violence.[18]

There are many factors which influence how children process violent media images including: age, gender, socioeconomic status, race, family constellation, level of emotional wellbeing, brain chemistry, intelligence, media literacy, how strongly a child identifies with violent characters, and so forth. Girls are less likely to act aggressively after watching violent media, and boys who were instructed to think about the victim before watching a violent cartoon, were less likely to behave aggressively after the show than the boys who had not been instructed to think about the victim.[19] Talking to children about violent representations in the news or media also helps them process the images.

## CELL PHONES

Most women said their children loved having a cell phone, although a few mothers said their children were indifferent to having a phone. The three main reasons women gave for getting their child a cell phone were: communication, safety, and because they did not want their child to be left out of their friend group if everyone else had cell phones. Parents generally paid for their child's cell phone plan, citing that it did not cost them much to add a phone to their plan, or they opted to get their kids the cheaper pay-as-you-go phones. Some parents had their children buy their own phone, and some had their child do household chores to reimburse them for the phone or monthly service charge. Many families no longer had a landline, so as soon as kids were old enough to be home alone parents felt a cell phone was a necessity.

Parents had different rules for what apps their children could have, ranging from no app could be downloaded without parent approval, that children must have and use educational apps, to kids being able to choose their own apps. In general, women liked that when their child had a cell phone they could easily get a hold of them or let them know if plans changed at the last minute. Most women also felt that their child was safer with a cell phone, and many loved that they could allow their child more freedom since their child could text them periodically to check in. Some parents occasionally used the phone to track their child's whereabouts.

Many parents had a rule that they could look at their child's phone at any time, especially if they were paying for the plan. Some parents checked their kids' texts on the Cloud, or had occasional spot checks, others only read them if they felt there was a problem, and some never read their kids' texts. Parents with elementary or middle school children were the most likely to monitor their child's texts. Mothers tended to think the messages they read were boring and innocuous, but some found issues they needed to address. Women were less likely to read their high school students' texts, especially if there were no signs of trouble. "The position I've taken is that kids need some privacy and space," said Rachel. "I liken it to, 'Would I have wanted my mom to listen in to every phone call that I had with my friends?' No." A few women reported calling school counselors when their teenager confided in them that a friend or acquaintance was texting them about serious issues such as wanting to hurt or kill themselves.

When Lindsay's daughter started texting her at work to ask her things like whether she could skip choir practice to hang out with a friend, Lindsay had to set some texting boundaries.

"It's not another way for you to nag me," she explained to her daughter, "it's a way to communicate with me if you need me." Lindsay thinks it is important for her daughter to understand "I have a life outside of being a mom, and I'm not constantly wondering what's she doing now?" Lindsay also feels that not texting throughout the day "improves dinnertime conversation because when I say, 'What did you do today?' I don't already know because I have a photo of everything she has done." She also does not like it when her daughter texts her when she is out with friends because she feels that her daughter should "get off the phone and be with her friends."

In hindsight, Eva thinks it was a mistake to get her middle school daughter a smartphone because now she is "on it all the time." Eva feels she needs to sign her daughter up for more activities that will "withdraw her from the phone." Dana Boyd argues that parents may think that their children are "addicted" to their phones or computers, when actually teenagers just see texting or social networking as a way to stay connected with their friends when it is impossible to get together with them in person. Sofia got her daughter a cell phone in junior high because she noticed that everyone in her daughter's friend group had them. "When she'd be with them they'd all be texting each other and she'd be left out. That's the only reason I did it. Then I realized what a nightmare they are, so my younger two are the only kids at the junior high who don't have phones." She believes cell phones are a nightmare because "their moods get so affected by things that are being texted to them." Gloria feels that cell phones and social media can accelerate regular teen things, because of "the speed at which somebody can be ostracized." She feels like things can feel bigger faster because there is no wait time between when people react to something.

The majority of mothers took an active role in teaching their children texting safety and etiquette. Mothers often reminded kids that what they said or sent in a text was not private. One mother saw naked pictures of her son's high school girlfriend on his phone. When someone stole his phone, which did not have password protection, she felt he did not understand the greater ramifications that the naked pictures of his girlfriend "could be all over the internet." Most women had a rule that their children could not look at their cell phone during dinner. Many women felt frustrated when their children would be looking at their phone when they were at a family gathering, and often reminded their kids not to be on their phone when they were with others in person. Several women said their kids did not like it when their friends were on their phone while they were hanging out together, so some women collected the phones of their kid's friends when they come over to play or attend a party. Many women had a strict rule that their children could not have their phone in their bedroom at night. "We have a year round rule that at night all the phones get plugged into a strip in the kitchen," commented Rachel. Kristina started making sure her sons did not have their phone in their bedroom at night, after her friend who is a child psychologist adamantly told her, "The best thing you can do as a parent is to never let them have electronics in their room at night."

## SOCIAL MEDIA

Dana Boyd argues that social media is not that much different from the public spaces that teenagers used to hang out in previous generations. For this generation of teenagers, the "cool" place to hang out together is on line. From a psychological development perspective, adolescence is a time where youth are concerned with their identity, establishing autonomy, creating intimacy, and exploring sexuality.[20] Boyd observes that social media is also a vehicle by which teens compete for social status, and oftentimes there are online conflicts as "teens participate in battles over reputation, status, and popularity."[21] She argues that such interactions are likely to occur outside of social media as well.

Boyd also notes that teens need to remember that what they post online is never really private, and can be visible by more people than their intended audience especially if someone shares their post or is doing a search on them. Most mothers were mindful of the pitfalls of social media and reminded their children to think before they posted anything. Several recalled dumb or immature things they did in high school, and felt it was unfortunate for this generation of kids that things they posted as teens could be retrieved later. Many women brought up the scenario where their child's future mother-in-law or boss would be able to search aspects of their high school or college life they may not want others to see.

Some kids asked their mother for permission to be on social media platforms but many women did not know the extent of their children's social media activities. Some were okay with their child under age 13 having a Facebook account, whereas others, like Alex, "refused to lie" for her daughter to be on Facebook. One mother was shocked to find that her second grader had followers on Twitter. If parents did know about their child's social media accounts they often attempted to monitor them to some degree. Rachel scrolls through her kids' Instagram pictures periodically, however she believes "they have to learn the rules of the road and in some ways suffer the consequences." Others were amazed by how quickly their children switched platforms to avoid being monitored, and some mothers had no idea how to access Instagram or Twitter.

Some kids were not into social media at all, other kids had fun connecting with their friends, and some had negative experiences. "My daughter is affected by Instagram," explained Sofia. "She thinks she's missing out on everything in the world. Everyone is having a great time. Everyone's lives are beautiful and perfect. I try to convince her that everyone is probably at home with their parents." Some women found it annoying that their kids would be posting photos from vacation, and being "extremely serious about how many people had liked it and how fast." While other women recalled that external social validation was important to them in junior high and high school, and that they never wanted to be out of the loop. "The thing that drives me crazy," exclaimed one mother "is the number of self-ies my daughter takes." Whereas another mother thought it was "actually kind of nice" that her daughters "send out the ugliest pictures of themselves." Nicole, whose teenage daughter makes videos of herself doing her nails or baking cookies, constantly tells her daughter, "You cannot put that out there, it might get in the wrong person's hands. She's one of those kids that wants to be on TV, and I worry that one day she will quit listening to me." A few mothers had serious issues come up with their kids, like bullying and harassment, which prompted them to work with school counselors.

Mothers deal with a whole gamut of issues related to their children watching TV shows and movies, being on the internet, gaming, texting, and participating in social media. Every mother must come to terms with the contradiction between our ideal that kids should have less than two hours of screen time a day, with the reality that that the growing number of devices and platforms kids have access to makes controlling screen time, especially for older children, really difficult. Many parents are figuring out workable and realistic solutions to monitoring screen time, and teaching kids good habits when they are young in hopes that their children will be able to enjoy the benefits of media and technology, without the negative impact. This can be time consuming and exhausting. Every mother who had a large age span between their oldest and youngest child felt it was significantly harder to manage screen time now than it was ten or fifteen years ago. It will probably become even more difficult as marketing analysts show that tablet use for kids 8 and under is growing rapidly, and smartphone ownership for kids eleven and younger will gradually increase each year.[22] This is one area where figuring out cultural solutions to lift some of the burden from parents is more challenging.

# Chapter 9

## "I just shout 'No' a lot."
### HOW MOTHERS RESPOND TO THEIR CHILDREN'S CONSUMER DESIRES

When I asked Carla if she thought our consumer culture had an affect on her preschool daughter, she replied, "Absolutely! My best example is Hannah Montana. My four-year-old has never seen or heard her on TV because we have never watched the show yet she has been obsessed with her for many months and wants to dress up as Hannah Montana for Halloween." Her daughter's obsession with Hannah Montana is driving Carla "absolutely crazy. When you walk through Target, she's on pajamas, she's on yogurt containers, she's on graham cracker boxes. It seems like Hannah Montana is on everything, and I'm waiting for her horrible downfall." Although "Hannah Montana" is long gone, merchandising of favorite television or movie characters to sell a wide variety of food and other products continues to be the norm. Like so many mothers, Carla feels frustrated with constantly combating advertising and marketing messages directed toward children.

Every mother I interviewed spent time and energy figuring out strategies to deal with their child's consumer desires: helping them learn to delay gratification; teaching them that advertisements are misleading; fielding requests for products; and telling kids that "things" will not make them happy. Even though we live in a free-market society that encourages consumerism, no mother wants to raise an overly materialistic child. Helping kids navigate our consumer culture has become increasingly difficult for mothers as consumer pressure on children has grown and as our society as a whole has become more materialistic.

## THE GROWTH OF THE CHILDREN'S CONSUMER MARKET

Advertising and marketing to children is a global phenomenon, with companies spending billions of dollars annually to get their share of the lucrative kid's market.[1] American children represent 4% of the global child population, however, Americans spend about $30 billion annually purchasing 40% of the world's toys. The average American child sees from 25,000 to 40,000 advertisements a year, and gets seventy new toys each year.[2,3] American children under 12 spend approximately $18 billion a year; 8- to 12-year-old "tweens" spend $30 billion annually; and teens spend approximately $160 billion per year. The direct influence of American children under 18 on family spending is close to $188 billion.[4]

James McNeal, a professor and children's marketing expert, identifies eight forces, starting in the late 1980s that have had a tremendous impact on the rise of children's consumer power. These include: dual income families; smaller families; older parents with more money; a higher divorce rate; more single parent families; more involved grandparents; higher levels of parental guilt in part due to less time; and the tendency for parents to be more worried about the future prospects of their children. During the 1980s, middle-class childrearing patterns also shifted away from expecting children to be obedient and respectful of parental authority, toward a style where parents seek out children's opinions, and are more likely to negotiate with their children.[5] Marketers categorize parents into categories such as: the "indulgers;" "kids' pal;" "conflicted" (parents more prone to guilt); and "bare necessities" (who are least influenced by nagging.)[6]

Children are especially appealing to advertisers because they represent a "3 in 1" market. They buy things themselves, they influence parental spending, and they are future customers.[7]

Children often accompany parents on shopping trips and exert considerable influence on household spending, especially for products they consume, like cereal, but they also influence larger purchases such as appliances, cars, hotels, and vacation venues.[8] Marketers call this, "pester power," or "the nag factor."[9] Children between the ages of 4 and 12 make about 15 requests in an average shopping trip, and approximately 3,000 requests per year.

Mothers do not need researchers to tell them that kids make many requests in stores. Maria tries not to bring her children along when she goes to the store. "They can't go into Target without wanting something, and they have more toys than they could ever play with. I just shout 'No' a lot (laughter)." Caroline only lets her children watch PBS, however she notices that when "they go stay with grandma and grandpa, then they're asking for the Jewel Gem Barbie. When they spend time watching commercial TV, their wants shoot up, and if they don't, it's not an issue. It's crazy how well it works, so we avoid it." Abby, who was soft-spoken throughout the interview, became agitated as she exclaimed, 'It really bothers me that all of the companies market to children. They know better. Don't they have children? It bothers me that we have to deal with that, and it bothers me that you go into a store and all of the candy is at their level. I feel like I'm constantly fighting that battle." Sweden not only bans advertising to children under twelve, they also prohibit the display of candy in stores near the check out lines to make it easier on parents when they have to wait in line.[10]

## CHILDREN'S ABILITY TO UNDERSTAND ADS / EFFECT OF ADS

Numerous studies conclude that advertising influences children's product preferences; their desire for advertised food, beverages, or other items; their requests for products; and sales.[11] Other studies indicate that children's advertising can promote racial stereotypes, materialism, obesity, and other health problems.[12] There is compelling evidence that children under the age of eight do not understand the persuasive intent of advertising, and view commercial claims as informative, accurate, and truthful.[13] James McNeal summarized the limitations of children by describing them as literal and gullible.[14] By age eight, most children recognize that ads are trying to get them to buy something, and do not always tell the truth.[15] The American Psychological Association concludes that children under eight "are uniquely vulnerable to commercial persuasion," and therefore recommends that that government "protect the interests of children" by restricting "advertising to children too young to recognize advertising's persuasive intent." They further argue that expecting young children to be media literate places "too much responsibility on children."[16] This raises the dual questions of whether or not children need to be "protected" from advertising, and if so, whose responsibility is it to protect them?

## GOVERNMENT REGULATION, CORPORATE RESPONSIBILITY, AND PARENTAL RESPONSIBILITY

Advertisers established the Children's Advertising Review Unit (CARU) in 1974, which sets voluntary self-regulation standards in order to avoid government regulation.[17] Congress did pass legislation in the 1970s that limited commercials during children's shows to ten and a half minutes per hour on weekdays, and twelve minutes per hour on weekend, and restricted advertising practices such as "host" selling and program-length commercials.[18] These bans are in effect today, but they do not apply to the Internet, or other "new" media advertising.[19] Other countries such as Australia, Belgium, Canada, Great Britain, Greece, Finland, Norway, and Sweden have enacted much stricter regulation on children's advertising.

Boston College sociology professor Juliet Schor, who has done extensive research on children and consumer culture, argues that public policies to protect children, which have been our traditional societal response to these types of issues, "will not be forthcoming," especially since multi-billion dollar corporations who do the bulk of children's advertising, have tremendous economic power and political influence. She cautions that bans on advertising could create "unintended consequences" such as the decline in quality children's programming, and would be logistically hard to coordinate in an era where there are so many mediums of advertising.[20] This suggests that the question of our government's responsibility to protect children from advertising has become an obsolete issue in our current political and legal environment.

Whether or not corporations have any moral obligations when it comes to advertising to young children becomes a more salient question. The corporate response is that parents have the responsibility to oversee their child's media usage, not the government.[21] Many corporations claim that by adhering to CARU guidelines and other forms of self-regulation, and by sponsoring public service advertising that promote healthy behaviors, they are fulfilling their corporate moral obligations to children. They further argue that children relate to, and use commercial culture in complex ways, and therefore are not passive victims.[22] Researchers suggest that corporations do these things to avoid the threat of regulation and bad publicity, while routinely figuring out ways to get around some of the voluntary standards.[23]

James McNeal contends that parents, and not marketers, are responsible for the expansion of children's consumption. McNeal notes that forty years ago, children were encouraged to save their money, however he argues that "children are turned into consumers at a very early age in our society through the desires and encouragement of parents, who also provide the youngsters with the necessary financial support."[24] "If parents insist on their children being consumers by giving them money and encouraging them to spend it," writes McNeal, "are they also giving approval to marketers to court their children as potential customers?"[25] He believes there is little evidence that parents are teaching their children responsible consumer behavior.

Most mothers stated that they actively try to teach their children to save their money and be responsible consumers. People had several strategies for giving their children an allowance, ranging from no allowance, to children getting an allowance with no strings attached, to children getting an allowance with the expectation that they will do household chores, and children doing household chores to "pay" for things such as a cell phone plan.[26] Several parents were inconsistent with giving an allowance, and some kids earned extra money for doing additional chores like mowing or shoveling, or for getting good grades. Of those that gave an allowance, many insisted that their children set aside a percentage for saving and giving. Tory explained their 30/30/30/10 breakdown for "every dime" their children received. "Thirty percent is for short-term spending, 30% long-term spending such as something you're saving for, and 30% goes into savings that you are never going to touch because it's for college, and then 10% is for charity." Parents generally exercised control over what their children could purchase with their own money.

Many parents who gave their child an allowance thought it helped their children learn to save while also curbing their spending. "I give my oldest $9 a week, and he has been saving for five weeks now to get a $55 Viking's jersey which I would never in a million years buy for him," explained Jackie. "That means when we go to Walgreen's he doesn't get candy, because if you want the $3 stupid sucker at Walgreen's, it's coming off of your allowance, so all of that spending has stopped." Parents also talked about the differences in their children's spending habits, where one child would consistently save their money and another would want to spend their money as quickly as they got it. Some women had conflict with their spouse or partner related to teaching their children about money and possessions. "We grew up different," explained Sofia, "so it's a bigger deal for my husband to make sure they have things and he will go behind my back and get them things."

## MATERIALISM

One of the biggest concerns researchers and parents have about the high levels of advertising exposure American children routinely experience is that ads promote materialism by implying that the right "thing" will make a person feel happy, fulfilled, "cool," or successful.[27] In *The Cultural Contradictions of Motherhood*, Sharon Hays notes that mothers have become more "intensive" at the same rate that our society has become more market-driven. She argues that when mothers willingly devote their time, attention, and financial resources to childrearing, without expecting anything in return, this suggests that they are participating in an "implicit rejection of the ethos of rationalized market society" because they are fundamentally ambivalent about a "society based solely on the competitive pursuit of self-interest."[28]

Studies throughout the world consistently find that people with high materialistic values, in other words, people who believe that acquiring "money and possessions that convey status" is "important and key to happiness and success" report "less happiness and life satisfaction, lower levels of vitality and self-actualization, and more depression, anxiety, and general psychopathology."[29] There is also a correlation between materialism and negative outcomes such as "lower social and personal well-being, compulsive and impulsive spending, increased debt, decreased savings, depression, social anxiety, decreased subjective well-being, less psychological need satisfaction, and other undesirable outcomes."[30] These effects are amplified for materialistic people living in materialistic cultures, such as the United States.[31] No study found any "positive associations between materialism and wellbeing."[32]

Juliet Schor, author of *Born to Buy: The Commercialized Child and the New Consumer Culture*, found that high levels of media exposure predict high levels of consumer involvement, and "consumer involvement predicts high rates of depression, anxiety, and psychosomatic complaints such as headache, stomachache and boredom, as well as lower self-esteem."[33] Schor states that, "contemporary American tweens and teens have emerged as the most brand-oriented, consumer-involved, and materialistic generation in history. And they top the list globally."[34]

When I asked women with "tweens" and teenagers if they felt this quote was an accurate representation of their child and their child's peer group, I got many different responses. Some women felt their kids are no more materialistic than they were growing up, commenting on how important it was for them to have Jordache, Girbaud, or Calvin Klein jeans as a teenager. Others felt their child's brand awareness reached a peak during junior high, when everyone is trying to fit in. Women who lived in solid middle-class or poorer neighborhoods did not think their kids, or their kids' friends, were particularly materialistic. "My daughter and her friends go to a Minneapolis Public School, they're not overdressed, and their parents are pretty decent," commented Eva. She realizes that there probably is some peer pressure at the school, but her daughter "knows what we can afford."

"As long as my son has his basic technology needs met, and really good shoes, he's okay," commented one mother. Kendra shops at thrift stores with her children and has tried to deter them from brand names. However, she feels that "regardless of what you do, when your kid watches Disney shows they're exposed to a different lifestyle, and I feel like in their minds we should have a nicer car, we should live in a nicer house, we should have nicer clothes, and we should be able to go on four or five vacations a year." Other mothers thought that reality shows gave their children a skewed perspective. "I've told my kids 1,000 times that television does not reflect real life," commented Tory. Some kids identify with a "media peer group" which makes them want to fit in with the people they see on television.[35]

Several parents talked about the challenges of living in wealthy communities. Bridget's children are friends with "kids who get laptops for their birthday, three play station games, a bicycle, and five other things, and that's just from their parents!"

Bridget keeps reminding her kids, "It doesn't matter how big your house is. It doesn't matter if you live on the water and have a boat." She also tells her children, "I could get a job at a firm where I could work a zillion hours, and we could have a whole lot more money, but I would never be there." Bridget's comments support the recurring theme I heard from so many mothers that spending time with children should take precedence over excessive material gain.

Rachel also lives in a wealthy suburb, and her children's friends all have more money than they do. She feels it is a "constant struggle to keep them grounded." Rachel tries to give her children a sense of the where they fall on the continuum by giving them exposure to people who are less fortunate, but she also realizes that people could look at their life style and say, "Oh my God, these people are over the top. They give their kids everything." She feels that teaching her children values amidst the backdrop of their wealthy community "is probably my single biggest personal challenge." She feels that "as a parent you have to really work hard not to get sucked into it and stay firm to what you think is right and wrong. And it's kind of a slippery slope." One of Rachel's children is a "giant consumer, and he's very brand aware, and he runs with kids that are all brand aware because he's in a crowd where his friends are million dollar kids."[36]

I heard repeatedly that children had different personalities in relation to being grateful for what they had, or always wanting more things. "You can smooth edges around your kids, but genetically, I think some of its natural," commented Emily. "Consumerism doesn't really affect my oldest; but my middle child is influenced by what she sees on TV and what she hears other people talking about. Things and acquiring things are important to her and bring her happiness." Emily thinks her daughter's desire is also driven by our culture. "Kids are so catered to these days. When they were little, they would get toys when they went to a fast food restaurant. It breeds a sense of entitlement. 'Hey, we're going somewhere, what are we going to get? What's in it for me?'" She and her husband try to counter-act the cultural messages, however she feels that they talk until "we're blue in the face but really that doesn't do much. We talk about trying to share what we have, trying to limit possessions, trying to plan ahead, trying to save, but for my girls there's a lot of need for immediate gratification, saving is just not satisfactory to them."

For Ellen's daughter who attends the public school in a wealthy suburb there is always pressure about: "Where are you going on vacation? Who are you going on vacation with? What kind of iPhone do you have? What kind of boots do you wear?" She does not see the same pressure in the private Catholic school where her son goes to high school. Women who lived in school districts with a wide economic base felt there was a broad range of attitudes and behaviors. "My daughter tells me that some of the girls at her school go shopping with their mom to buy new clothes all the time. She never had Uggs when the other girls had Uggs. She hasn't really cared very much," commented Jill. Another mother noticed that some of her daughter's friends "are really into what they look like and what they're wearing, then you meet their mother and you get it." Lynette found it interesting that when a girl in her daughter's school posted pictures of all the clothes and gifts she got for Valentine's Day, there was a lot of negative feedback for her "bragging." Lynette felt this helped to set a standard in their school that conspicuous consumption was gross. Amy sometimes feels guilty because her daughter's friends have so many things her daughter does not have. "Even though I know it's not important, I also think about how easily kids' self-esteem can just get ravaged." She worries that kids will exclude children who "don't have the right clothes."

## STRATEGIES MOTHERS USE TO COMBAT MATERIALISM

Our country has traditionally depended on mothers to protect children from taking on negative personality characteristics inspired by materialism. In the mid-1800s, French Historian

Alexis de Tocqueville observed that American mothers tended to discourage "sheer privatized selfishness" in their husband and children, and were one of three cultural forces, along with volunteerism and religion, that curbed our cultural tendencies toward isolation and rampant individualism.[37] Mothers continue to have that responsibility today, and have figured out many different strategies to combat materialism.

### Delayed Gratification

Like many mothers, Caroline deals with her children's requests for toys by telling them to put it on their wish list. When her kids ask her for something in a store, she replies, "Is today your birthday? Is today Christmas?" When Melinda and her four-year-old daughter recently walked through a store her daughter said, "Look at that pretty dress, maybe I can get that for my birthday." Melinda told the salesperson that she would have to wait another eleven months until her birthday. "She's heard me say, 'Maybe for your birthday,' or 'maybe for Christmas' so many times that now she answers her own questions. I've got her trained."

### The Importance of Working to Get Something and Cultivating Gratitude

When Bridget's son wanted the latest PlayStation, she told him he would have to use his own money to buy it, and could only get it if he got straight As in school. He worked hard in school and did chores around the house in order to get the PlayStation3. Bridget feels that it meant a lot more to him than just having it handed it to him. Abby, like many mothers, frequently reminds her children, "You have to work for things, and you don't get everything you want, and everything isn't good for you." Mothers also tried to instill gratitude by making their kids say thank-you, write thank-you notes, or "explode" when they are being ungrateful. "If I catch the kids disrespecting any of their toys or their possessions it gets taken away temporarily," commented Alex. "I explain to my kids, that is not how we treat our stuff because someone took the time and energy to pick that out for you because they thought you would like it. If you can't respect it, you don't get to play with it."

### Giving Back, Volunteering, and Religion

Jan feels that her kids don't need anything, so she suggested that for their birthday parties they should ask friends to bring a canned good instead of a gift, which "they haven't quite bought into yet." She knows they have "good hearts and they like to give," so she periodically has her children go through their toys and clothes to see what they could give away. She also brings her kids to volunteer at "Feed My Starving Children." Jan believes that they are learning the importance of giving back, but she is always trying to balance it with the "pressures of their friends, and wanting to get the cool stuff." Jackie feels it is important to teach her kids how to have a generous spirit, so they had a family discussion about how they can give without spending any money. "My oldest came up with the idea to babysit someone's kids so that the mom and dad could go out for a date." Kim wants to figure out how to "give back as a family," so they joined a church that has a strong giving and social justice message. Many mothers commented that they rely on religion and volunteerism, the same two forces the de Tocqueville described in the 1800s, in order to instill values that counter materialistic values.

### Living in a Middle-Class Neighborhood and Being a Good Role Model

Several women felt that living in neighborhoods where people are not materialistic helped their children stay grounded. When Jenna's son went to a private school where he was around kids who had bigger houses, he noticed the difference, but "what spoke more loudly to him was the example of the people we're surrounded by and how we live." Andrea is grateful that all her friends "live according to a certain ethic of not being wasteful, being mindful, and being generous." She feels this sets a strong example for her children. Women also felt it was important to be a role model for responsible spending habits. "When I pay the bills each month," asserted Lynette, "I make sure my kids hear me say, it feels so good to be able to pay your bills." Jill remarked, "My children see a mom who packs her lunch for work every day, makes her own chicken stock, and shops at Aldi."

### Talking Openly About Money Decisions, Creative Present Giving, and Spending Time Together

When Alex's husband unexpectedly lost his job, they told their children, "We need to tighten the belt buckles and a lot of the extra stuff that you guys are used to is going away. Presents are going to be more practical because that's the way it has to be." Alex believes her family has really benefited by this mindset because they have started going to the park and having picnic lunches by the lake. "Spending time together as a family has become more important than material things." Another family started making presents for each other at Christmas. "We started it one year when our finances were really tight," commented Lydia, "but we have kept it going because everyone loves giving and receiving homemade gifts."

After Andrea's husband died, she felt a lot of anxiety about how she was going to make it financially. I told my kids, 'This is our budget and we need to live within our means." As a result, her kids know "in a very real way" that if they want choices in life they have to do well in school. "They've also had to pay for some of their activities, and that's really different from their peers. Sometimes they're resentful, but I also see their pride." Some parents who did not have financial pressure also talked to their children about consumer choices. Ellen and her husband use family purchases as a teaching example.

> When we were going to buy a car we had a family dis-
> cussion about what we needed, how we're going to save
> money, were we going to take out a loan, were we going
> to pay cash for this car, what were the benefits of doing
> both? How do we save to pay cash so we don't have these
> loans and don't have to pay interest? Do we want to get a
> car that's brand new or one that is one-year-old?

Financial experts suggest that it is "crucial" for parents to talk
to their children about money "given the epidemic of silence
around money that persists within many families."[38]

### Lifestyles of Anti-Consumerism

Several women went to great lengths not to be materialistic.
Marie exclaims that her children think they live with the "anti-
consumer terrorist!" "I've been in the mall twice with my children.
They've probably been to McDonalds with us two or three times
in their life for an ice-cream cone. We just don't do those kind
of things." Her children have "not done a lot of demanding" for
things because they know that their family "values putting extra
money toward an experience verses a thing."

### Consuming to Create Connections

Most mothers want their children to know that their worth
stems from who they are, not from what they have; and they
also want to provide their children with material goods that
will make them happy, entertain them, enrich their lives, and
make them fit in with their peers. Ninety-seven percent of the
women I surveyed usually or always buy clothes for their children. Most women really enjoyed shopping for school clothes
with their kids and many had figured out how to stick to their
budget, no matter how small. Several women shopped at thrift
stores. "I would take my daughter to Goodwill when she was
young," Danielle explained, "and I would show her the difference

in how much you can get if you're buying here." Now that her daughter is older, she encourages her to think about "who's making the clothes and where they are made." Other women gave their children a specific budget, which made it easier not to overspend, while giving the kids a better understanding of how to make choices. Several mothers also had their kids buy their own high-end clothes. "I have a moral objection with the CEO of Lululemon," explained Ellen. "I told my daughter, 'I'm not going to buy you anything from there. You can save your babysitting money and buy a Lululemon shirt if that's where you want to put your money,' and she spent $65 on a t-shirt."

When we hear reports that children of this generation are adopting materialistic values, people blame parents, and in particular mothers, for raising materialistic children. We do not recognize how difficult it is to single-handedly attempt to counter consumer pressure. Many women thought their children had too many things, and often made comparisons with more materially privileged families to help them feel that they had maintained a reasonable limit to their children's possessions. The stories in this chapter clearly illustrate the hard work involved by both financially well off and financially struggling women as they attempt to strike a balance between buffering their children from the negative aspects of consumer culture, teaching children responsible consumer behavior, and allowing their kids to enjoy the things and experiences one can get in a consumer culture. This raises the question of why we so easily let the government and big corporations off the hook for being part of the solution to reduce the negative impact of materialism.

# Chapter 10

## The New Second Shift

### ACTIVITIES AND ACHIEVEMENT

Jenna vividly recalls attending her son's first pre-school conference, fully expecting to get a good report. She was surprised by her strong reaction when the teacher said her son was "having some issues" at school. "It was so painful because it started my awareness of how much is my identity tied up with my son? How much do I judge myself, or deem myself worthy or unworthy depending on how he's turning out?" Her son struggled academically throughout high school and decided that he did not want to attend college right away. "I have learned to have faith that my identity is not totally connected to my son's achievement," observed Jenna. "I have learned to hold the paradox that I am responsible for who he is in a certain way because I am his mom, and at the same time, he is making his own decisions."

Jenna's comments get to a core issue: how responsible are mothers for who their children are, how their children act, and what their children achieve? There is not a cut-and-dried answer to these questions. Even so, there is an undeniable tendency in our culture to blame mothers if a child has behavioral or academic problems, or struggles in any way.[1] Mothers cannot help but internalize some of the criticism and judgment on mothers, and most women felt anxious, or guilty, or responsible, if their child had problems. Even though women acknowledged that their children came into the world with their own personality tendencies, they also believed that parenting does matter and conscientiously tried to do their best to meet the needs of their children.

## Changes in Middle Class Parenting Norms

Most women described differences between her parenting style and her mother's style of parenting. Many noted that they spend more time playing with their children, make more of an effort to connect with their kids, and are more likely to talk about feelings with their children. Women also felt they were more involved with their children's academics and activities. Most also thought they were less strict, and really "enjoyed" their kids in a way that their parents did not. Women believed their own mother was following the mothering norm of her era, just as they are following current parenting expectations.

Scholars define middle-class parenting norms in a variety of ways. Sharon Hays contends that "intensive mothering" is the dominant parenting model of our culture, where we assume children are "innocent" and "priceless," and expect that mothers will devote a tremendous amount of time, energy, and money to raise their children, consulting expert advice when necessary.[2] Susan Douglas and Meredith Michaels note that the "new momism" is a media-driven insistence that mothers need to prove that they are a perfect, and totally involved mother. Annette Lareau uses the term "concerted cultivation" to describe the middle-class parenting style where parents have open discussions with their children, and "organized activities established and controlled by mothers and fathers" often dominate children's lives.[3] This style of childrearing "places intense labor demands on busy parents, exhausts children, and emphasizes the development of individualism, at times at the expense of the development of the notion of the family group."[4]

Adrie Kusserow observed that middle and upper middle-class parents who live in safe neighborhoods socialize their children in "soft" individualism, where a parent's job is to nurture a child's uniqueness by helping them uncover their inner thoughts, feelings, desires, talents, and creativity so they can "flower" into their full potential. Parents do this by praising and encouraging their child, allowing them emotional expression, enhancing their self-esteem, and fostering creativity. These parents value "success, achievement, and leadership in a competitive society" and believe that cultivating a child's uniqueness will set her apart from others, while "the energy of true desire, authentic preference, feelings, and tastes will naturally motivate her to be good at what she loves."[5]

Melissa Milkie and Catharine Warner suggest that middle-class mothers invest a great deal of time and energy in "status-safeguarding" to ensure that their "child's future social and economic status in a competitive marketplace is sustained or improved." [6] Mothers focus their safeguarding efforts in three realms. "Academic safeguarding," where mothers choose the school their child will attend and get involved in school improvement efforts. They also consistently analyze "whether a child has the right teacher, an appropriately challenging curriculum, acceptable homework material, and able and appropriate peers."[7] "Talent safeguarding" takes place when a mother makes sure that "each child has unique talents and experiences," which "may be developed through extracurricular activities, work in the community or with religious organizations, or with the family through traveling to new places." This involves testing out a variety of options to see "which ones become passions or talents."[8] "Emotional safeguarding" occurs when "mothers make extensive efforts to protect children's happiness and self-esteem, while also reducing any anxieties a child might experience." The long-term goal of emotional safeguarding is to "instill a sense of enjoyment in daily life, particularly school, that will translate to long term success and economic mobility."[9] They believe that "status-safeguarding" is a way to weave children an "individualized safety net" to thrive in our increasingly competitive country.[10]

Women's descriptions of their interactions with their own children reflected the current middle-class norms for intensive

mothering, concerted cultivation, safeguarding, and instilling "soft" individualism. In contrast, women's descriptions of
their own childhood experiences sounded strikingly similar to
Annette Lareau's definition of the "accomplishment of natural
growth" model of parenting, which she contends is currently
used by lower and working class parents. In this model, parents do not try to elicit "their children's feelings, opinions, and
thoughts." Instead, they "see a clear boundary between adults
and children." Parents directly "tell their children what to do,"
instead of "persuading them with reasoning." Children do not
"have a steady diet of adult-organized activities," but rather have
"more control" over their leisure time and "are free to go out and
play with friends."[11]

This significant shift in parenting styles suggests that most
middle-class American parents no longer believe their children
will "naturally" be okay without a lot of parental involvement.
Many other market-driven countries are experiencing a similar
explosion in children's activity participation, which some scholars
indicate is a reflection of our belief in the importance of "liberal
individualism," where we expect individuals to stand out in order
to be recognized for what makes them unique.[12]

Some women grew up in homes that fostered "hard" individualism, which Kusserow defines as a style of socialization used by
lower and working class parents to help kids develop "thick skin."
Hard individualism offers kids "protection" from the realities of
"violence, poverty, and misfortune," and "emphasizes the ability
to project themselves to better circumstances."[13] When women
described recurrent conflict they had with their spouse, partner,
or child's father over child-rearing, it seemed like it often related
to a fundamental difference in their beliefs about the importance of instilling "hard" individualism or "soft" individualism, or
whether they thought that kids should be "cultivated" or would
"naturally" grow up to be fine.

## LESSONS, ACTIVITIES, AND SPORTS

Many women expressed a love-hate relationship with their children's activities. Women liked activities because they served many positive functions. They keep kids active, reduce screen time, develop skills, expose kids to new friends, facilitate teamwork, provide adult role models, give kids discipline, boost self-esteem, help children prioritize commitments, and create opportunities for parental socialization. Above all, many liked that activities and sports were fun for their children. The down side of activities for many mothers was the tremendous time commitment and the expense. If a child was in a competitive sport, some mothers felt frustrated by the intensity and politics within a particular team.

A stay-at-home mother, whose four children are all in activities, exclaimed, "Their activities are my schedule!" Celeste noted, "We have three kids with three different sports to manage. I'm tired at the end of the day because I've given it my mental all, and it's like, 'Oh my God, I have a whole other session,' and then the laundry, and I've got to get dinner on the table, but it's my own fault." Jennifer, whose husband travels frequently said, "I was hanging by a thread because it was me and three schedules, and it was just too much." She finally quit her job because she felt she was "constantly leaning on everybody else, and you're always thinking you're never available to give back." Jennifer feels that her kids are in too many activities and she is not keeping up with everything, but she concluded, "I'm doing that to myself by allowing that." Eighty-six percent of the women surveyed "always" or "usually" chose the activities in which their children participated, or were the gatekeeper for kids' requests to do a particular activity, so most women who felt their schedules were too busy also felt responsible.

Ellen, who sets boundaries with how much time she will spend at her kids' events, remarked, "I'm probably not as good of a parent as one of my colleagues that will take time off work and spend three days at an out of town baseball tournament. I don't let my kids play in those tournaments." Several women mentioned that attending games and events on weekends is especially time-consuming. "The worst weekend I have had was when we had 17 games in a weekend," commented Rachel. "I thought, 'What are we doing?' And now sports are dropping off right and left and I didn't have a tournament last weekend, and I hardly knew what to do with myself." A few women felt badly that Sunday tournaments always took precedence over going to church.

Many women enjoyed attending their children's events. "Nobody can tell you how fun and exhilarating it is to watch your kids do stuff," commented Gloria. Brittany, whose daughter is in college, felt "wistful" when she was recently in a restaurant where high school athletes and their parents were eating. "As much as my life was wrapped around my daughter's 10-month dance season, and I had no weekends to myself for years, I sat there wishing it back because it was so fleeting." One mother, whose children have tournaments in different states with their club sports teams, observed that a major difference between her and her parents is that her social life revolves around what her kids are involved in. "It was not that way for my parents. I never wanted my mom to come to any of my athletic events, and she came to one or two a year, but all our vacations seem to be tied up to my kids' sports." Many parents liked the fact that being involved in a child's activities is also a way to spend time together as a family and connect with other families; while some liked that dropping their kids off at activities gave them some personal down time.

Women were especially happy to commit to lessons or sports if their child loved what they were doing. "A lot of the things they do are very expensive, but if they really want to do it, I will figure it out, which is sometimes really hard as a single mom," commented Danielle. "It's important to me to put my life a little bit on hold. I know that sounds terrible, but I think that for the next five years my job is to finish what I've started, and if that's to give my kids opportunities in life once they're out in the world, then that's what I need to do." The main area where mothers pushed their children to do something they did not want to do was music lessons. "I'm a bad mom because I told my boys early on that they are going to do music outside of school," exclaimed Jennifer. "I also told them if you want to quit music, that' fine, but then you also have to quit your sport, so they stayed in music because they loved sports. My son is thankful now, which surprises me, but at the time, it was painful and not fun for anyone." Some women let their children quit music lessons when their children did not like it, and some withdrew their children because lessons were too expensive, or inconvenient, or because their children would not practice enough.

Many women were also mindful of not letting activities and sports consume too much family time. Tara and her husband struggle with the fact that their daughter's swim schedule takes up four nights a week and many weekends. "She loves practice, but she does not like the meets. She does not have the competitive soul of a swimmer. My husband and I are asking ourselves, 'Is that okay to spend this much time for our whole family to do this thing that she is good at, but not great at?'" This fits with an aspect of "talent safeguarding" where parents assess how the time commitment or intensity of an activity "weighs against the 'talent' the child demonstrates now and potentially can convert to future status."[14]

The expense of lessons, activities, or sports was a limiting factor for many families. Some people do not enroll their kids in activities, others have children who are not particularly interested in participating in anything, and some intentionally limit their children's activities so their family can have more down time. Ashley looks at other moms who "bring their kids to swimming lessons and all this other junk, and my kids are chilling at home. If I would have done things in a more traditional order, then my kids wouldn't have to be making sacrifices for my goals." Women who were trying to better their circumstances by getting a college degree after they had children, often felt guilty that they were not able to afford the time or expense of enrolling their children in activities.

Emily believes that children's sports have been "ramped up" because "we want our kids to succeed. We want to make sure we give them every advantage we can." She feels it is competitive in "a keeping up with the Jones' kind of way. If they're starting their kids at soccer at ten, maybe if we start at nine we'll have a little bit of an advantage. It just keeps going back until you have three-year-olds out there." Women who had kids who were good athletes felt there was pressure to specialize at a young age because making varsity, or the top team, requires year-round training. One mother lamented, "I don't know how you go back from where we are now. I don't know that you can, but I think it's really bad." Diana felt it was a "blessing" that her son was a "B+ athlete" because he could participate in multiple team sports without feeling pressure to specialize. Others were disappointed that their kids who were average athletes did not have a chance of making a competitive sports team. This often meant they were no longer able to play a sport that they loved. Many were grateful there were still sports like Track and Field that did not require previous experience and did not cut anyone.

Some mothers worried about overuse injuries and burn-out, which are on the rise for children.[15] "I was an elite athlete, and I know what injury looks like at a young age, and I know what it does to you long term," commented Leslie.

> My son's coach expects him to run 400 miles over the summer, which I don't think is healthy for a growing body, especially considering he is doing other things as well. The other parents are very much on board, but I feel like it's my job to protect him from the things he hasn't learned on his own yet, so we're trying to come up with a happy medium.

Mothers varied in the level of intensity in which they approach lessons, activities, and sports, as well as their vision of how important it is for a child to excel in a particular domain. Some women had kids who were self-motivated to take part in an activity, whereas others pushed their reluctant kids to practice and participate. Some women let their children quit a sport or class mid-season if they did not like it, whereas others felt strongly that it was important for their child not to quit. Women also had different beliefs about the impact that lessons, activities, and sports will have on their child's future. Some were hopeful it would lead to something big, or at least to a college scholarship, whereas others realized their kids would probably not participate in their activity or sport in college, but felt that it was a great thing to be involved in growing up. While some studies suggest that kids are over-scheduled, other researchers note that many children are energetic and have fun being involved in various activities, so it boils down to parents deciding what is best for their particular child.[16] In general, women were mindful of making sure that the activity load matched their children's personality and energy level, and their family dynamic.

Low-income parents have similar desires for how their children should spend their free time, but oftentimes are not able to provide their children with enrichment activities.[17] Researchers note that:

> Social class differences in the quality and quantity of children's activities do not stem largely from fundamental differences in parents' desire to help children cultivate their skills and talents. Instead, these differences stem from parents' differential access to a wide range of resources, including money, the human capital to know best how to cultivate children's talents, and the social capital to learn about and gain access to programs and activities.[18]

As our expectations for children's achievement have expanded, and colleges seek "well-rounded" students, the ability for middle-class parents to afford the time and expense of "cultivating" their child's talent through participation in lessons, activities, and sports, gives them a tremendous advantage over children who do not have equivalent access to enrichment opportunities.

## ACADEMIC ACHIEVEMENT

When I asked women about their children's academic achievement, I heard stories laced with humor, anxiety, pride, and exasperation. Every woman believed that education was important, and many families chose where they lived based on the positive reputation of the public school district. Some enrolled their children in private school if they could afford one. Many women volunteered at their child's elementary school, and most attended conferences and school events in which their child participated. Mothers also went to great lengths to help a child who was struggling academically.

A review of 50 studies on academic achievement indicates that: "parental involvement was positively associated with achievement, with the exception of parental help with homework."[19] The link between parent involvement and school success is so strong that school reforms targeting the achievement gap strive to get parents to be more involved.[20] During elementary school, parent involvement means that parents interact with the school and their child to support their child's academic success.[21] During middle-school, parents should: convey the benefit of education; help their child build habits for doing homework; offer clarification or help with understanding homework if needed; encourage their child's own motivation to do well in school; provide their child with extra experiences that promote knowledge and achievement; and help their child develop plans for their future.[22] Parents of successful high school students across race and class lines have "high levels of educational expectations, consistent encouragement, and actions that enhance the learning opportunities of children."[23] Psychologist Madeline Levine notes that high expectations for children are good, however, "it is when a parent's love is experienced as conditional on achievement that kids are at risk for serious emotional problems."[24]

Some women explicitly verbalized their academic expectations to their children. "We have made it absolutely clear," commented Tara, "that we don't care what they do with their life, but they are going to college. It is not a question." Some felt that even though they may not verbalize their expectations, children were good at picking them up. "We don't say, 'We expect you to get an A,'" commented Gloria, "but I'm pretty sure it oozes out of us." Ashley, was a "hop, skip, and a jump" away from foster care, "so my parents set the bar a little low for me." She realizes how much further she would have been if she had "any help whatsoever," so she tries "really hard" to make sure her kids understand how important it is to do well in school. Angela, who grew up as a "free-range child" and figured out many things for herself believes she could have done better had her parents pushed her a little harder. "I tell my 16-year-old that all the time. 'I'm pushing you because I love you. Just realize that'. Could he do better than he does? Yes! So I push a little bit, and he resists a lot a bit." Andrea is glad her children are self-motivated because she does not keep track of their schoolwork, however, she sometimes wonders what they could have achieved if they had more support. "I see kids with more support, and I think, 'That would be great', but what my kids have done is their own."

Mothers reported that they supported their children in doing homework when they were younger, but did not do the homework for their child. "Did I answer questions? Absolutely. Did I guide them and have resources in my home? Absolutely. But I did not do the work," commented Lynette. "If they forgot something at home, they would have to face the music because I would not bring it up to school for them. Maybe it's too hard

core, but my husband and I really felt it builds responsibility."
Tory laughed when she said how different things were for her
oldest child compared to her younger ones. "I didn't do papers
for her, but if she was supposed to do an edit, we did that edit,
and if I didn't think she was doing a really good job, I'd say, 'You
have to sit down and try again', and there were tears. I don't treat
my younger kids like the project I treated my oldest." Danielle
made sure her kids did their own work from the beginning. "I
didn't believe in going to the 1st grade science fair with a laptop
and PowerPoint. My kids had their poster board and things were
spelled wrong, and I was okay with that because that was how I
wanted to raise my kids."

Mothers were for the most part pro-active in making sure
their child attended a good school, which usually meant living
in an area with good public schools. Women who did not think
their local public school was a good fit for their child tried to
figure out an affordable alternative. Jordan, who lived in a poor
city neighborhood got her daughter into a good private school.
"I didn't want to send her to an inner-city school because I know
it's a meat grinder because I work there." She felt the private
school had enough people of color so her daughter "didn't stick
out like a sore thumb," but it was a big shift in culture for her
daughter. "It's not that I wanted to pick her friends," explained
Jordan. "I wanted to pick the people she could pick from." She is
proud that her daughter was successful in school and learned to
interact with kids who are "stinking rich" while still staying connected to some of her friends from the neighborhood.

Women had different experiences with having a "parent portal" to see their children's grades. Some did not have one, some
never checked it, some only checked it before conferences, and
others were on it daily. Anger or anxiety was the most common response from mothers who noticed a problem. "I see them
going off the rails," joked Sofia. "I would get so angry, but then
I learned that some of the anger was misplaced because teachers
didn't always put in stuff. I feel like the parent portal is there to

make us do their job." Emily laughed when she said, "We usually look at it right before conferences, which then usually results in us yelling, 'Didn't you learn from last quarter that you can't let yourself get behind and expect to catch up.'" One mother, whose oldest son was beginning high school, started looking at the portal daily, reminding her son, "It's all counting now, and mom's stressing." To which her son replied, "Mom, back off. I've got it. Don't look at it again." She did quit verbalizing her anxiety to her son, and was proud that he set a goal for himself and managed his daily work. Mothers were especially frustrated with kids who did not turn in assignments that they had done. "There were many times where it was very painful," commented Jenna. "Every time I would look at the portal, my son would brace himself because I would get so upset and ask him, 'Why didn't you turn that assignment in?'"

While many women liked the fact that technology made communication with teachers much easier, many felt that having access to their children's grades put pressure on them to monitor their child's daily progress. Some felt that having a parent portal was a bad idea because high school kids should be responsible for managing their own grades, and giving parents that kind of daily access makes it more likely that parents will micro-manage their kids.

Mothers who had older students who were not self-motivated, or where school did not come easily, felt it was stressful to oversee their child's academic achievement. One mother expects a 3.0 from her son, however "it is a real struggle" for that 3.0. "Between 4th and 7th grade there was such a clash between me and him or him and his father that we got a math tutor. I think my younger one is exceptionally smart, but it doesn't transfer academically." They eventually enrolled their son in a private school. Jenna, whose son was not a high-achieving student because he had "problems with organizing and paying attention," tried to be helpful, but her son saw her as being "over-controlling."

Women noticed differences in their children's academic strengths or shortcomings. "My kids are so completely different," commented one mother. "One manages everything on his own, and does well, even though it does not come easily for him. One I have to monitor every day because he has ADHD and struggles with knowing what his assignments are and turning them in. The other is in-between." She feels that school is not the best set-up for her son with ADHD because he used to love learning just for the sake of learning, but now his attitude is, "I need this many points to get the grade I need." Others felt their children had different personalities. "Our daughter is a focused, driven, hard-working, high achiever, and our son is content to get a B," noted another mother.

Mothers of high-achieving high school students indicated that their child was self-motivated to do well, and they were no longer involved in overseeing their child's homework. Their children were usually in a peer group of students who also excelled in school. Women believed there is significantly more academic pressure on their children than they had growing up, and many mothers were worried about the college admission process. Some mothers had been thinking about it for years, making sure their kids were well prepared with the right volunteer and extracurricular activities, while most mothers had let their children choose their own classes and activities.

"My kids are in high school, and there's such a pressure cooker around that achievement piece, the grades, the academic performance, the test scores, the college conversations," commented Sylvia. "My son will go to college. Is he going to go to Harvard? No. Is he going to go to a decent school and have a productive life? Yes. But, I think, 'Geez, maybe I wasn't on top of him enough in junior high to build his study habits', and now he's done with his junior year." When Kristina took her son on his first college visit, her son worried that he should be doing more. "If they don't want you, screw them," Kristina told her son. "You can't live your life based on what some imaginary college admission officer thinks you should do because number one, you can't predict it, and number two, for better or worse you're a white male, and number three, it's your life."

Ellen recalls that her mom told her, "You've got to go to college, so figure out how to make that happen." She arranged her own rides to tour campuses by herself. "Now it's so much more competitive. The kids who have to figure it out on their own are at a disadvantage because they are competing against kids who have very involved parents and lots of resources. I don't know if that's a good thing or a bad thing. It's just reality." Parents of all classes want their children to go to college, but middle-class children are more likely than lower-class children to achieve this goal, mainly because of parental involvement, and because school environments and college admission standards are based on middle-class parenting norms.[25] Leslie, whose son "may go to Harvard," is in "the middle of the meat and potatoes of looking at schools" and is surprised by how everything feels so "monumental and tantamount to what will happen in their life. All of a sudden, it just happens, and you have to be on it from such an early time." This speaks to the pressure many parents feel that making sure their children get into a good college is imperative to them having a successful future. "The college machine didn't exist when we were going to school," commented Brittany. To which Kristina replied, "It's such a screwed up model. It's got to break." While some women knew parents who were "resume building" for their children, most tried to keep everything in perspective, and believed that their child was capable of having a good experience at any number of schools.

Former Stanford Dean of Freshman and Undergraduates Julie Lythcott-Haims noticed that as Stanford's incoming freshman became more accomplished, "they seemed increasingly reliant on their parents in a way that felt simply off."[26] She often saw that students' first impulse was to turn to their parents when something little went wrong instead of figuring things out for themselves. Middle-class over-parenting practices aim to give kids an advantage, she argues, but ultimately stunt kids' independence because it sends a message that they are not good enough on their own, and will always need their parents.

Many of the highest-achieving young adults get into competitive colleges because of the tremendous time and resources their parents have invested in coaching them to work hard to achieve distinction. The pressure to ensure a child's future continually increases because "the more mothers labor to build children's portfolios," suggest Milkie and Warner, "the harder it becomes for any one child to stand out, pushing the cultural bar for what counts as unique achievements even higher."[27] This is a clear example of how "liberal individualism" fuels extreme parenting.

Lythcott-Haims notes that parenting a child to be independent someday starts young, and offers parents steps for the process, which include: "give them unstructured time; teach life skills; teach them how to think; prepare them for hard work; let them chart their own path; normalize struggle; have a wider mind-set about colleges; and listen to them."[28] Throughout the interviews, I heard many parenting stories reflecting these steps, which seem grounded in common sense.

Middle-class mothers want to do "right" by their children in ways that reflect our current high expectations for middle-class parents. Women recognize that each child is unique, and that a child's personality, ability, drive, school environment, opportunities, and peer group influence their achievement. They also feel it is important to make sure their kids have access to the education and opportunities that will give them the life skills necessary to "make it" in an increasingly competitive global economy, where even a college degree no longer guarantees a good job. Mothers learn to hold the paradox, as Jenna did, that they are responsible for their children to a point, but as kids grow up, they also make their own decisions. And even though many women took delight in their child's accomplishments, they usually gave their children full credit for their own success.

# Chapter 11

## Raising Good Kids

"We all want the same things for our kids," commented Leslie during a focus group one beautiful June evening. "We want them to be extraordinary. We don't want them to be ordinary. We don't want them to be half as good as anybody else." After reflecting for a moment, Lindsay replied,

> How about if we just want our kids to be happy, and grow up and find meaning and be resilient. Why is there so much pressure to be the best? I think it sets them up for this distorted viewpoint of how life really is. College kids are messed up because parents have never taught them that they're regular people. They're special, but they're regular.

Chloe exclaimed, "We can't all be the best!" Penny, who works closely with students at an urban private college, laughed as she quickly added that college freshman have to come to grips with the fact that "now you're with a lot of special people. Your mom is the only one you're special to because everyone is equally special."

What do we want for our kids? Given that the United States is a competitive society that places a high value on individualism, do we want our kids to be extraordinary, like Leslie suggests? Do we want kids to know that everyone is equally special like the other women suggest? We have traditionally held mothers responsible for socializing their children to grow up to be future productive members of society. How do today's mothers go about doing this, and what makes them feel like they have been a successful parent?

## QUALITIES MOTHERS HOPE TO INSTILL IN THEIR CHILDREN

We live in a society where there is polarizing conflict and inequality. Members of Congress, who arguably should be role models for American youth, routinely treat their colleagues from another party with blatant disrespect. There is a growing gap between wealthy Americans and poor Americans, and racial tension continues throughout our country. In light of the strain we are experiencing in our nation, women felt it was incredibly important to actively teach their children to recognize that people are different, but everyone is equal and deserves respect and kindness.

Mothers felt it was important to teach their children to be respectful, honest, polite, kind, hard-working, loving, empathetic, trustworthy, compassionate, confident, caring, happy, and generous.[1] They wanted their kids to have "good manners," a "good character," "good morals," and "good sportsmanship." They encouraged them to be a "good listener," and be "good to others," and hoped they would grow up to be a "good member of society." They also wanted their kids to be self-motivated, self-reliant, self-sufficient, and have self-esteem, self-love, and self-respect. Many mothers thought it was imperative to teach their daughters to be "emotionally strong," to either protect them from some of the hardships young women face, "like the eating thing," or to "not be a doormat," or to help them be competitive enough so they could do well in school and project themselves into a good career path.

Individualism "binds itself to other racial and ethnic aspects of local worlds, taking on the particular flavor or spice of a rural or urban media-soaked, or media-damped community," writes

Adrie Kusserow.[2] The qualities and behaviors mothers identified as being important suggest that the Minneapolis and St. Paul metro area has a culture that values pro-social behavior, which fits with the colloquial concept of "Minnesota Nice."[3] Parents throughout our country model pro-social behavior when they cooperate with other parents to trade off babysitting and play dates, coordinate carpools, and the countless other ways parents support each other. The United States can be a society that overtly values independence and individualism over cooperation and interdependence because mothers, fathers, grandparents, caregivers, and teachers counter this tendency at the individual level by promoting behavior that facilitates relational connections.[4]

## RELIGION

Religion and spirituality are fundamental ways in which humans address existential questions, create meaning in their lives, receive moral guidance, find comfort, and reinforce a sense of belonging and community. In the mid-1800s, Alexis de Tocqueville identified three cultural forces that curbed American tendencies toward rampant individualism: mothers, religion, and volunteerism.[5] The United States, which is one of the most religious countries in the world, is currently undergoing a shift in religious preferences and affiliations.[6]

Several mothers had a deep commitment to instilling religious beliefs and values in order to give their child a foundation, which they hoped would support them throughout their lives. Ellen feels it is important to teach her children that when you are having "huge successes and epic failures, there's something bigger than you to get through the good and the bad." Emily believes giving her children "that central grounding" is one of the most important aspects of her parenting role. Robin wants her children to grow up with a religious background and have a strong Jewish faith. Her children have attended Jewish preschool and Jewish elementary school because she wants her children to "understand who they are and what religion they come from before they spread out."

Tory, like several women I interviewed, felt that religion was an important component in helping her parent. "I don't know how I would have raised kids without a religion to keep me focused. I wouldn't know how to center myself. It's really helped me to teach my children what is important in life." She noted that, "Raising my kids Catholic as they go through their teen years has been harder because they are aware of the primary issues that the Catholic faith is being criticized for and they're critical of that. I keep telling them, 'Your faith is bigger than those two or three issues.'" She felt critical of the faith herself when her children were young, but "I remember consciously saying to myself, 'What else am I going to do? What faith would I pick instead? I'm going to stick with the one I know and that my ancestors have passed down.'"

For over fifteen years, Jenna has met with a small group of women who pray together. "Our group has been the strongest support for my parenting. We support each other, encourage each other, pray for each other, and feel safe talking about hard things when they happen." Leah said that praying with other mothers has been the main thing that keeps her "sane and hopeful."

Many women felt that belonging to a church or synagogue was a great way to teach their children the importance of helping those in need and giving back to the community. Janet likes the fact that Judaism is "really strong on restoring the earth, which means payback, community service, and giving back to the community." Erica, who grew up Born Again Christian, asserts that religion is a "thorny" issue for her because she has "rejected" so much of fundamentalism. She does not want her children to contend with the feelings of guilt she had because of her religion, and as a result, she is very tentative about how she instills religious beliefs. Erica's family attends a church with a strong social justice message. Erica hopes her children will "see that other people need to be helped, and need to be protected, and respected." She also wants them to understand that "not everyone is treated equal in our world, and that we need to work to change that." Ultimately she thinks that if her children learn to "treat everybody with respect, no matter their gender, their race, or who they choose to love, and believe that everybody is important and equal in the eyes of God, then everything else will follow."

When I asked Abby if she felt that her spirituality or religion affects her parenting, she immediately turned the question around, "Or does being a parent affect your religion?" She went on to explain that she grew up Lutheran, but did not join a church as an adult until her children were born. She feels that growing up in a church environment did not make her a very religious person, but she feels that she is a good person. Abby, like many mothers I spoke with, was involved in her church's youth group when she was a teenager, and wants her children to be active in a church youth group when they are teens. This is in line with Emile Durkheim's assertion that one of the fundamental aspects of religion is its facilitation of a moral community.[7] Abby sometimes feels like "a little bit of a hypocrite because I'm going through the actions but I'm not really all that religious." Charles Lippy notes that many people in the United States have a practical relationship to religion, and tend to be involved in formalized religious institutions when they are raising their children.[8]

Several women had gone to church or synagogue growing up, but were not raising their children within a religious tradition. The main reasons were that: they no longer believed in organized religion; they had moral problems with their religion; they did not believe in God; they had a spouse with a different religious upbringing; they felt that church or synagogue was judgmental; they had not found a church or synagogue they liked; and they did not have the time. Not raising religious kids made some women feel guilty, others felt empowered by freeing themselves from their religious upbringing, many did not think too much about it one way or the other, and some taught their children spiritual values and practices.

Jackie, who had a strong religious upbringing, has chosen not to bring her kids to church. "I think it's all just a made up story to tell you the truth. You get rich white men telling everybody what the stories are, and I think there's something wrong with that, and the older I get, the more firmly I believe there's something wrong with that." Jackie decided, "I don't have to be in this building called church to have my kids get God and have a relationship with God, so I created a religious home school curriculum." Jackie organizes teaching her children about God around monthly themes such as helping others, being grateful, karma, family commandments, and other religious traditions.

Vanessa prays to her children's angels for them, and tells them that they have angels and spirit guides. She has introduced her children to the concept of animal spirit guides because she wanted them to learn about "that whole piece of magic that is yours to be had if you know about it." In *Spiritual, But Not Religious: Understanding Unchurched America*, Robert Fuller notes that unchurched spirituality is a growing trend in the U.S. even amongst people who attend church.[9] He observes that unchurched forms of spirituality "often have a pronounced mystical dimension, which meets the important spiritual need of having a felt-sense of the sacred."[10] He believes this is in part because "many Americans are dissatisfied with our material culture and long for an existentially significant spiritual path."[11]

## PROMOTING AUTONOMY VS. HELICOPTER PARENTING

Most women attempt to strike a balance between being an involved enough parent to ensure their child's wellbeing, and to fit in with current middle-class norms of parenting, without over-managing their child, or inhibiting their child's ability to do things for themselves. Appropriate parental involvement facilitates healthy child development and contributes to positive academic, emotional, and social outcomes for children.[12] Caring parents who support their children by teaching them skills to solve their own problems, to be independent and self-sufficient at a proper level for their age, and to make good decisions and choices, have a positive effect on the overall wellbeing of their child by helping children become autonomous and feel competent in their abilities.[13]

Many women thought the cultural norm is for people to over-parent their kids, and stated that they did not want to be a "helicopter" parent.[14, 15] Even though the phenomenon of "helicopter" parenting is widely reported in the media, there has been little academic research on the subject, with only a handful of studies looking at parents of college-age students.[16] One article describes a helicopter parent as "a mother, father, or even a grandparent who 'hovers' over a student of any age by being involved—sometimes overly so—in student/school, student/employer, or student/societal relationships." The article notes that "positive results accrue when the 'hovering' is age-appropriate; when students and parents engage in a dialogue; when the student is empowered to act; and when parents intercede only if the student needs additional help."[17]

Being an overly controlling, or over-involved parent, may result in a child feeling less capable of managing problems; hinder psychosocial development during adolescence; and has also been associated with higher levels of anxiety, depression, and acting out behavior, combined with lower levels of satisfaction with their family life.[18] It can also lead to lower levels of life satisfaction for the controlling parent.[19] Some studies indicate that middle-class and upper-middle-class white mothers are most likely to be overly involved in their child's life, whereas other studies found that "helicopter parents are male and female and come from all racial, economic, and ethnic groups."[20]

A study of 9,000 college students found that 13% of first year college students replied that their parents helped them solve problems at college "often" or "very often," and 25% stated their parents "sometimes" intervened. These percentages for seniors were 8% and 21%, respectively.[21] This indicates that 87% of first year college students, and 92% of senior college students in this study do *not* feel that their parents frequently step into to solve problems for them.[22] Another study found that parents who show interest in their child's college experience and are supportive of them have a positive impact on their child's decision-making skills and autonomy.[23] Other researchers interviewed 190 academic and student affairs administrators and found that their estimates of college helicopter parents were in the 40 to 60 percent range, with most helicopter parents being a "consumer advocate," "fairness advocate," or a "safety patrol parent."[24]

Mothers wanted to encourage their child to be independent, and figure things out on their own, although many felt it was harder for kids to be independent than it was when they were growing up. Many women believed that safety concerns inhibited a child and teen's ability to roam freely, and some thought the current norm of parental involvement means that kids get less autonomy. "When we had out-of-town meets in high school," commented Emily, "we'd just go and stay in a hotel with our team. Now, it's the whole family. Kids do not get the chance to branch out." Others thought cell phones made parents and kids too closely connected. "I know a lot of moms who text their kids during school," one mother observed. A woman who works closely with college students has noticed that many freshmen have problems dealing with roommate conflict, which she thinks is because most kids have not learned basic conflict resolution skills. She makes her daughters share a bedroom because she feels "it is one of the little things I can do to help them learn to communicate and deal with conflict."

Several women felt their kids' experiences with failure were important in helping them learn coping skills. One mother reminds her kids that, "Failure is an opportunity for a fresh start." Another mother wants her children to know that, "It's okay if you fall apart, and it's okay if you make mistakes," but at the same time, she wants to "manage them so they don't make big mistakes." Even though most mothers thought it was important for their child to experience failure in some things, I consistently found that women wanted to be involved enough to make sure their child did not make a mistake so big that it would have serious or long-term consequences. "In some ways I am a hovering mom," remarked one woman, "because during my son's senior year I drove him to school every day because I was going to do whatever it took to get him through his senior year." Danielle held her hands far apart as she explained, "The best thing I did was to have these boundaries of what was acceptable and what wasn't, and it is a very wide path. I'm giving my kids space all along the spectrum, but the minute they go outside the boundary I've defined is when there's an issue."

Mothers knew it was important to give kids household responsibility and chores, however women had different levels of follow-through with this. Some expected their kids to contribute on a daily basis. "My mantra to my kids is that I have a full time job, your dad has a full time job, we don't have time, so you have to contribute and pick up your crap," commented Penny. "Everyday there's a dishwasher to empty and other chores they have to get done." Some mothers had chore charts with daily responsibilities, and others had the expectation that their kids would help clean whenever the house needed cleaning. Others felt that assigning chores was one more thing they had to manage. "I've had to let go of the stress of assigning chores around the house and making sure they do them, because I'm just too tired to do that," commented one mother. Some felt their kids were so busy with homework and activities, or employment, that there was no time for them to do daily chores.

In one focus group, a woman was critical of her sister because her niece was about to go to college and had never washed a load of laundry. Nicole replied, "I'm guilty of that." She went on to explain, "I have ways I like my household run, and I'm anal in that way. I don't want my washing machine messed up. My mom did my laundry until I moved out, so I don't think there's a right

way or a wrong way, it is just something that has worked for us."
Nicole feels her son is self-sufficient in many ways and can do
things like change his own oil, but she is always asking herself:

> Is my son ready for the real world? Can I teach him
> something else? When he decides to marry and take on a
> family, is he going to be able to take care of them? Is he a
> solid man to run a household and to be there for his wife
> as a companion and helpmate? Is he going to be a stand
> up dad for his kids if he gives me grandkids? I know
> there are things he'll learn on the way, but as a mom I
> want to send him out in the world correctly.

Every mother believed it was important to teach their children
skills and attitudes so they could function on their own when
they left home.

## CONNECTED AUTONOMY

Mothers want to raise children to be independent and self-sufficient adults, yet they also want to maintain a sense of connection
to their kids, even after they leave home. I use the term "connected autonomy" to describe this new expectation, which
several women remarked is very different from their own parents. "My parents raised us to leave," observed Gloria. "I don't
know anymore what the end game is. Are we raising more of a
community of connected people? That would be much more like
the rest of the world, where the expectation is that you're going
to be part of my life." Jenna said, "I don't think my parents had
any expectation of being involved with me when I went off to
college." Lynette exclaimed, "We were dropped at 18!"

Lynnette's older children, who are out of college, continue to
check in with her almost daily. She wishes there were a new word
for her relationship with her older daughters. "I'm not the mom,
and I'm not a friend. I'm in between there someplace. I'm more
of a confidant." Beth, who talks to her college daughters more
than she ever talked with her own parents, wonders if frequent

communication is healthy, or if it is prolonging a dependent relationship.

> There is this whole phenomenon of the crisis phone call. I get 100% of the 10% that's wrong in her life. It distorts my overall sense of how she is. I'd call home once a week on Sunday when the rates were down, so I had a week to deal with any crisis and get perspective, and I get the instant phone call, so it's curious to me.

Even though it is easy to communicate with children after they leave home, most mothers want their children to become autonomous. Many women gave their young adult children space by not calling or texting frequently; several reported that their children did things to claim their own independence, like not checking in as often, or blocking them from social media platforms; and some felt their child was able to become independent amidst frequent communication.

## WHAT MAKES A MOTHER FEEL SUCCESSFUL?

When I asked mothers, "What have you been successful at as a mother?" an uncomfortable silence *always* followed this question, unless someone joked, "My kids are alive," which many did. Throughout the interviews, women were hard on themselves for things they could have done better or differently, or for not doing things they knew they "should" do. Ellen recalled a conversation she had with her 82-year-old neighbor.

> My neighbor told me, 'You're doing a great job, and your kids are wonderful.' I said, 'Really? I think the jury is still out. I'm not sure. I never feel secure about this.' Then I asked her, 'When do you know that you've been successful as a parent?' She replied, 'When they're 35.' I said, 'So we're only half way there!' (Laughter.)

How do mothers measure their success? It is a difficult question to answer because there is no cut-and-dried standard for what constitutes doing a good job as a parent. Our cultural focus is often on what parents do wrong, as opposed to what they are getting right; and if success is measured solely by the adult a child becomes, then it is definitely is a long-term prospect, as Ellen's neighbor observes.

It took most women awhile to answer the question, and many ultimately answered the question by describing their parenting failures. "A lot of times, you have a bad day, you've yelled at the kids, and everyone is pushing buttons," commented one mother, "and at the end of the day you think, 'I'm such a horrible parent' and you lose track of things you did right." Another mother said, "Some days I feel like I haven't been successful at anything, but every year when we leave family camp I feel like this is the one thing we did right this year." One mother sighed as she said, "I certainly have a very realistic view of my parenting ability and if anything, I've struggled with being a bad mom, but my son knows I care."

Several women measured their success by seeing behaviors and traits in their children they thought were important such as: manners, respect, curiosity, empathy, being thoughtful, non-judgmental, accepting of others, not self-centered, independent, and self-sufficient. Women also felt successful because their kids were good students, or well rounded, or comfortable in their own skin, and many were grateful their kids did not smoke, drink, or do drugs. Others were proud they had provided their children with opportunities, experiences, and a good home life; and many mentioned that they loved their children unconditionally, with no favorites. Some felt they were successful at role modeling how to meet the big and small challenges in life, and teaching their kids how to get through their own failures and challenges.

"I feel like they could function, God forbid, if I wasn't there," remarked Sylvia. Penny commented, "My daughter is willing to forge her own path. She does not get stuck in this box of what you have to do because you're a girl, and I love that about her. When I see that, I think, 'Okay, I did something right.'" Ashley exclaimed, "My kids are aware of class and gender and social and race issues because they get to hear it from me all the damn time!" Sofia felt successful because she thought a couple of her children would take care of her when she was old.

"I did not see a lot of anger or emotional variation in our Norwegian household," commented Holly. "I try to see the upside of demonstrating anger sometimes (laughter) and having arguments and strong emotions, and getting through them, and showing my kids that we still love each other and can move on." Beth said, "I have modeled saying I'm sorry first because it is hard to offer a humble apology, but I feel like it has been one successful thing I've done because it's helped my relationships with these strong-willed emerging adults." Some women were happy that their kids could be honest with them. "I like how my kids tell me everything straight up," said one mother. "They can also cuss like sailors, which I think is adorable because I don't think vulgar language is entirely a bad thing."

Many women who described their children as "good" kids attributed it to luck or biology, and one woman felt she could not take responsibility for how her children turned out, good or bad. Others felt that having a community of people who loved their kids was the most important thing they had provided. "I grew up so isolated," remarked Kristina, "and my kids understand there are many grown ups who love them and care for them, and they have so many people they are accountable to." One woman cried as she said:

> I'm grateful to have a community where my kids have tasted what is lovely, good, and true. I'm scared about where they're at and the choices they're making. It took becoming a parent to recognize that my parents did the best they could with what they had. I've failed in so many ways, but I've done my best. We get our parents neurosis and we impart our neurosis. They know they're loved and they're part of a stable community, and if they get

themselves to a place where they are not knowing this, I hope they will come back to it.

Several mothers were grateful that they had been successful at changing a generational family message. One mother reflected:

> I can remember such a seminal moment when my therapist said to me, so many of the things you're dealing with are because your whole life you have always felt that you were a burden, and if you could change that for your children, their lives and the world will be transformed. I get chills when I say that because my kids know that they're a blessing, and even when I'm pissed as hell at them, they know that I love them and believe that my life and the world is better because they are on this planet. I didn't have that, and I am so grateful to be able to give that to them.

Another mother commented:

> When I was growing up, my mother would often say to us, 'My life would be so much better if I hadn't had you guys'. When I had my daughter, it was clear to me that she's the best thing that ever happened to me, and I might not always like her, but I absolutely love her, and I can say without hesitation that she believes that. I succeeded there.

One woman, who was "not planned," knew her entire life that her mother was resentful that she had to get married at 21 because her mother constantly threatened to leave the family. "I have made a conscious effort to make sure my kids know I enjoy them, and that watching them do gymnastics makes me happy and is fun. I've been trying to be less hard on myself, but I do feel good about this."

Both of Erin's parents have been dead for several years, but she is comforted just "knowing" that they would be proud of her accomplishments.

Sometimes I don't feel like I'm successful, but ultimately my kids know I love them unconditionally. I hope when I'm gone the love and anchoring I gave them will make them feel proud of themselves and make them walk through the world knowing that you're a good person, knowing that you have love, and that you're not walking alone, even if that person isn't there anymore. I hope I am that person for them when I'm gone.

These women's responses show that women want different things for their kids, and do their best to ensure their kids have the beliefs, skills, and qualities they personally feel are important to be successful in life. The daily challenges of raising children, combined with the fact that women frequently have to let some of their parenting ideals go, makes mothers more likely to be self-critical. Yet, when mothers reluctantly identified what makes them feel successful, we see the many ways in which mothers are doing a great job of raising good kids.

# Chapter 12

# Where Do We Go from Here?

This book has provided a snapshot of the diverse thoughts, feelings, and experiences of a cohort of Minnesota middle-class mothers as they juggle and balance their various roles and responsibilities. It has shown how cultural changes over the last generation have increased the workload and stress level of mothers who are responsible for protecting their children from negative cultural influences, while preparing their kids for an increasingly competitive world.[1] It has also revealed the tremendous thoughtfulness, time, and effort women put into parenting, along with the pressure and guilt mothers often experience on a daily basis.

The majority of women who participated in this study had a college degree, adequate resources to support their family, and many even had an above-average standard of living. Most lived in safe neighborhoods, and were in stable marriages, or shared custody with a child's father.[2] In turn, these mothers are able to provide their children with good educational opportunities, access to various enrichment activities, and quality time. The stories of these women reveal that even privileged mothers are under a lot of pressure in our culture, while mothers who have access to fewer resources experience even greater challenges. This begs the question: What can we do to create more support for all parents and children in our culture?

Over the past several decades, there have been numerous scholarly books and articles written about mothers, and many have suggested that we implement public policies to assist parents. To date, we have no broad scale social policies that have made it easier for parents, and in our current political environment, it is unlikely that sweeping government changes will happen anytime soon. Americans have different visions of the government's responsibility to our children; our fiscal crisis makes creating new programs problematic; powerful corporations are influential in lobbying against regulation; and our current congress has repeatedly demonstrated the limits of its ability to reach a consensus on anything. We need to think of other solutions.

We are at a turning point in our culture. We can continue to place much of the responsibility for managing the effects of social change on mothers' plates; or alternatively, we could re-envision our cultural beliefs and practices to better support all parents raising children. In *Switch: How to Change Things When Change is Hard*, authors Chip and Dan Heath argue that it is imperative to focus on the "bright spots," or the ways in which people are creating solutions to a problem, which can be replicated by others.[3] The women's stories reflected many "bright spots" in creating individual, family, community, workplace, and cultural changes that support parents.

## REVEALING "BRIGHT SPOTS"

### *Creating Realistic Expectations for Good Parenting*

The good news for all mothers is that no one aspires to be a "perfect supermom." Instead, women have realistic and practical ideas about what makes someone a good mother. As more women recognize that there is wide scale rejection that a "perfect supermom" is a "good" mother, the idealized images of motherhood will begin to lose their power. As individuals, and as a culture, we can more fully embrace the idea of the "good enough mother," and we can acknowledge that there are no universal rules that all American parents follow, and no one right way to parent. This gives parents a fair amount of freedom in how they raise their children, as long as they are not hurting, neglecting, or endangering a child.

Since measuring one's overall parenting success is elusive, and our cultural focus tends to be on what mothers do wrong, women can be proactive in defining ways in which they are successful. Mothers who are in the habit of rehashing their parenting failures at the end of the day can experiment with switching their point of view to focus on small daily successes rather than perceived shortcomings. Some women reduce their guilt by framing the things they do for themselves in a positive light. Others make sure they make time to replenish themselves periodically, which reduces their overall stress.

## Support for New Parents

Several Minneapolis and St. Paul hospitals are updating maternity wards and offering services to create better birthing and postpartum experiences for new parents, which may make the physical, emotional, and psychological transition to parenthood easier. In-home nurse visits following the birth of a child have a positive effect on the wellbeing of both the mother and child, and decrease the severity of depressive symptoms for women experiencing postpartum depression.[4] Minnesota's Early Childhood Family Education (ECFE) program provides family education classes taught by licensed educators for children and parents from birth until a child enters kindergarten. These classes provide support, education, and enrichment by helping parents develop their parenting skills, increase their knowledge of child development, and navigate potential parenting stressors. Minnesota is the only state in the country that offers these classes through each school district. ECFE classes have a sliding fee scale, and no family is turned away because of cost. In 2010 alone, ECFE classes throughout the state served more than 120,000 children and nearly 130,000 parents.[5]

Many women felt lucky for all the ways friends, family, and co-workers supported them as they made the transition to parenthood, and were committed to pass on acts of kindness to other new parents. Having a child is a big transition in the lives of individuals and couples. Realistic information about the broad range of normal experiences, including sleep deprivation, postpartum depression, or relationship difficulties, will make it easier for people to honestly talk about their experiences with friends, family, or healthcare providers so that they can receive help if they need it. Couples can be proactive in figuring out strategies to have regular date nights, incorporate their new parenting roles into their relationship, and stay connected to each other as they embark on the project of raising children together.

### Creating an Equitable Division of Labor

The division of labor is a significant issue that many couples fight about. Women in heterosexual relationships are usually the partner most dissatisfied with the division of labor because they are more likely to have a heavier workload if a couple has children. Couples who have an egalitarian division of labor tend to have three things in common. 1) They commit to organizing household and childcare tasks in a non-gendered way. 2) The male partner has primary responsibility for childcare at some point. 3) Couples trust their partner's parenting decisions, and do not try to control how their partner parents.

Our historical cultural practices that make it seem "natural" for women to be responsible for childcare, domestic responsibilities, and "the work of kinship," and for men to be "breadwinners" create conditions that stack the deck against achieving gender equality in the home. While there are some commercials representing men as being responsible for cleaning or childcare, more representations of men as being *competent* in cleaning and caring for children may normalize men's housework and childcare participation. Several women noted that their husbands were taking on some of the "work of kinship," such as arranging play dates, planning birthday parties, and buying presents for extended family members.

## Supporting Working Mothers and Stay-At-Home Mothers

We can recognize that the "Mommy Wars" does not literally exist because working mothers and stay-at-home mothers are not homogenous groups of women unified in a battle against another group of women. What does exist, are negative cultural stereotypes of both working mothers and stay-at-home mothers, which set up artificial divides and fuel judgments many women have internalized. All mothers would benefit from dismantling our stereotypes of marginalized groups of mothers and creating a broader awareness of the multiple constraints American mothers face. At the community level, there are countless practical ways mothers support each other on a daily basis. Community expectations for how families will manage working and taking care of children are diverse, and women who lived in neighborhoods that were supportive of people doing what was best for their family appreciated this atmosphere.

The majority of women, regardless of whether they worked or stayed home with children full time, made career sacrifices. Research indicates that young single women expect that they will have to "interrupt their work" when they have children, whereas young men do not.[6] Studies consistently show that creating family-friendly workplace environments, which offer benefits such as flextime and onsite daycare, create greater job, family, and life satisfaction for all employees.[7] These policies are also effective in sustaining employee engagement and are a draw for recruiting and retaining talent.[8] The women whose employers made it easier to create work-life balance were incredibly loyal to their organization. Organizations that have employees who are "invested and enthusiastic" increase an organization's success in measurable ways. Happy employees are "more productive, more creative, and provide better client service." They are also less likely to quit or call in sick.[9]

## Safety

Our perception that the world is inherently less safe for children is in part a response to our increased cultural awareness of risk combined with the high prevalence of media stories and images designed to promote fear.[10] Dan Gardner notes that people need to rationally correct for the ways in which their perception of danger has been skewed by exposure to anxiety-provoking media images.[11] Jared Diamond suggests that people should be more mindful of risks they can actually control instead of worrying about unlikely scenarios.[12] One mother made a conscious decision to focus on seatbelts, helmets, and sunscreen, because these were three things in her control.

Lenore Skenazy's *Freerange Kids* has created a movement where many parents are intentionally giving their children more freedom. Women described different community norms, which were influential in determining how much freedom their kids had to roam the neighborhood. However, the widely publicized recent arrests of parents who let their children go to the park by themselves, made many women less inclined to let their children go to the park on their own. Several mothers wished their community had clear rules for the age in which a child can go to the park alone, or with other kids. Women who lived in unsafe, or economically disadvantaged neighborhoods wished there were safe neighborhood recreation options for their children. Several women were involved in neighborhood groups that organized events to bring community members together.

## Nutrition, Exercise, and Body Image

Programs such as *Let's Move*, and many others like it, are creating a sense of shared responsibility amongst families, schools, and communities for creating opportunities and infrastructure for exercise, and healthy food choices. Mothers appreciated the ways in which schools are incorporating healthier food options and more exercise into their kids' daily routine. CDC Director,

Thomas Freidan has proposed several ideas for implementing public policies to reduce obesity rates. Although government regulation has become unlikely, consumers have gained some power in pressuring big food companies to make changes. For example, Minnesota-based General Mills has pledged to remove artificial colors and flavors from its cereal, and have already reduced the amount of sugar in some of its kid brands in response to changing public attitudes. Many mothers are making an effort to help their daughters have a positive body image by being mindful not to say negative things about their own body in front of their daughter.

## Screen Time

This is one of the harder areas for cultural and community interventions as kids have increased access to technology through smartphones and other devices. The U.S. Task Force on Community Preventive Services, which is a panel of public health experts appointed by the CDC, believes there is sufficient evidence to recommend that communities and schools roll out more programs aimed at reducing screen time, while encouraging physical activity.[13]

## Advertising and Consumerism

Parents are on the frontlines in buffering their children from the negative aspects of consumer culture, while also teaching children responsible consumer behavior, and allowing them to enjoy the things and experiences one can get in our culture. Every mother employed strategies such as: limiting television and trips to the store, teaching children the importance of working to get things, having children learn about money management with an allowance, talking to their children about needs verses wants, teaching their children to delay gratification, modeling lifestyles of anti-consumerism, and exposing their children to those who have less through volunteering. One woman's tweet about gender-based signage in an Ohio Target store prompted a national conversation. In response to guests' opinions that gender-based labeling is unnecessary, Target announced that it will phase out gender-based labeling in many departments.[14] In an era where the government is unlikely to regulate corporations, exerting consumer power has become a potential avenue for creating change.

## Achievement and Activities

Children's lessons, activities, and sports, which can require a significant amount of parental time and resources, are functional in helping kids get exercise, develop skills, reduce screen time, promote friendships, and so forth. One Minnesota suburb teamed up with the YMCA to offer immigrants who lived in low-income housing free youth summer programs, which provided games, activities, and crafts. Creating on-site youth programming eliminates "barriers such as cost, technology, and transportation issues."[15] A recent report noted that 263,443 kids, which is about one-third of the children living in Minnesota, would participate in an after school program if there was one available to them.[16] Creating more access to enrichment opportunities that eliminate barriers to participation will help level the playing field for all kids who want to participate in activities. There are also several community-based afterschool programs that serve children in "low performing schools" located in high poverty neighborhoods.[17] A national study of high-quality after-school programs for low-income children found that children who attended these programs over a two-year time period made significant academic and behavior improvements, increased their standardized math test scores, and had fewer incidences of misconduct and substance abuse than their peers who were not involved in after-school programming.[18] Funding and creating more after-school programs that offer kids enrichment opportunities and resources to be academically successful is a step towards closing the achievement gap.[19]

## SUPPORTING THE WORK OF MOTHERS

Many of the "intensive mothering norms" women have adapted are a response to our changing cultural environment, where mothers are responsible for keeping their kids safe and healthy, buffering children from market forces and inappropriate media, and preparing them to be successful in our increasingly competitive global economy. If we want to reduce the pressure many mothers routinely feel, foster an environment where mothers are better able to balance work, family, and leisure pursuits, and create equal opportunities for all American children to succeed, then we need to hold fathers, workplaces, schools, communities, corporations, and our government accountable for taking some of the responsibility off mothers' plates. The actions we take today will have an impact on the next generation of parents and children. Cultural change is daunting, but family, workplace, and community change is definitely achievable. As the words of Margaret Mead remind us: "Never doubt that a small group of thoughtful, committed citizens can change the world; indeed it is the only thing that ever has."

## THE WISDOM OF AMERICAN MOTHERS

At the end of every interview and focus group, I asked women what their advice would be to a new mother just starting out. I close this book by sharing the collective counsel of Minnesota Mothers:

- Accept that your life is going to be different after you have kids, and enjoy the process. Enjoy every phase, even the hard ones, because everything is temporary. Even when it is not fun, try to be in the moment, and do not over-think it. Do not wish any part of your life away because it goes fast, and you will never get that time again. It will just be a fleeting memory someday.

- Go easy on yourself, because everyone has bad days. There is no right way. Your children don't always have to be perfectly dressed, perfectly fed, perfectly anything. You are not going to be on top of your game every day, so learn to forgive yourself. If you have a bad day, tell your kids, "I'm sorry," because they need to know that it is okay to make mistakes, and that everyone makes mistakes. Doing that will help them understand that you will still love them even when they make mistakes.

- Follow your gut, and don't worry about how others perceive you. If your head is getting wrapped up in something, and it's not feeling right, you're probably not supposed to be focusing on it. Know that you are going to have challenges and that it might not be smooth sailing from A to B, but chances are your kids are going to turn out just fine. You may not feel that way when you're in the midst of a hard time, but it does all work out. If something terrible happens, and your kid doesn't turn out, whatever that means, it is not your fault.

- Acknowledge that motherhood can be isolating, and try not to isolate yourself, even if you are shy. Don't be afraid to take your children places when they're babies, and don't be afraid to go out and do things with them. Find a group of parents with children your age. If you don't know anyone, join an ECFE class. Talk to other moms when it is hard, and don't pretend like your life is okay when it is not. The second you have a group of parents you can talk to, it puts everything in perspective because someone else's baby may be even more difficult than yours, and you will hear some version of what you are going through for better or worse. Don't be afraid to ask questions, and don't be afraid to ask for help from other Moms and Dads. Surround yourself with people who are good for you and helpful, and if some parents are stressing you out, then don't pay attention to what they are doing.

- Do things to make your family work. Have Sunday night meetings where everyone in the family comes together with the calendar, and weekly to-do lists, and any other issues. Make sure your kids contribute when they are old enough to do chores. Even if some things would be easier to do yourself, children need to understand that pitching in is part of being a family and that Mom doesn't do everything. Put your phones away during meals.

- Give your children a wide path of what is acceptable, let them make mistakes within that path, and pick your battles. Control the controllable, and don't worry about the other stuff. There is so much conflicting information, and everyone gives you advice, so you have to develop the ability to take it in, filter what you think might work for you, and ignore the rest.

- Wear the macaroni necklace your child makes for you. Hang their artwork on the fridge. Play with them, spend time with them, and don't over-indulge them. Buy fewer toys, because your kids don't need as many things as you think they do. Try your best to be patient, even if you're not a patient person. When you feel yourself getting angry, count to ten in your head before you respond. Remember that kids go through phases, and they are doing what they are supposed to be doing, and the behaviors you can't stand will pass. Don't keep signing them up for soccer, especially if they never once kick a soccer ball in the yard. In fact, you don't even have an obligation to do soccer in the first place.

- Let your kids know that they matter. Let them see your eyes light up when they walk into a room.

- Get as much sleep as you can, take good care of yourself, and make sure you get your own emotional needs met. Take some time for yourself and for you and your husband. Make sure you and your partner are in a good place before you start having kids. Try to make yourself happy because it will ultimately make you a better person, and able to give more to your children.

- Do not look at parenting as a job because, if it is a job, then in the end you're going to wonder whether you were successful or whether you failed. Don't do it for the recognition and admiration from outsiders. Put your heart and soul into it because it is the human interaction that really matters in the end. Love your kids like crazy, let them be who they are, do not judge them, and enjoy who they are at this very moment.

# APPENDIX 1:
# RESEARCH METHODOLOGY

*All On One Plate: Cultural Expectations on American Mothers* is an ethnography which highlights the thoughts, feelings, and experiences of self-described middle-class, upper-middle-class, and lower-middle-class mothers in the Minneapolis-St. Paul metropolitan area (MSP). There are several ways of defining social class depending on the weighting of professional prestige, educational attainment, income, and family wealth. I relied on individual women's self-assessment of their class status. Many women had a difficult time deciding what class they were. Additionally, two women described themselves as upper class, two women described themselves as lower class, and one participant did not live in MSP.

The first phase of research for this project took place between April 2007 and November 2008. I used this research to complete my doctoral dissertation in anthropology at the University of Minnesota. The University of Minnesota Institutional Review Board approved this study. To recruit participants during Phase 1, I distributed five-page detailed questionnaires to daycare centers, pre-schools, and Early Childhood Family and Education classes in MSP. I also had people from different neighborhoods in MSP distribute no more than five surveys to mothers in their area. The questionnaires included return postage-paid envelopes addressed to me. I continued distributing surveys until I received 80 responses. This technique is called "snowball sampling."[1] Snowball sampling provides practical advantages in reaching target populations for qualitative and descriptive social science research. Snowball sampling is considered an "ascending methodology" that is especially useful for locating the subjects needed to provide comprehensive data on specific research questions. One of the drawbacks of snowball sampling is the problem of selection bias. I offset this by using many "chains" of subject referrals with fewer links per chain.

In the questionnaires, women filled in a chart indicating who is responsible for 32 common household and childcare tasks; answered 18 questions to assess their beliefs about parenting; answered eight open-ended questions on topics related to parenting; and filled in demographic information. Women could indicate if they were interested in participating in a one-on-one interview. Twenty participants who completed the survey also participated in an interview. However, these women are only included one time in the total number of participants. Every woman who participated in the first phase of research had at least one child under the age of 10, with the range being from four months to nineteen years, with a mean age of four. I gave women who participated in an interview a $15 gift card, and for every 10 questionnaires I received in the mail, I randomly drew one questionnaire and mailed that person a $10 gift card.

The second phase of research took place in the spring of 2014, and the final phase occurred in June and July of 2015. I used snowball sampling to recruit participants for these phases, and interviewed 46 mothers in individual interviews, or small focus groups of not more than six people. Six of the mothers in this cohort had participated in a phase 1 interview, but I only include them once in counting the total number of participants. In phase 3, I primarily recruited women who had at least one child in middle school, junior high, and high school. I recorded and transcribed all interviews and focus groups, which lasted anywhere from 45 minutes to three hours. I offered no monetary compensation for women who participated in phase 2 and 3, however I did promise to send them a copy of this book.

Overall, 140 women from 40 zip codes participated in this study. Of the 80 women who participated in an interview or focus group: 12.5% identified themselves as African American; 3.75% identified themselves as Asian American; 3.75% identified themselves as bi-racial; 73.75% identified themselves as

Caucasian; 5% identified themselves as Latino; and 1.25 percent identified themselves as "other," but did not specify their racial category. Women had a variety of work experiences, ranging from being home full time with their children, working part-time, working full-time, and some were the primary breadwinner for the household. The majority of women were married or living with a partner at the time of the interview, and the majority of these partnerships were heterosexual. Approximately 15 percent of the interview sample were single, or had been single for a significant amount of time while raising children. Women were single because of divorce, being widowed, or because they had never been married. Every participant had a high school degree, and some college or technical training. The majority of women had a college degree, and at least 25% of the sample reported having a graduate degree or some graduate training.

I use grounded theory methodology for my data analysis because it can generate, expand, and validate social science theory.[2] In the first level of analysis, I read the transcription of every interview and focus group several times in order to identify salient themes, and core categories. Then I assigned codes for core themes and categories, and coded the transcripts accordingly. In the second level of analysis, I used grounded theory "memoing" technique to write memos about each core category and sorted the memos in relation to the core categories they addressed. In the third level of analysis, I analyzed the data to look for coherency, differences, and structures of meaning within each interview, and across all interviews. Ultimately, I was looking for "data saturation" for each category. Data saturation occurs when interview data add no new concepts to a particular category.

Using qualitative data in social science research has many advantages. "Qualitative data, with their emphasis on people's 'lived experience,' are fundamentally well suited for locating the *meanings* people place on the events, processes, and structures of their lives; their 'perceptions, assumptions, prejudgments, presuppositions' and for connecting these meanings to the *social world* around them."[3] In some chapters, I supplement qualitative data with quantitative data based on the answers to the questionnaires I distributed.

# APPENDIX 2:
# THE TOP TEN ATTRIBUTES OF AN
# IDEAL AMERICAN MOTHER

| Rank | Overall Description | Specific Resposes |
|---|---|---|
| 1 | Perfect Supermom | perfect, does it all; Supermom; does everything perfectly; handles everything (full time work, household, childcare) without anyone feeling shorted; a perfect wife, mother, lover, housekeeper, entertainer |
| 2 (tied) | Self-Sacrificing | self-sacrificing; sacrificing; selfless, puts needs of family before her own; puts children's needs above everything |
| 2 (tied) | Calm, Happy, Never Stressed | calm; always calm; even-tempered; never frustrated; never stressed; has no visible stress; always cheery; always smiling; always happy; completely fulfilled by role as a mom |
| 4 | Patient | patient; always patient; never ending patience |
| 5 (tied) | Looks Good | looks good; looks great; looks sassy; put-together; beautiful; looks fit; trim; dresses nice; should look like single self; wears make-up |
| 5 (tied) | Great Cook | great cook; prepares delicious meals; prepares well-balanced meals; feeds organic food; provides good food; bakes cookies |
| 5 (tied) | Good Housekeeper | homemaker; keeps house clean; does laundry; takes lead with all domestic needs; manages house |
| 8(tied) | Stay-At-Home Mom | stays home with her children; quits her job |

| 8 (tied) | Working Mom | works full time; advances career; brings home the bacon; contributes to the household income; balances work and family; provides financially; works some outside the home but puts her kids first |
|---|---|---|
| 8 (tied) | Perfect Children | children are: perfect; well-behaved; smart; good; happy; well-mannered; polite; respectful; sleeping through the night; wearing nice clothes; involved in a lot of extra-curricular activities that she is happy to drive them to in her mini-van; happy to listen to her and she never has to raise her voice. |

# APPENDIX 3:
# THE TOP TEN ATTRIBUTES OF MOTHERS' PERSONAL VIEW OF A GOOD MOTHER

| Rank | Category | Description |
|---|---|---|
| 1 | Loves Child Unconditionally | loves child unconditionally; makes child feel loved; helps child realize their uniqueness and loves them for who they are; lots of love |
| 2 (tied) | Setting Rules & Limits; Discipline | setting rules and limits; providing discipline; setting boundaries |
| 2 (tied) | Teaching Child | teach child: values; morals; responsibility; compassion; right from wrong; respect; honesty; to work hard; to live on one's own some day; good personal habits; healthy eating; how to clean a bathroom |
| 4 | Balance | balance; balance between self-centered and child-centered; creates balance for self so I am best able to raise happy, self-directed children/adults; takes time for self so enjoys being a mom; a balanced person who pursues their "before kids" interests and stays current; respectful to child's needs while keeping herself happy and healthy; doing the best they can for the well being of their children while not sacrificing themselves to do so |
| 4 (tied) | Emotionally Present | emotionally present; take time to 'be' with child; one who is 'there' paying attention and energy to child; is always there for kids when they need her; attentive to child's needs, not desires and whims; attends to child's needs as they really are, not from societal pressure or an idea; knows individual kid's needs; gives undivided attention; tries her best to be available |

| Rank | Category | Description |
|------|----------|-------------|
| 6 | **Spending Time With Child** | spends time with children; spends quality time with children; spends time with each child to talk, play, and laugh; spends quality time playing and reading |
| 7 | **Patient** | patient; patience |
| 8 | **Choosing Work Status** | one person said that "a good mother can balance working outside the home on a part time basis while being there for her children;" the others stated that one's work status did not affect one's ability to be a good mother |
| 9 (tied) | **Providing a Safe Environment** | provides safe, consistent environment; provides security for each child (emotional and physical); keeps kids safe; makes child feel safe and secure; makes child feel safe and loved |
| 9 (tied) | **Being a Good Role Model** | is a good role model for her children; makes good choices to be a positive role model for her kids; models deliberate, conscious life; healthy social behavior; sets a good example |

# ENDNOTES

## NOTES FOR INTRODUCTION

1. See: C. Ogden et al., "Prevalence of Obesity in the United States, 2009-2010," *National Center for Health Statistics Data Brief* no. 82 (January 2012). H. Colten and B. Altevogt, eds., *Sleep Disorders and Sleep Deprivation: An Unmet Public Health Problem* (National Academies Press, 2006). J. Song, "How Sleep Loss Affects Women More Than Men," *WEB MD - Women's Health* (n.d.), accessed June 17, 2013, http://women.webmd.com/features/how-sleep-loss-affects-women-more-than-men. L. Pratt, D. Brody and Q. Gu, "Antidepressant Use in Persons Aged 12 and Over: United States, 2005–2008," *National Center for Health Statistics Data Brief* no. 76 (October 2011). K. Bindley, "Women and Prescription Drugs: One in Four Takes Mental Health Meds," *The Huffington Post*, November 16, 2011, http://www.huffingtonpost.com/2011/11/16/women-and-prescription-drug-use_n_1098023.html.

2. J. Williams, *Unbending Gender: Why Family and Work Conflict and What to Do About It* (Oxford University Press, 1999).

3. This belief is evident in the speeches of women in politics. For example, Hillary Rodham Clinton opened her speech to the 2008 Democratic National Convention, "I am honored to be here tonight. A proud mother. A proud Democrat. A proud American. And a proud supporter of Barack Obama." Throughout the 2008 presidential campaign, Sarah Palin often referred to herself as "an average hockey mom," and after her campaign, she called herself and other candidates "Mama Grizzlies." In Ann Romney's 2012 speech to the Republican National Convention, she talked about the difficulties people have in making it through each day. "And if you listen carefully, you'll hear the women sighing a little bit more than the men. It's how it is, isn't it? It's the moms who have always had to work a little harder to make everything right. It's the mom's of this nation, single, married, widowed, who really hold the country together." Michelle Obama wrapped up her 2012 convention speech by saying, "You see, at the end of the day, my most important title is still 'Mom-in-Chief.' My daughters are still the heart of my heart and the center of my world."

4. Helicopter parents, see: R. Alsop, *The Trophy Kids Grow Up: How the Millennial Generation is Shaking up the Workplace*, (John Wiley & Sons, 2008). P. Druckerman, *Bringing Up Bébé: One American Mother Discovers the Wisdom of French Parenting* (Penguin, 2014). J. Lythcot-Haims, *How to*

*Raise an Adult: Break Free of the Overparenting Trap and Prepare Your Kids for Success* (Henry Holt, 2015). Spoiled, see: E. Kolbert, "Spoiled Rotten," *New Yorker*, July 2, 2012. R. Lieber, *The Opposite of Spoiled: Raising Kids who are Grounded, Generous, and Smart about Money* (HarperCollins, 2015). Privileged, see: M. Levine, *The Price of Privilege: How Parental Pressure and Material Advantage are Creating a Generation of Disconnected and Unhappy Kids* (HarperCollins, 2006). Narcissistic, see: J. Twenge and W. Campbell, *The Narcissism Epidemic: Living in the Age of Entitlement* (Simon and Schuster, 2009). J. Twenge, *Generation Me-Revised and Updated: Why Today's Young Americans Are More Confident, Assertive, Entitled—and More Miserable Than Ever Before* (Simon and Schuster, 2014). Lazy/Materialistic, see: J. Arnold, et al., *Life at Home in the Twenty-First Century: 32 Families Open Their Doors* (University of California-Los Angles Press, 2012). It is still impossible to simultaneously have a successful career, marriage, and young children, see: A. Slaughter, "Why Women Still Can't Have it All," *Atlantic Monthly* (July/ August, 2012). American mothers are enslaved by oppressive childrearing norms, see: E. Badinter, *The Conflict: How Modern Motherhood Undermines the Status of Women* (Macmillan, 2012).

5. For scholarship on women who mother outside of the dominant white, middle-class, heterosexual norm, see: P. Collins, "The Meaning of Motherhood in Black Culture and Black Mother/Daughter Relationships," in *Toward a New Psychology of Gender*, ed. M. Gergen and S. Davis (New York: Routledge, 1997). K. Edin and M. Kefalas, *Promises I Can Keep: Why Poor Women Put Motherhood Before Marriage*, (Berkeley: University of California Press, 2006). K. Edin and L. Lein, *Making Ends Meet: How Single Mothers Survive Welfare and Low-Wage Work*, (New York: Russell Sage Foundation Publications, 1997). B. Ehrenreich, *Nickel and Dimed: On (Not) Getting by in America* (New York: Holt Paperbacks, 2001). B. Ehrenrich and A. Hochschild, ed., *Global Woman: Nannies, Maids and Sex Workers in the New Economy* (Henry Holt, 2004). D. Eicher-Catt, "A Communicology of Female/Feminine Embodiment: The Case of Non-Custodial Mothering," *American Journal of Semiotics* 17, no. 4 (2001): 93-130. S. Hays, *Flat Broke with Children: Women in the Age of Welfare Reform* (Oxford University Press, 2003). P. Hondagneu-Sotelo, *Domestica: Immigrant Workers Cleaning and Caring in the Shadow of Affluence* (Berkeley: University of California Press, 2001). A. Kusserow, *American Individualisms: Child Rearing and Social Class in Three Neighborhoods* (New York: Palgrave Macmillan, 2004). M. Ladd-Taylor and L. Umansky, *"Bad" Mothers: The Politics of Blame in Twentieth-Century America* (New York: NYU Press, 1998). A. Lareau, *Unequal Childhoods: Class, Race, and Family Life* (Berkeley: University of California Press, 2003). A.

Tsing, "Monster Stories: Women Charged with Perinatal Endangerment," in *Uncertain Terms: Negotiating Gender in American Culture*, ed. F. Ginsburg and A. Tsing (Boston:Beacon Press, 1990), 282-99. L. West, *Soccer Moms, Welfare Queens, Waitress Moms and Super Moms: Myths of Motherhood in State Media Coverage of Childcare* (Atlanta: Emory University Press, 2002).

6. In *The Cultural Contradictions of Motherhood*, Sharon Hays argues that the cultural model of "intensive mothering," based on native-born, white, middle-class practices, is America's most recognizable, powerful, and articulated model of motherhood. S. Hays, *The Cultural Contradictions of Motherhood* (Yale University Press, 1998). For media images, see D. Johnston and D. Swanson, "Invisible mothers: A Content Analysis of Motherhood Ideologies and Myths in Magazines," in *Sex Roles* 49, no. 1 (2003): 21-33.

7. For a discussion of the increased parenting demands on fathers see: H. Palladino, "The Cultural Contradictions of Fatherhood: Is there an Ideology of Intensive Fathering? in *Intensive Mothering: The Cultural Contradictions of Modern Motherhood*, ed. L. Ennis (Bradford, ON: Demeter, 2014).

## NOTES ON CHAPTER ONE

1. Early Childhood and Family Education (ECFE) Classes are prevalent throughout the Minneapolis-St. Paul metro area. The ECFE program provides weekly classes during the school year for parents and children from birth to kindergarten. Oftentimes parents and children will meet together for socializing and songs, and then parents will go off with a licensed teacher to talk about issues related to childrearing, while teachers lead the children in group time.

2. White, middle-to-upper class, able-bodied, heterosexual, married women are generally revered as "good" mothers; while the culture's focus on "bad" mothers elicits stereotypes of African American welfare mothers, immigrant mothers, teen mothers, drug-using mothers, lesbian mothers, non-custodial mothers, voluntarily childless women, and career women who put their jobs before their children, to name a few. See S. Douglas and M. Michaels, *The Mommy Myth: The Idealization of Motherhood and How it has Undermined All Women* (Simon and Schuster, 2005). D. Eicher-Catt, "Noncustodial Mothering A Cultural Paradox of Competent Performance–Performative Competence," in *Journal of Contemporary Ethnography* 33, no. 1 (2004): 72-108. S. Hays, *The Cultural Contradictions of Motherhood* (Yale University Press, 1998). M. Ladd-Taylor and L. Umansky, eds., *"Bad" Mothers: The Politics of Blame in Twentieth-Century America* (NYU Press, 1998). E. T. May, *Barren in the Promised Land: Childless Americans and the Pursuit of*

*Happiness* (Harvard University Press, 1997). D. Roberts, "Unshackling Black Motherhood," *Michigan Law Review* (1997): 938-964.

3. The description of a "good" mother based on the top ten responses is consistent with the social science literature, which describes the American cultural ideal of a "good" mother, as being selfless, idealized, unrealistic, and unattainable. Scholars also contend that the cultural standard for a "good" mother is someone who is white, heterosexual, middle or upper-middle class, married, and not working outside the home. None of the women in my sample mentioned race, class, sexual preference, or marital status in their description of the cultural ideal of a "good" mother. This could be because these attributes are so normalized in our culture that they become invisible and taken for granted as the standard, or because using the word "what" instead of "who" to phrase the question did not make people think about identifying features such as race and class. Alternatively, perhaps the women in my sample do not consciously think that a woman's race, class, sexual preference, or marital status excludes her from being a "good" mom by our cultural standards. For scholarly discussions of a good mother, see: T. Arendell, "Conceiving and Investigating Motherhood: The Decade's Scholarship," *Journal of Marriage and Family* 62, no. 4 (2000): 1192-1207. H. Dillaway and E. Paré, "Locating Mothers: How Cultural Debates About Stay-at-Home Versus Working Mothers Define Women and Home," *Journal of Family Issues* 29, no. 4 (2008): 437-464. Douglas and Michaels, *Mommy Myth*. Hays, *Cultural Contradictions*. A. O'Reilly, "Ain't That Love? Antiracism and Racial Constructions of Motherhood," in *Everyday Acts Against Racism: Raising Children in a Multicultural World* ed. M. Reddy (Seal Press, 1996), 88-98. D. Smith, "The Standard North American Family (SNAF) as an Ideological Code," in *Journal of Family Issues* 14, no. 1 (1993): 50-65.

4. This suggests that our culture ideal of a "good" mother is no longer exclusively a stay-at-home mother, at least in the Minneapolis/St. Paul Metropolitan area.

5. Douglas and Michaels, *Mommy Myth*, 12.

6. Anthropologist Sarah Hrdy notes that human mothers differ from primate mothers in two important respects: the great deal of variation in maternal care patterns across our species (i.e. there are no "fixed action patterns" exhibited by human mothers); and the fact that "women imagine ahead of time what it will be like to give birth and to be a mother." Women base their expectations of motherhood on personal observations of other mothers, interaction with babies, and "from what others (especially other women) tell them it *should* be like." See S. Hrdy, *Mother Nature: Maternal Instincts and How They Shape the Human Species* (Ballantine Books, 2000), 164, 167. There

have been several studies, which demonstrate that media images of mothers are idealized in our culture. See Douglas and Michaels, *Mommy Myth*; D. Johnston and D. Swanson, "Invisible Mothers: A Content Analysis of Motherhood Ideologies and Myths in Magazines," *Sex Roles* 49, no. 1 (2003): 21-33.

7. Douglas and Michaels, *The Mommy Myth*.

8. M. Milkie, "Social Comparisons, Reflected Appraisals, and Mass Media: The Impact of Pervasive Beauty Images on Black and White Girls' Self-Concepts," *Social Psychology Quarterly* (1999): 190-210, 192.

9. Ibid., 192.

10. Women articulated their emotions with such candor. One mother wrote: "Wow! Every one in the book! Overflowing love, joy, pride, nervousness, fear, anger, guilt, pain, regret, relief, hope, concern, worry, disbelief, empathy, sympathy, boredom (when you're reading a story for the 100th time), excitement."

11. For example, Anthropologist Kathleen Barlow observed that in Murik society, the mothering role emphasizes "nurturance, protection, teaching and generosity," which provides clear expectations for young mothers' actions. See K. Barlow, "Working Mothers and the Work of Culture in a Papua New Guinea Society," *Ethos* 29, no. 1 (2001): 78-107, 84.

12. In *Bringing Up Bébé: One American Mother Discovers the Wisdom of French Parenting*, Pamela Druckerman notes that French parents do not have to choose "a parenting philosophy" because "everybody takes the basic rules for granted." She observed that there is more consistency in how French parents act because everyone agrees that parents should teach their children delayed gratification and to eat a variety of food. P. Druckerman, *Bringing Up Bébé: One American Mother Discovers the Wisdom of French Parenting* (Penguin, 2014), 6.

13. Hays *Cultural Contradictions*, 122.

14. Claire talked about how it took her awhile to figure out her own style of mothering because she has observed and respected so many different models of parenting. "I would see so many models of people that I thought had it down. Like the chubby mom that's so doughy and comforting and is a great cook and is joyful all the time like my great aunt Eleanor. Being at her house was so fun, so I thought maybe I need to be more like that, but I'm skinny and kind of nervous (laughter) it's not working for me (laughter). Then there's my mom, the educator, who's very calm all the time. I tried that and I'm a little too goofy for that. So it's taken me awhile to just come to the new me with the new peace about where I'm at and accepting of things like my husband and I are going to have different expectations."

15. For example, how children address adults varies by neighborhood in the Twin Cities. In some neighborhoods, children informally call adults by their first name, whereas in other neighborhoods, children use Mr. or Mrs., with the adult last name. When friends from Maryland visit us, their children called me Miss Solveig, and my husband Mr. Sean, which is the norm for children in the south, but rarely heard in Minneapolis outside of a pre-school or daycare setting.

16. I think her lawn example is interesting because it is one rather obvious indicator of the variation in neighborhood community cultures within an urban area. Whereas Valerie felt pressure not to chemically treat her lawn, there are suburban areas where there is pressure to have a weed-free lawn, so chemical treatment is the norm.

17. Minnesota has the second highest female labor force participation in the United States, with 66.4% of women over 16 employed outside the home. See N.A., "Employment and Earnings," *Status of Women in the States*, accessed November 30, 2015, http://statusofwomendata.org/explore-the-data/state-data/minnesota/#employment-earnings.

## Notes for Chapter 2

1. A. Harris, *Future Girl: Young Women in the Twenty-First Century* (New York: Routledge, 2004), 3-4.

2. A. Giddens, *Modernity and Self-Identity: Self and Society in the Late Modern Age* (Stanford University Press, 1991), 70.

3. A. Lareau, *Unequal Childhoods: Class, Race, and Family Life* (University of California Press, 2011).

4. Anthropologists studying American mothers in the 1950s and 1960s also found that not having a single set of parenting norms created "anxiety about conforming to ideal norms that are culturally unclear." See L. Minturn and W. Lambert, *Mothers of Six Cultures* (New York: John Wiley and Sons, 1964), 198.

5. Ibid., 190.

6. Psychologists note that social comparison is "is phylogenetically very old, biologically very powerful and is recognizable in many species." B. Buunk, F. Gibbons and A. Buunk, "Health, Coping, and Well-Being: Perspectives from Social Comparison Theory," *Psychology Press* (2013): 15-18.

7. Ibid., 18.

8. Ibid.

9. See K. McHenry and D. Schultz, "Skinny Jeans: Perfection and Competition in Motherhood," in *Intensive Mothering: The Cultural Contradictions of Modern Motherhood*, ed. L. Ennis (Bradford, ON: Demeter, 2014), 301-302.

10. Ibid.

11. A. Henderson, S. Harmon and J. Houser, "A New State of Surveillance? Applying Michel Foucault to Modern Motherhood," *Surveillance & Society* 7, no. 34 (2010): 231-247.

12. D. W. Winnicott, *The Child, the Family and the Outside World* (Perseus, 1964).

13. E. Galinsky and J. David, *Ask the Children: The Breakthrough Study That Reveals How to Succeed at Work and Parenting* (HarperCollins, 2010).

14. For a great discussion of mother blame, see M. Ladd-Taylor and L. Umansky, *"Bad" Mothers: The Politics of Blame in Twentieth-Century America* (New York: NYU Press, 1998).

15. Schizophrenia: T. Lidz, *The Origin and Treatment of Schizophrenic Disorders* (Basic Books, 1973). Anorexia: J. Brumberg, *Fasting Girls: The Emergence of Anorexia Nervosa as a Modern Disease* (Harvard University Press, 1988). Autism: Ladd-Taylor and Umansky *"Bad" Mothers*, 4.; J. Allan, "Mother Blaming: a Covert Practice in Therapeutic Intervention," *Australian Social Work* 57, no. 1 (2004): 57-70.

16. We also retroactively blame mothers, such as the recent articles asserting that 1950s mothers are responsible for our current obesity epidemic. See N. Wurtzel, "Obesity Epidemic: Is Your Mother to Blame?" *The Huffington Post*, February 16, 2012, <http://www.huffingtonpost.com/nancy-wurtzel/thank-goodness-i-can-blam_b_1281887.html>.

17. Government definitions of a stay-at-home mother require that they be in a heterosexual marriage.

18. C. Gross, et al., "State Intervention in Intensive Mothering: Neo-Liberalism, New Paternalism and Poor Mothers in Ohio," in *Intensive Mothering: The Cultural Contradictions of Modern Motherhood*, ed. L. Ennis (Bradford, ON: Demeter, 2014), 163-179.

19. M. Levine, *The Price of Privilege: How Parental Pressure and Material Advantage are Creating a Generation of Disconnected and Unhappy Kids* (New York: HarperCollins, 2006), 30-31.

20. R. Frank, *Falling Behind: How Rising Inequality Harms the Middle Class, Vol. 4* (University of California Press, 2013), vii.

21. See K. Edin and M. Kefalas, *Promises I Can Keep: Why Poor Women Put Motherhood Before Marriage*, (Berkeley: University of California Press, 2006). B. Ehrenrich and A. Hochschild, ed., *Global Woman: Nannies, Maids and Sex Workers in the New Economy* (New York: Henry Holt, 2004). D. Eicher-Catt, "A Communicology of Female/Feminine Embodiment: The Case of Non-Custodial Mothering," *American Journal of Semiotics* 17, no. 4 (2001): 93-130. F. Ginsburg and R. Rapp, ed., *Conceiving the New World Order: The Global*

*Politics of Reproduction* (University of California Press, 1995). J. Hanigsberg and S. Ruddick, ed., *Mother Troubles: Rethinking Contemporary Maternal Dilemmas* (Beacon Press, 1999). S. Hays, *Flat Broke with Children: Women in the Age of Welfare Reform* (Oxford University Press, 2003). R. Hertz, *Single by Chance, Mothers by Choice: How Women are Choosing Parenthood Without Marriage and Creating the New American Family* (Oxford University Press, 2006). P. Hondagneu-Sotelo, *Domestica: Immigrant Workers Cleaning and Caring in the Shadow of Affluence* (Berkeley: University of California Press, 2001). A. Kusserow, *American Individualisms: Child Rearing and Social Class in Three Neighborhoods* (Palgrave Macmillan, 2004). E. Lewin, "On the Outside Looking In: The Politics of Lesbian Motherhood," in *Conceiving the New World Order: The Global Politics of Reproduction*, ed. F. Ginsburg and R. Rapp (University of California Press, 1995), 103-121.

22. Giddens, *Modernity and Self-Identity*, 9. As Max Weber presciently observed over a century ago, "in the United States, the pursuit of wealth, stripped of its religious and ethical meaning, tends to become associated with purely mundane passions." M. Weber, *The Protestant Ethic and the Spirit of Capitalism* (Dover, 2003), 182.

## NOTES FOR CHAPTER 3

1. Oftentimes, a new mother is marked by a change in status or appearance as a way to facilitate her psychological transition to her new role. In many cultures there are postpartum ceremonies, rituals, proscribed periods of seclusion and rest, and social assistance given to new mothers. See V. Turner, *The Ritual Process: Structure and Anti-Structure* (Transaction Publishers, 1995). A. Van Gennep, *The Rites of Passage* (University of Chicago Press, 2011).

2. Gwen Stern and Laurence Kruckman identify six postpartum social structures present to some degree in many non-western societies. These structures include: (1) Cultural patterning of a distinct post-partum period; (2) protective measures designed to reflect the vulnerability of the new mother; (3) social seclusion; (4) mandated rest; (5) assistance in tasks from relatives and/or midwife; (6) social recognition of new social status through rituals, gifts or other means. See G. Stern and L. Kruckman, "Multi-Disciplinary Perspectives on Post-Partum Depression: an Anthropological Critique," *Social Science & Medicine* 17, no. 15 (1983): 1027-1041.

3. The former became popular for the middle class after World War II when consumerism began to take hold in the United States. See K. Vander Straeten, "The American Baby Shower," *Suite 101*. April 25, 2012. Web. Accessed March 22, 2015, <http://katrien-vander-straeten.suite101.

com/the-american-baby-shower-a12164>. The latter, Robbie David-Floyd argues, is a powerful American ritual that is meant to physically, emotionally, and symbolically affirm our society's core belief in the primacy of science, technology, and patriarchy. See R. Davis-Floyd, "The Technocratic Body: American Childbirth as Cultural Expression," *Social Science & Medicine* 38, no. 8 (1994): 1125-1140.

4. R. Ray, J. Gornick and J. Schmitt, *Parental Leave Policies in 21 Countries: Assessing Generosity and Gender Equality* (Washington, D.C.: Center for Economic Policy Research, 2009). See also G. Livingston, "Among 38 Nations, US is the Outlier When it Comes to Paid Parental Leave," (Pew Research Center, December 12, 2013).

5. Only one woman in my sample, who immigrated to Minnesota as an adult, believed she had a clear idea of what to expect. "No time for your-self anymore, no more freedom, and you have to be responsible twenty-four hours a day." She knew exactly what parenting entailed because she essentially raised her younger brother while her mother worked on their family farm in her native country, which gave her experience with all facets of childrearing to which most middle class American women are not normally exposed.

6. See N. Bashiri and A. Spielvogel, "Postpartum Depression: A Cross-Cultural Perspective," in *Primary Care Update for OB/GYNS* 6, no. 3 (1999): 82-87. Also see C. Westdahl, et al, "Social Support and Social Conflict as Predictors of Prenatal Depression," *Obstetrics and Gynecology* 110, no. 1 (2007): 134. S. Milan, et al. "Prevalence, Course, and Predictors of Emotional Distress in Pregnant and Parenting Adolescents," *Journal of Consulting and Clinical Psychology* 72, no. 2 (2004): 328.

7. While there is not a clear consensus of what exactly constitutes "baby blues," many researchers conclude that it is a time when there is a heightened sensitivity to emotional connotations. For a full review of studies, see L. Miller and M. Rukstalis, "Beyond the Blues: Hypotheses About Postpartum Reactivity," *Postpartum Mood Disorder* (1999): 3-19.

8. Miller argues that the term "blues" is a misnomer and suggests a more accurate label to describe this condition would be "postpartum reactivity." Ibid., 8. Stein argues, "that psychosocial factors may influence what a women with the blues says or does, but not whether the blues occur." See G. Stein, A. Marsh and J. Morton, "Mental Symptoms, Weight Changes, and Electrolyte Excretion in the First Post Partum Week," *Journal of Psychosomatic Research* 25, no. 5 (1981): 395-408.

9. Currently there are two theories about the genesis of postpartum blues. The hormonal hypothesis postulates that change in hormone levels in the days after a woman gives birth—in particular the dramatic decrease in estrogen,

progesterone, prolactin, cortisol and fluctuations of oxytocin levels—manifest in the symptoms associated with post partum blues. The biological attachment hypothesis suggests that post partum blues are a normal mammalian response to giving birth and facilitate bonding and attachment. Research on non-human mammals shows that the mammalian limbic system contains an "anterior cingulated gyrus" (ACG), which is a unique structure associated with maternal behavior in other mammals. It appears that the ACG has a heightened reactivity in postpartum women, associated with increased levels of oxytocin, in order to promote attachment. While the biological attachment theory has not been empirically tested on humans, the hypothesis "is consistent with all known systematic data about the nature of postpartum blues." Overall, the biological attachment hypothesis argues that postpartum blues are a normative response to childbirth and are not a form of depression, although women who develop post partum depression may experience the post partum blues as depressing. See Miller and Rukstalis, "Beyond the Blues," 15.

10. C. Beck, "Postpartum Depression: A Metasynthesis," *Qualitative Health Research* 12, no. 4 (2002): 453-472. C. Beck, "Predictors of Postpartum Depression: An Update," *Nursing Research* 50, no. 5 (2001): 275-285.

11. See A. Keshen and J. MacDonald, "Case Report: Postpartum Depression: Making the Case for Routine Screening," *Case Report - McGill Journal of Medicine* (2004), <http://www.medicine.mcgill.ca/MJM/issues/v07n01/case_rep/case_rep.htm>.

12. I spoke with a veteran nurse practitioner at a major Minneapolis OB/Gyn practice about postpartum depression and she stated that she and her colleagues have noticed a dramatic increase in women who are on anti-depressant medication while they are pregnant. She said that they are particularly careful to monitor women for postpartum depression who have issues with depression prior to pregnancy and during their pregnancy.

13. When Erica was pregnant with her second child she read Brooke Shields' book, *Down Came the Rain*, (Penguin, 2007) because she thought it was likely that the postpartum depression would reoccur. Erica felt such a sense of relief when she read the book because it confirmed for her that she had classic symptoms of post-partum depression. It made her feel more comfortable with what she had gone through.

14. Currently there is debate as to whether postpartum depression is caused by biological factors, such as dramatic hormonal fluctuations, or whether it is related to the presence or absence of specific psychosocial factors. See A. Georgiopoulos et al., "Population-Based Screening for Postpartum Depression" in *Obstetrics & Gynecology* 93, no. 5 (1999): 653-657.

The scholarship that focuses on the biological foundation of postpartum depression investigates the role of hormonal fluctuations associated with the onset of postpartum depression. Initially, many researchers speculated that the dramatic reduction of estradiol levels inhibited the breakdown of serotonin, contributing to depressive symptoms. However, a comprehensive review of the research pertaining to the biological component of postpartum depression reveals that identifying causal effects of specific biological components has been elusive and concludes that, "the literature to date does not consistently support any single biological etiology for post partum depression." See V. Hendrick, L. Altshuler and R. Suri, "Hormonal Changes in the Postpartum and Implications for Postpartum Depression," *Psychosomatics* 39, no. 2 (1998): 93-101. C. Beck reviewed eighty-four studies, conducted in nineteen countries, and compiled a list of psychological and social variables that the literature reported as risk factors for postpartum depression. The psychosocial variables associated with postpartum depression (listed in their order of associated risk, with the highest risk first) are as follows: "prenatal depression,...self-esteem,...child care stress,...prenatal anxiety,... life stress,...social support,...marital relationship,...history of previous depression,...infant temperament, ... maternity blues,...marital status,... socioeconomic status,...and unplanned/unwanted pregnancy." See C. Beck, "Predictors of Postpartum Depression: An Update," *Nursing Research* 50, no. 5 (2001): 275.

15. A British study of women with postpartum depression found that a model of bereavement or loss fits well with postpartum depression because it involves re-configuring aspects of a woman's identity. See P. Nicolson, "Understanding Postnatal Depression: a Mother-Centred Approach,"*Journal of Advanced Nursing* 15, no. 6 (1990): 689-695.

16. See Stern and Kruckman, "Multi-Disciplinary Perspectives." S. Harkness, "The Cultural Mediation of Postpartum Depression," *Medical Anthropology Quarterly* 1, no. 2 (1987): 194-209.

17. W. Dement and C. Vaughan, *The Promise of Sleep: A Pioneer in Sleep Medicine Explores the Vital Connection Between Health, Happiness, and a Good Night's Sleep* (Dell Publishing Co, 1999), 233.

18. There have been several sleep studies relating to pregnant and postpartum women. One study of new mothers and new fathers reported that both mothers and fathers experienced sleep disruption and fatigue during the postpartum period. C. Gay, K. Lee and S. Lee, "Sleep Patterns and Fatigue in New Mothers and Fathers," *Biological Research for Nursing* 5, no. 4 (2004): 311-318. Some researchers have noted that maternal depression is associated with infants who have sleeping problems. As the child's sleep patterns improved, so did

the maternal depression, leading some researchers to hypothesize that reducing a new mothers' sleep deprivation could potentially help her with symptoms of depression. See L. Ross, B. Murray and M. Steiner, "Sleep and Perinatal Mood Disorders: a Critical Review," *Journal of Psychiatry and Neuroscience* 30, no. 4 (2005): 247. Researchers also suggest "maternal role 'acquisition,' experienced by first-time mothers results in more fatigue and sleep disruption than does maternal role 'expansion.'" M. Waters and K. Lee, "Differences Between Primigravidae and Multigravidae Mothers in Sleep Disturbances, Fatigue, and Functional Status," *Journal of Nurse-Midwifery* 41, no. 5 (1996): 364-367.

19. D. Lawrence, K. Nylen and R. Cobb, "Prenatal Expectations and Marital Satisfaction Over the Transition to Parenthood," *Journal of Family Psychology* 21, no. 2 (2007): 155. Lawrence, E., et al., "Marital Satisfaction Across the Transition to Parenthood," *Journal of Family Psychology* 22.1 (2008): 41.

20. Lawrence et al. followed 172 married couples for four years starting before the birth or adoption of their first child. They found that before a couple had children, marital satisfaction was stable for men, and declined slightly for women. However, in the postpartum period, there was a dramatic decline in satisfaction for both partners, followed by husbands regaining relatively stable levels of satisfaction, while wives maintained stable levels of low-grade dissatisfaction. Overall, husbands had lower prenatal expectations about parenthood than did wives, which contributed to their feelings of greater satisfaction. The couples that had low expectations about the transition to parenting maintained higher levels of satisfaction. The wives who had the highest expectations about parenting were more likely to be the least satisfied with the marital relationship after having children. Thus, this study found support for a link between unfulfilled expectations about parenting roles and the marital relationship with increased levels of marital dissatisfaction. Ibid.

21. The *Oprah* show to which this woman is referring was filmed in response to an essay entitled, "Modern Love Truly, Madly, Guiltily" written by Ayelet Waldman for a *New York Times* column in 2005. The essay was an observation about how in the variety of Mother's Groups in which Ms. Waldman was a member, she seemed to be the only mother who had a satisfying sex life with her spouse. Waldman states that women are exhausted from childcare responsibilities, however, she argues: "but the real reason for this lack of sex, or at least the most profound, is that the wife's passion has been refocused. Instead of concentrating her ardor on her husband, she concentrates it on her babies. Where once her husband was the center of her passionate universe, there is now a new sun in whose orbit she revolves. Libido, as she once knew it, is gone, and in its place is all-consuming maternal desire. In the

column, Waldman makes the distinction that while she loves her children, she is not "in love" with her children. She goes on to clarify her feelings. "If a good mother is one who loves her child more than anyone else in the world, I am not a good mother. I am in fact a bad mother. I love my husband more than I love my children." It was the last line of this quote, "I love my husband more than I love my children," which set off a national frenzy of criticism and debate as to whether a "good" mother could possibly love her husband more than she loves her children. See A. Waldman, "Truly, Madly, Guiltily," *New York Times*, March 27, 2005. http://www.nytimes.com/2005/03/27/fashion/truly-madly-guiltily.html.

## NOTES FOR CHAPTER 4

1. E. Kluwer, J. Heesink and E. Van de Vliert, "Marital Conflict About the Division of Household Labor and Paid Work," *Journal of Marriage and the Family* 58, no. 11 (1996): 958-69. See also J. Gottman, "The Roles of Conflict Engagement, Escalation, and Avoidance in Marital Interaction: A Longitudinal View of Five Types of Couples," *Journal of Consulting and Clinical Psychology* 61, no. 1 (1993): 6.

2. R. Konigsberg, "Chore Wars," *Time*, July 21, 2011, 44-49.

3. These are descriptive statistics for this sample only. However, this finding is consistent with other studies. T. Arendell, "Conceiving and Investigating Motherhood: The Decade's Scholarship," *Journal of Marriage and Family* 62, no. 4 (2000): 1192-1207. S. Coltrane, "Research on Household Labor: Modeling and Measuring the Social Embeddedness of Routine Family Work," *Journal of Marriage and Family* 62, no. 4 (2000): 1208-1233. A. Hochschild and A. Machung, *The Second Shift: Working Families and the Revolution at Home* (Penguin, 2012). For a review of the research on the household division of labor see: M. Lachance-Grzela and G. Bouchard, "Why Do Women Do the Lion's Share of Housework? A Decade of Research," *Sex Roles* 63, no. 11-12 (2010): 767-780.

4. As a comparison, the only task of the 32 tasks that 11% or less of the women did not "always" or "usually" do was take out the garbage.

5. There was little difference in the number of tasks more than half of the full-time working mothers, part-time working mothers, or stay-at-home mothers "always" or "usually" did: 23 tasks for stay-at-home mothers; 22 tasks for part-time working mothers; and 20 tasks for full-time working mothers. Furthermore, half of full-time working mothers only reported sharing three tasks equally with their husband or partner, compared to part-time working mothers, who reported sharing 5 tasks equally, and stay-at-home mothers who reported sharing 4 tasks equally.

6. See S. Davis, T. Greenstein and J. Gerteisen-Marks, "Effects of Union Type on Division of Household Labor Do Cohabiting Men Really Perform More Housework?" *Journal of Family Issues* 28, no. 9 (2007): 1246-1272. Also see, H. Diefenbach, "Gender Ideologies, Relative Resources, and the Division of Housework in Intimate Relationships: A Test of Hyman Rodman's Theory of Resources in Cultural Context," *International Journal of Comparative Sociology* 43, no. 1 (2002): 45-64.

7. See Arendell "Conceiving Motherhood." S. Walzer, *Thinking About the Baby: Gender and Transitions into Parenthood* (Philadelphia: Temple University Press, 1998). One study found that married fathers who expressed beliefs in women's equality did "only four more *minutes* of domestic labor daily...then traditional men." See N. Wolf, *Misconceptions: Truth, Lies and the Unexpected on the Journey to Motherhood* (Vintage/Ebury, 2002), 233-234.

8. Kelly's story also highlights potential gender differences when there is work and family conflict (WFC). One study showed that when a man experienced higher levels of WFC, his wife would assume more responsibility at home. However, when a woman experienced higher levels of WFC, her husband did not increase his domestic contribution. See J. Hoobler, J. Hu and M. Wilson, "Do Workers Who Experience Conflict Between the Work and Family Domains Hit a "Glass Ceiling?": A Meta-Analytic Examination," Journal of Vocational Behavior 77, no. 3 (2010): 481-494.

9. Large corporations such as Timberland, IBM, and Microsoft offer fathers two weeks leave, and Merrill Lynch offers one week of paid paternity leave. K. Abel, "Dads and Paternity Leave," *Family Education* (n.d.) accessed 3/15/2012, http://life.familyeducation.com/working-parents/fathers-day/36483.html.

10. L. Rudman and K. Mescher, "Penalizing Men Who Request a Family Leave: Is Flexibility Stigma a Femininity Stigma?" *Journal of Social Issues* 69, no. 2 (2013): 322-340.

11. A. Doucet, "You See the Need Perhaps More Clearly Than I Have: Exploring Gendered Processes of Domestic Responsibility," *Journal of Family Issues* 22 (2001): 328-357.

12. V. Mackintosh, M. Liss and H. Schiffrin, "Using a Quantitative Measure to Explore Intensive Mothering Ideology" in *Intensive Mothering: The Cultural Contradictions of Modern Motherhood*, ed. L. Ennis (Bradford, ON: Demeter, 2014), 142-159.

13. M. Di Leonardo, "The Female World of Cards and Holidays: Women, Families, and the Work of Kinship," *Signs* 12, no. 3 (1987): 440-53, 443.

14. Ibid., p. 441.

15. E. Zaretsky, *Capitalism, the Family and Personal Life* (HarperCollins, 1973).

## NOTES FOR CHAPTER 5

1. This is why it seems normal to ask first time mothers, and not first time fathers, whether they plan to keep working after their baby is born or adopted. It is why one stay-at-home dad I spoke with often hears the comment, "oh, you have the kids for the day," or why people sometimes say that a father is "babysitting" his own children. This assumption also explains why it is more common for mothers to make daycare arrangements and career sacrifices to raise children than it is for fathers.

2. The government bears "little or no obligation to assist with the costs, unless childcare is necessary to help a low-income parent remain employed or unless an early intervention program is necessary to prepare a disabled or disadvantaged child for school." The US spends on average $600 per year for pre-school education and childcare, with most of this funding being in the form of tax credits for parents who pay for private childcare. Many Nordic and European countries spend more than five times this on early childcare because it is "seen as a public responsibility and a public good like elementary and secondary education." J. Waldfogel, "International Policies Toward Parental Leave and Child Care," in *The Future of Children* (2001): 99-111.

3. For a more in-depth discussion of this topic, see J. Williams, *Unbending Gender: Why Family and Work Conflict and What to Do About It* (Oxford University Press, 1999). We rank 20th out of 21 rich countries for parental leave policies after the birth or adoption of a child. See R. Ray, J. Gornick and J. Schmitt, "Parental Leave Policies in 21 Countries: Assessing Generosity and Gender Equality" (Center for Economic Policy and Research, 2008). For a discussion of America's low ranking on employee vacation time see R. Ray, M. Sanes and J. Schmitt, "No-Vacation Nation Revisited" (*Center for Economic and Policy Research*, 2013).

4. Our negative stereotype about stay-at-home mothers is that we do not consider what they do as work that counts, which means that they run the risk of being seen as an irrelevant person, because our society privileges participation in market labor. The negative stereotype of working mothers is that if they prioritize work over their children, then they run the risk of not being viewed as a "good" mother.

5. See R, Marcus, "Palin Hits the Motherload," *Washington Post*, September 10, 2008, <http://www.washingtonpost.com/wp-dyn/content/article/2008/09/09/AR2008090902521.html>.

6. Hillary Rosen wrote, "And what about the argument that she is a negligent mother who will be distracted from her important role? I am a mother who constantly feels the pressure from others about whether I am fit to be a parent, whether I put my kids first often enough and whether my

children get enough of my attention. Who has the right to judge my family?" H. Rosen, "Am I 'Off Message' on Sarah Palin?" *The Huffington Post*, October 4, 2008, <http://www.huffingtonpost.com/hilary-rosen/am-i-off-message-on-sarah_b_123540.html>.

7. Catherine Hakim, a senior research fellow at the London School of Economics, notes that women have varied preferences and priorities in managing the conflict between family work and outside employment, which leads to significant variation in women's employment patterns. Hakim analyzed women's employment patterns since 1965 and found that approximately twenty percent of women focus their time and energy on home-centered, family work ("Home-Centered"); roughly twenty percent of women prioritize market work related activities ("Work-Centered"); and the majority of women are a diverse group of women who want to prioritize both family work and market work ("Adaptive"). See C. Hakim, *Work-Lifestyle Choices in the 21st Century: Preference Theory* (Oxford University Press, 2000).

8. Higher quality of daycare is associated with smaller group sizes, low children to staff ratios, and caregiver interactions that are responsive and sensitive to children's needs. See J. Love, P. Schochet and A. Meckstroth, "Are They in Any Real Danger? What Research Does--and Doesn't--Tell Us about Child Care Quality and Children's Well-Being" (Child Care Research and Policy Papers 1996).

9. In 2010, it was $1,800 per month. Minnesota ranks third nationally in the cost of accredited childcare, which means that for many Minnesota families childcare is an economic hardship. See *Status of Women and Girls in Minnesota: Full Report* (University of MN Humphrey Institute's Center on Women & Public Policy in partnership with The Women's Foundation of Minnesota, June 2010), <http://www.wfmn.org/research/2010Reports/2010SWGM_FullReport.pdf>.

10. J. Kimmel, "Child Care Costs as a Barrier to Employment for Single and Married Mothers," *Review of Economics and Statistics* 80, no. 2 (1998): 287-299.

11. Her commentary reflects the trend that Caryn Medved and Erika Kirby noticed where college educated women use corporate terminology to describe and legitimize their home labor. C. Medved and E. Kirby, "Family CEOs: A Feminist Analysis of Corporate Mothering Discourses," *Management Communication Quarterly* 18, no. 4 (2005): 435-478.

12. Sharon Hays found that regardless of a woman's work status, she tends to justify it through the lens of intensive mothering. In other words, most women who work part-time or full-time believe that working makes them a better mother, likewise most stay-at-home mothers believe that

staying home is good for their children. I noticed the same trend with the women I interviewed. See S. Hays, *The Cultural Contradictions of Motherhood* (Yale University Press, 1998).

13. Preference Theory predicts that women in modern, affluent societies will be heterogeneous in their preferences, priorities, work histories, and employment patterns, especially with regard to negotiating the conflicting domains of family work and market work. See Hakim, *Work-Lifestyle Choices*. I found that some stay-at-home mothers made an agonizing decision to leave a job that was deeply rewarding to stay home with children, whereas other women were happy to quit their job. Some women were home because they lost their job, which was a hardship for some, and a relief to others. Some women leave the work force because their job, or their spouse's job, has a demanding schedule that is not conducive to family life. Some women love their career and feel great about their work; others have to work and wish they did not have to work. Some women work to make ends meet, others work because they enjoy what they do. Some couples agree that having one parent stay home with children is a good thing; whereas, others fight when one parent thinks someone should stay home, and the other believes both partners should work. Some stay-at-home mothers whose spouse works wish that they had a job that made enough money where they could be the sole breadwinner; whereas other stay-at-home mothers are happy to be home with kids. Some women stay home because they have a spouse or partner who makes enough money to support the family comfortably; others struggle financially to stay at home. Some mothers stay home because they fear putting their child in daycare; other women stay home (especially after a second child is born) because they cannot afford to pay for daycare.

14. L. West, "Soccer Moms, Welfare Queens, Waitress Moms, and Super Moms: Myths of Motherhood in State Media Coverage of Child Care," *MARIAL Centre, Emory University, Working Paper* 16 (2002).

15. For a review of the numerous studies, see J. Shelley et al., "Getting a Job: Is There a Motherhood Penalty?" *American Journal of Sociology*, 112, no. 5 (March 2007): 1297-1339.

16. Ibid.

17. S. Sandberg, *Lean In: Women, Work, and the Will to Lead* (Random House, 2013), 7.

## NOTES FOR PART 2, INTRODUCTION

1. P. Druckerman, *Bringing Up Bébé: One American Mother Discovers the Wisdom of French Parenting* (Penguin, 2014), 4.

2. R. Alsop, *The Trophy Kids Grow Up: How the Millennial Generation*

*is Shaking Up the Workplace*, (John Wiley & Sons, 2008). H. Marano, "A Nation of Wimps," *Psychology Today* 37, no. 6 (2004): 58-70. S. Tingley *How to Handle Difficult Parents: Proven Solutions for Teachers* (Waco, TX: Prufrock, 2012).

3. B. English, "'Snowplow Parents' Overly Involved in College Students' Lives," *The Boston Globe*, November 9, 2013, <http://www.bostonglobe.com/arts/2013/11/09/parents-overly-involved-college-students-lives/mfYvA5R-9IhRpJytEbFpxUP/story.html>. A. Braner, "Soccer Mom, Helicopter Mom or Snow Plow Mom?" *The Huffington Post*, April 24, 2014, <http://www.huffingtonpost.com/andy-braner/soccer-mom-helicopter-mom-or-snow-plow-mom_b_5206924.html>. J. Lythcott-Haims, *How to Raise an Adult: Break Free of the Over-Parenting Trap and Prepare Your Kid for Success* (Henry Holt & Co., 2015). A. Rosenfeld and N. Wise, *The Over-Scheduled Child: Avoiding the Hyper-Parenting Trap* (Macmillan, 2010).

4. E. Kolbert, "Spoiled Rotten," *New Yorker*, July 2, 2012. Lieber, R. *The Opposite of Spoiled: Raising Kids who are Grounded, Generous, and Smart about Money* (HarperCollins, 2015).

5. R. Eyre and L. Eyre, *The Entitlement Trap: How to Rescue Your Child with a New Family System of Choosing, Earning, and Ownership* (New York: Avery, 2011).

6. J. Arnold, et al., *Life at Home in the Twenty-First Century: 32 Families Open Their Doors* (Los Angeles: University of California-Los Angles Press, 2012).

7. J. Twenge and W. Campbell, *The Narcissism Epidemic: Living in the Age of Entitlement* (Simon and Schuster, 2009). J. Twenge, *Generation Me-Revised and Updated: Why Today's Young Americans Are More Confident, Assertive, Entitled—and More Miserable Than Ever Before* (Simon and Schuster, 2014).

8. Arnold et al., "Life at Home," Kolbert, "Spoiled Rotten."

## Notes for Chapter 6

1. B. Whiting and C. Edwards, *Children of Different Worlds: The Formation of Social Behavior* (Harvard University Press, 1992).

2. I think that 1950s and 1960s mothers had other things to worry about that are not covered in the anthropological ethnographies of this era. The late 1950s was a time when millions of women were prescribed a tranquilizer called Miltown, also known as "mother's little helper." See T. Dokoupul, "America's Long Love-Affair with Anti-Anxiety Drugs," *Newsweek* January 21, 2009, http://www.newsweek.com/americas-long-love-affair-anti-anxiety-drugs-77967. Betty Friedan's *The Feminine Mystyque* uncovers some of the complexities women of this era faced who wanted something more than

being homemakers. See B. Friedan, *The Feminine Mystique* (WW Norton & Company, 2010).

3. In fact, during this era, the awareness of traffic safety as a danger to children was a catalyst for local communities to build parks and playgrounds so children could have a safe place to play away from traffic. This was also a time when the Cold War with Russia escalated, and our national fear of Russia dropping a hydrogen bomb on the United States motivated many families to build bomb shelters, while schools carried out routine bomb drills where children were taught to duck and cover.

4. Think about how much time MSNBC, FOX, and CNN infotainment news broadcasts spend offering predictions about elections that may be years away.

5. Most parents know not to leave their child unattended on a changing table, in a tub, or swimming pool. People are aware that they should cut food such as apples, carrots, and grapes into small pieces to reduce the risk of choking. There are warnings that tell of the dangers of babies suffocating from plastic bags, or being strangled, if their crib is near blinds that have cords. Parents try to remember to turn pot and pan handles in when they are cooking on the stove. We no longer have walkers where a child could accidentally propel themselves down a flight of stairs. We have gates, outlet covers, cupboard latches, toilet locks, and many other things to child proof our homes. We have mandatory car seat laws, and most parents require their children to wear helmets when biking or doing any other sports where there is a risk of head injury.

6. "Constructive Paranoia" is the term Diamond uses for Papua New Guinea people's "hypervigilent attitude toward repeated low risks," which he believes makes good sense. J. Diamond, "That Daily Shower Can Be a Killer," *The New York Times*, January 28, 2013, <http://www.nytimes.com/2013/01/29/science/jared-diamonds-guide-to-reducing-lifes-risks.html>.

7. Ibid.

8. D. Gardner, *The Science of Fear* (New York: Dutton, 2008), 10.

9. Ibid.

10. Ibid.

11. Allen Feldman observes that the accelerated mass media circulation, distribution, and consumption has created a space and time compression which he defines as "the implosion of perceptual simultaneity—the abutment of persons, things, and events from a plurality of locales, chronologies, and levels of experience once discrete and separate." A. Feldman, "On Cultural Anesthesia: From Desert Storm to Rodney King," *American Ethnologist* 21, no. 2 (1994): 404-418, 407.

12. C. Rivers, *Selling Anxiety: How the News Media Scare Women* (Upne, 2008).

13. For an excellent discussion of how media stories of safety increased during the 1980s and 1990s, see S. Douglas and M. Michaels, *The Mommy Myth: The Idealization of Motherhood and How it has Undermined All Women* (Simon and Schuster, 2005).

14. "Raising Awareness of Sexual Abuse: Facts and Statistics," The U.S. Department of Justice National Sex Offender Public Website, accessed September 25, 2014, https://www.nsopw.gov/en/Education/FactsStatistics.

15. M. Peterson, "What is a de Minimis Risk?" *Risk Management* (2002): 47-55, 47.

16. Gardner states that "Most experts have come to the sensible conclusion that it goes both ways: If you read and watch more, you fear more; and if you fear more, you read and watch more." Gardner, *Science of Fear*, 196.

17. Gardner, *Science of Fear*, 10.

18. Pamela Druckerman states, "I'm hardly the first to point out that middle class America has a parenting problem. In hundreds of books and articles, this problem has been painstakingly diagnosed, critiqued, and named: over-parenting, hyperparenting, helicopter-parenting, and my personal favorite, the kindergarchy." Druckerman, *Bringing Up Bébé*, 4.

19. See R. Clements, "An Investigation of the State of Outdoor Play," *Contemporary Issues in Early Childhood*, 5, no. 1 (2004): 68-80. See also L. Karsten, "It All Used to be Better? Different Generations on Continuity and Change in Urban Children's Use of Space," *Children's Geographies*, 3, no. 3 (2005): 275-290.

## Notes for Chapter 7

1. D. Neumark-Sztainer, *I'm, Like, SO Fat!: Helping Your Teen Make Healthy Choices about Eating and Exercise in a Weight-obsessed World* (Guilford Press, 2005).

2. Between 1963 and 1970, 4.2% of 6- to 11-year-olds, and 4.6% of 12- to 19-year-olds were obese. From 1976 to 1980, 6.5 % of 6- to 11-year-old children, and 5% of 12- to 19-year-old children were obese. C. Ogden and M. Carroll, "Prevalence of Obesity Among Children and Adolescent: United States, Trends 1963-1965 Through 2007-2008," *Center for Disease Control and Prevention*, (n.d.), http://www.cdc.gov/nchs/data/hestat/obesity_child_07_08/obesity_child_07_08.htm.

3. C. Ogden et al., "Prevalence of Childhood and Adult Obesity in the United States, 2011-2012," *Jama* 311, no. 8 (2014): 806-814.

4. "Childhood Obesity Facts," Center for Disease Control and Prevention (n.d.), http://www.cdc.gov/healthyyouth/obesity/facts.html.

5. A. Farrell, *Fat Shame: Stigma and the Fat Body in American Culture* (NYU Press, 2011), 9. Farrell also cautions that, "the war against fat can become, too easily and too rapidly, a war against fat people." In *Illness as Metaphor*, Susan Sontag contends that the metaphors our culture uses for disease blame and shame the person with the disease. S. Sontag, *Illness as Metaphor and AIDS and its Metaphors* (Macmillan, 2001).

6. Farrell, *Fat Shame*, 10.

7. Farrell notes that there are deeply rooted historical connotations of fatness with being "lazy, gluttonous, greedy, immoral, uncontrolled, stupid, ugly, and lacking in will power." Farrell, *Fat Shame*, 11.

8. Ibid, 5-6.

9. D. Neumark-Sztainer and P. Hannan, "Weight-Related Behaviors Among Adolescent Girls and Boys: A National Survey," *Archives of Pediatric and Adolescent Medicine*, 154, 569-577.

10. In 1969, 48% of children usually walked or biked to school, and 89% of children who lived a mile or less from school biked or walked. In 2009, only 13% of children walk or bike to school, and of the children who live a mile or less from school, only 35% of them walk or bike. See "The Decline of Walking and Bicycling," *Safe Routes to School Guide* (n.d.), http://guide. saferoutesinfo.org/introduction/the_decline_of_walking_and_bicycling. cfm.

11. S. Schultz, J. Anner, J. and A. Hills, "Paediatric Obesity, Physical Activity and the Musculoskeletal System," *Obesity Review* 10, no. 5 (2009 ): 576-82.

12. T. Frieden, et al., "Reducing Childhood Obesity Through Policy Change: Acting Now to Prevent Obesity," *Health Affairs* 29, no. 3 (March 2010): 357-363.

13. In 2009, the average American preschooler viewed around 3,800 food and beverage television ads during a one-year period, while 6- to 11-year-olds viewed over 4,400 food and beverage advertisements. See J. Harris et al., "Redefining 'Child-Directed Advertising' to Reduce Unhealthy Television Food Advertising," *American Journal of Preventive Medicine* 44, no. 4 (2013): 358-364. In 2006, food companies spent 1.6 billion dollars marketing sweetened beverages, snacks, and cereal, and fast food to children. See K. Marr, "Children Targets of 1.6 Bllion in Food Ads," *Washington Post*, July 30, 2008, http://www.washingtonpost.com/wp-dyn/content/article/2008/07/29/ AR2008072902293.html. The nutritional content of foods advertised to children is low, with 97.8% of foods advertised to 2- to 11-year-olds, and

89.4% of foods advertised to 12 to 17 being extremely "high in fat, sugar, or sodium." See J. Mayer, "Television and Children's Consumption Patterns. A Review of the Literature," *Minerva Pediatrica* 54, no. 5 (2002): 423-436. L. Powell et al. "Nutritional Content of Television Food Advertisements Seen by Children and Adolescents in the United States," *Pediatrics* 120, no. 3 (2007): 576-583. Studies show that children do request products they see advertised on television. L. Chamberlain et al., "Does Children's Screen Time Predict Requests for Advertised Products? Cross-Sectional and Prospective Analysis," *Archives of Pediatric Adolescent Medicine* 160 (2006): 363-368. T. Lobstein and S. Dibb, "Evidence of a Possible Link Between Obesogenic Food Advertising and Child Overweight," *Obesity Reviews* 6 (2005):203-208. An Australian study found that children who were overweight are more susceptible to food advertisements than children who were not overweight. This is in line with "externality" research, which hypothesizes that overweight people are more likely to eat because of external cues, as opposed to internal signals. See D. Kessler, D. 2009. *The End of Overeating: Taking Control of the Insatiable American Appetite* (New York: Rodale, 2009), 163.

14. S. Folta et al., "Food Advertising Targeted at School-Age Children: A Content Analysis," *Journal of Nutrition Education and Behavior* 38, no. 4 (July-August 2006): 244-248. Food ads targeted to preschoolers focused on "building brand recognition and positive associations, through the use of licensed characters, logos, and slogans." S. Connor, "Food Related Advertising on Preschool Television: Building Brand Recognition in Young Viewers," *Pediatrics* 118, no. 4 (October 1, 2006): 1478-1485.

15. E. Isganaitis and R. Lustig, "Fast Food, Central Nervous System Insulin Resistance, and Obesity," *Arteriosclerosis, Thrombosis, and Vascular Biology Journal of the American Heart Association* 25 (2005): 2451-2462.

16. Children ingest more calories, fat, carbohydrates, and sugar, while getting less fiber, milk, fruits and non-starchy vegetables on days when they eat fast food compared to days when they do not. S. Bowman et al. "Effects of Fast-Food Consumption on Energy Intake and Diet Quality Among Children in a National Household Survey," *Pediatrics* 113, no. 1 (January 1, 2004): 112-118.

17. "In 1953, fast food accounted for 4% of total sales of food outside the home; by 1997, it accounted for 34%....As a percentage of total energy intake, fast food quintupled from 2% in the 1970s, to 10% in 1995." Fast food is "energy dense," which can interfere with a person's "appetite control mechanisms," making it more likely for people to increase their consumption of food. Isganaitis and Lustig, "Fast Food," 2451. In 2010, revenues for fast food restaurants were over $180 billion. In 1977, the average fast-food

cheeseburger was 5.8 ounces and had 397 calories. By 1996, an average cheeseburger was 7.3 ounces, and 533 calories. See S. Dalton, *Our Overweight Children What Parents, Schools, and Communities can do to Control the Fatness Epidemic* (University of California Press, 2004). During 2006, 1.2 billion kids' meals consumed by children under the age of 12. See Federal Trade Commission, "Marketing Food to Children and Adolescents: A Review of Industry Expenditures, Activities, and Self Regulation," (2008), www.ftc.gov/os/2008/07/ P064504foodmktingreport.pdf.

18. Ibid.

19. Ibid.

20. M. Moss, *Salt, Sugar, Fat: How the Food Industry Hooked Us* (Random House: New York, 2013).

21. "Profiling Food Consumption in America," in *The Agricultural Fact Book* (US Government, 2002), http://www.usda.gov/factbook/chapter2.pdf.

22. Isganaitis and Lustig, "Fast Food."

23. C. Visness, et al., "Association of Obesity with IgE Levels and Allergy Symptoms in Children and Adolescents: Results from the National Health and Nutrition Examination Survey 2005-2006," *Journal of Allergy and Clinical Immunology* 123, no. 5 (2009): 1163-1169.

24. G. Singh, M. Siahpush and M. Kogan, "Neighborhood Socioeconomic Conditions, Built Environments, and Childhood Obesity," *Health Affairs* 29, no. 3 (2010): 503-512.

25. One study found that teenagers who go to a school within 1/10 of a mile of a fast food restaurant were more likely to be obese. Currently about 20% of America's schools offer Fast Food brands, such as McDonald's Taco Bell and Pizza Hut in their school cafeteria. J. Currie et al., "The Effect of Fast Food Restaurants on Obesity and Weight Gain," *American Economic Journal* 2, no. 3 (2010): 32-63.

26. J. Harris et al., "Priming Effects of Television Food Advertising on Eating Behavior," *Health Psychology* 28, no. 4 (July 2009): 404-413.

27. The American Heart Association recommends that women should consume no more than 24 grams, or 6 teaspoons of added sugar daily, and men no more than 36 grams, or 9 teaspoons, and children should consume even less than these amounts, depending on their age. See American Heart Association, www.heart.org.

28. Children between the ages of one and three typically consume 48 grams, or 12 teaspoons of added sugar daily; and four- to eight-year-olds consume 84 grams, or 21teaspoons daily. Fourteen- to eighteen-year-old girls consume approximately 100 grams, or 25 teaspoons a day, and boys in the same age range consume on average 136 grams, or 34 teaspoons of added

sugar daily. The average American adult consumes 88 grams, or ½ cup, of added sugar every day. See American Heart Association, www.heart.org.

29. On average, children consume approximately 224 calories from sugared beverages, which is approximately 63 grams of sugar, and 11% of the total calories in the average child's diet. This is a 70% increase from 1977, when sugared beverage consumption made up only 4% of a child's total calories. See Y. Wang, S. Bleich and S. Gortmaker, "Increasing Caloric Contribution from Sugar-Sweetened beverages and 100% fruit juices among US children and adolescents, 1988-2004," *Pediatrics* 121, no. 6 (2008): 1604-1614. See also Frieden, T. et al., "Reducing Childhood Obesity." Isganaitis and Lustig, "Fast Food."

30. M. Moss, *Salt, Sugar, Fat*, 19-21.

31. Ibid.

32. C. Ross, "Why Do Women Hate Their Bodies?" *Psych Central* (2012), http://psychcentral.com/blog/archives/2012/06/02/why-do-women-hate-their-bodies/.

33. Neumark-Sztainer, *I'm Like SO Fat*," 8.

34. M. McCabe and L. Ricciardelli, "Parent, Peer and Media Influences on Body Image and Strategies to Both Increase and Decrease Body Size Among Adolescent Boys and Girls," *Adolescence* 36, no. 142 (2001): 225-240.

35. Ibid.

36. J. Berge et al., "Parent Conversations About Healthful Eating and Weight: Associations with Adolescent Disordered Eating Behaviors," *JAMA Pediatrics* 167, no. 8 (2013): 746-753.

37. Ibid. See also H. Keery et al., "The Impact of Appearance-Related Teasing by Family Members," *Journal of Adolescent Health* 37, no. 2 (2005): 120-127.

38. These groups include Healthy People 2010; the NFL Play 60; the NBA and WNBA FIT; CATCH USA; Clinton Global Initiative; Alliance for a Healthier Generation; The Robert Wood Johnson Foundation; Nickelodeon's Public Service Announcements; Cartoon Network's "Move It Movement Tour" and We Can! There are also community and school-based programs all over the country doing their part to create a healthier environment for children.

39. There have been several school-based programs encouraging children to reduce screen time. One such program is the Washington Nutrition and Physical Activity Plan, which included screen time reduction in their education outreach efforts. Unplugged and Media Savvy, a Collaborative Project of the University of Washington Center for Public Health Nutrition and The Northwest Center for Excellence in Media Literacy, is funded by the National Institutes of Health, http://depts.washington.edu/waaction/action/

p2/c5.html

40. "Labeling and Nutrition Guidance Documents and Regulatory Information," Food and Drug Administration (October, 2009), http://www.fda.gov/Food/GuidanceRegulation/GuidanceDocumentsRegulatory Information/LabelingNutrition/ucm385663.htm.

41. "Children's Food and Beverage Advertising Initiative," (The National Partner Program), http://www.bbb.org/council/the-national-partner-program/national-advertising-review-services/childrens-food-and-beverage-advertising-initiative.

42. The members of the CFBAI include: Burger King, Campbell's, ConAgra Foods, Coca-Cola, Dannon, Ferrero, General Mills, Hershey's, Hillshire, Kellogg's, Kraft Foods, Mars, McDonald's, Mondelez, Nestle, Pepsico, Post, and Unilever. At a White House meeting in 2013, the CFBAI, reported that its members have committed to advertise healthy products, based on CFBAI nutrition criteria, *or* to not specifically target children in advertisements in media where the audience share of children aged 12 and under is greater than 35%. According to the report, the CFBAI independently monitors and scrutinizes members for compliance within all forms of media.

43. Restaurant chains in the group, such as McDonald's and Burger King, now offer healthier children's meals that include fruit and low fat milk choices, while also reducing the serving size of French fries. The cereals of CFBAI participants have reduced their levels of sugar while increasing their levels of whole grain. One third of CFBAI products still fail voluntary nutrition guidelines, but CFBAI contends that implementation of healthier options need to be gradual in order to be accepted by consumers. The CFBAI concluded their report at the White House meeting by reaffirming that their participants are committed to "being *part* of the multi-faceted solution needed to achieve healthy weights for children." See E. Kolish, "Self-Regulation Creates Significant Ongoing Progress in Foods Advertised to Children," *White House Convening on Food Marketing to Children*, (September 18, 2013), http://www.bbb.org/globalassets/local-bbbs/council-113/media/cfbai/cfbai-self-regulation-successes-white-house-sept-18-2013-final.pdf.

44. Contrary to CFBAI reports that indicate that self-regulation has been effective in reducing advertising of food with poor nutritional value to children, several studies note that there are many loopholes in the CFBAI self-regulation policies. An independent study published in *Obesity Reviews* contends there has been little change in advertising to children throughout the United States, Canada, Europe, Asia, and Australia. For example, there are many smaller food and beverage companies which are not members of

CFBAI and do not need to comply with voluntary restrictions. CFBAI member restrictions apply to television shows that have a greater than 35% viewing share of children 12 and under. However, independent researchers indicate that these standards are too lax, and suggest that restrictions that apply to shows that have a 20% share of child viewers, or more than 100,000 child viewers, would cover approximately 70% of the shows that children watch. Additionally, advertisers can market their brand, without advertising specific food products that are unhealthy. The International Association for the Study of Obesity (IASO) calls for "comprehensive rules, covering digital as well as broadcast media, with independent monitoring and costly penalties for non-compliance." See Harris et al., "Redefining 'Child-Directed Advertising." Also see E. Galbraith and T. Lobstein, "The Impact of Initiatives to Limit the Advertising of Food and Beverage Products to Children: A Systematic Review," *Obesity Reviews* 14, no. 12 (2013): 960-974.

45. T. Frieden et al., "Reducing Childhood Obesity." A review of children's food advertising in the United States, Australia, and eight European countries found a "significant association" between "the proportion of children overweight and the numbers of advertisements per hour on children's television, especially those advertisements that encourage the consumption of energy-dense, micronutrient-poor foods." See Lobstein and Dibb, "Evidence of a Possible Link," 203-208. Australian researchers constructed a mathematical model that predicted that eliminating food advertisements to children could reduce American children's obesity levels by one-third. See L. Veerman et al., "By How Much Would Limiting TV Food Advertising Reduce Childhood Obesity?" *European Journal of Public Health* (March 26, 2009).

46. Ibid.

47. One study found that teenagers who go to a school within 1/10 of a mile of a fast food restaurant were more likely to be obese. J. Currie, et al. "The Effect of Fast Food Restaurants on Obesity and Weight Gain," in *American Economics Journal* 2, no. 3 (2010): 32-63. In tandem with this, Friedan suggests governments should partner with grocery store chains to "expand full-service groceries in underserved neighborhoods." T. Frieden et al., "Reducing Childhood Obesity."

48. Such a tax would reduce average per capita consumption by 8,000 calories annually, potentially preventing about 2.3 pounds per year of weight gain." Ibid.

49. M. Gagnon and R. Freudenburg, "Slowing Down Fast Food: A Policy Guide for Healthier Kids and Families," Corporate Accountability International and City University School of Public Health at Hunter College (2012).

50. R. Edgerton, *Sick Societies* (Simon and Schuster, 2010), 215.

51. Ibid, 87.

## NOTES FOR CHAPTER 8

1. These estimates include time spent: watching TV; listening to music; being on the computer; playing video games; reading newspapers, magazines, and books; and watching movies. According to the Kaiser Family Foundation Study of Media in the Lives of 8- to 18-year-olds, there are demographic differences between children's average media use. African American and Latino children have higher average daily rates of total media use (approximately 13 hours) compared to white youth who average just over 8-1/2 hours. On average, boys spend about an hour more using media per day than girls, and 11- to 14-year-olds have higher rates of media use than 15- to 18-year-olds or 8- to 10-year-olds. Children whose parents have a college degree average 10 hours of media use per day, whereas children whose parents have a high school degree or some college average around 11-1/2 hours per day. See the full report at Henry Kaiser Foundation. *Generation M2* Media in the Lives of 8- to 18-year-olds. A Kaiser Family Foundation Study. See http://kff.org/disparities-policy/press-release/daily-media-use-among-children-and-teens-up-dramatically-from-five-years-ago/. See also: Kirkorian, H. et. al. "Media and Young Children's Learning." *The Future of Children* 18.1 (2008):40-61. Larson, et. al. "Combined Influence of Physical Activity and Screen Time Recommendations on Childhood Overweight." *Journal of Pediatrics* 158.2 (February 2011):297-300.

2. Sigman, A. "Well connected? The biological implications of 'social networking.' *Biologist* 56.1( February 2009). See also, Kraut, R. et. Al. "Internet Paradox: A Social Technology that Reduces Social Involvement and Psychological Wellbeing? *American Psychologist* 53.9 (September 1998):1017-1031.

3. See Strasburger V. et. al. "Health Effects of Media on Children and Adolescents." *Pediatrics* 125 (2010):756, originally published online March 1, 2010. See also Livingstone, S. and P. Smith. "Annual Research Review: Harms experienced by child users of online and mobile technologies: the nature, prevalence and management of sexual and aggressive risks in the digital age." *Journal of Child Psychology and Psychiatry* 55.6 (2014): 635-654.

4. The author uses the analogy of a telephone as a way for us to think about new media. "In this view, we may look back on digital technology like we do today about the telephone. It was revolutionizing and has become integral to everything we do, but it did not organize our thinking about youth development or social problems. Although it plays a part in sex and

aggressive behavior, we did not end up problematizing 'tele-bullying' or 'tele-predators.'" See Finkelhor, D. "Commentary: Cause for alarm? Youth and internet risk research—a commentary on Livingstone and Smith." *Journal of Child Psychology and Psychiatry* 55:6 (2014) :655-658.

5. In his commentary on Youth and Livingstone's internet risk research, David Finkelhor, concludes by asking, "Where is the research about the technology's virtues: making downtime less boring, helping stay in touch with friends and family, and managing social anxiety, participating in adult worlds, stoking imagination, giving a sense of mastery, and fueling optimism about the future?" See Finkelhor, D., 2014.

6. Ibid. Also see the original study, Zimmerman, F.J. and Christakis, D. "Associations between Content Types of Early Media Exposure and Subsequent Attentional Problems." *Pediatrics* 120(2007):986-992.

7. Wilson, Barbara. 2008. Educational programming can by promote pro-social behavior, such as honesty, respect, and sharing, and enhanceproblem solving skills and kindergarten readiness. For example, children who watched the pro-social "Mister Rogers Neighborhood" over a four-week time-period had a greater ability to regulate their behavior, follow rules, and be more persistent in completing a task, than children who watched violent cartoons during that same time-period, who showed a decreased ability to regulate their behavior. Some studies even show a positive association between watching educational shows at age five, and later high school achievement in math, science, and English. See Kirkorian, H. et. al. Wartella 2008. Also see the original study, Zimmerman and Christakis, 2007.

8. Tom Conley and John Ingham argue that there is tension between the domestic sphere and the market economy, which has increasingly commodified and eroticized childhood. See Conley, T., and J.M. Ingham. "Ideological Fantasy (PG-13): Lessons for Film Studies." Psychoanalysis, Culture & Society 38.10 (2005):286-298.

9. Roberts et. al., 2005.

10. See http://www.emarketer.com/Article/Digital-Set-Surpass-TV-Time-Spent-with-US-Media/1010096.

11. Ninety-seven percent of American teens report playing video games, and youth under age 18 represent 30% percent of all video gamers. In 2013, consumers spent 15.4 billion dollars purchasing games for various platforms, and an additional 6+ billion purchasing hardware and accessories. Boys spend more time than girls playing video games, and Black and Hispanic youth spend more time than white youth playing video games. Adolescents between 11 and 14 spend the most time playing video games. See Roberts, et. al., 2005. Also see http://www.emarketer.com/Article/

Digital-Set-Surpass-TV-Time-Spent-with-US-Media/1010096.

12. Some researchers argue that the dopamine release can also facilitate learning, especially if a child can transfer the problem solving skills learned in the game to new situations. See Koepp, Matthias J., et al. "Evidence for striatal dopamine release during a video game." *Nature* 393.6682 (1998): 266-268.

13. For example, children who played *Tetris*, scored better on paper and pencil tests that required mental rotation. See De Lisi, R. and J. L. Wolford, "Improving Children's Mental Rotation Accuracy with Computer Game Playing," *The Journal of Genetic Psychology* 163 (2002): 272–82.

14. Prensky, Marc. *Don't Bother Me, Mom, I'm Learning!: How Computer and Video Games are Preparing Your Kids for 21st Century Success and how You Can Help!* Paragon House, 2006. Also see, Green, C. Shawn, and D. Bavelier. "Action video game modifies visual selective attention." *Nature* 423.6939 (2003): 534-537.

15. Prensky, Marc, 2006. For a thorough description of "flow," see Csikszentmihalyi, Mihaly. *Flow.* Springer Netherlands, 2014.

16. The statement was issued by the American Academy of Pediatrics; American Academy of Child and Adolescent Psychiatry; American Psychological Association; American Medical Association; American Academy of Family Physicians; and American Psychiatric Association. See Wilson, B. 2008. Also see the original Source: Congressional Public Health Summit, "Joint Statement on the Impact of Entertainment Violence on Children," July 26, 2000.

17. Anderson et. al., 2007.

18. Ibid. See also, Escobar-Chavez, S. and C. Anderson, "Media and Risky Behaviors." The Future of Children. 18.1:147–180.

19. Ibid.

20. Hill, "Early Adolescence: A Framework," *Journal of Early Adolescence* 3.1 (1983): 1–21.

21. Boyd, D. 2014. *It's Complicated: The Social Lives of Networked Teens* Yale University Press. See chapter 5.

22. For tablet use see http://www.marketingprofs.com/charts/2013/12042/75-of-american-children-under-8-have-access-to-a-smart-phone-or-tablet. For smartphone use see http://www.emarketer.com/Article/Smartphones-Hands-of-Youngest-Demographic/1009915.

## NOTES FOR CHAPTER 9

1. McNeal, J. U. *The kids market: Myths and realities.* New York, Paramount Market, 1999, p. 17-18. Political Theorist Benjamin Barber contends that the global inequality of wealth creates a situation where there are not enough

enriched adults to buy commodities, so children become valuable consumers. See Barber, B. R. *Consumed: How markets corrupt children, infantilize adults, and swallow citizens whole.* WW Norton & Company, 2008, pp. 7-12. Another report notes that "Today's little kids and tweens have buying power to the tune of $1.2 trillion per year," stated a report from one of the world's largest advertising agencies. This includes the amount they purchase on their own, and the spending they "influence." See "Kids Spending and Influence Power: $1.2 Trillion Says Leading Ad Firm." *Center for Digital Democracy.* N.p., 1 Nov. 11. Web. 26 Jan. 2015. <http://www.democraticmedia.org/kids-spending-and-influencing-power-12-trillion-says-leading-ad-firm>. In the United States alone, advertising to children ranges from $1.6 billion to more than $15 billion annually. The $1.6 billion estimate is based only on food and beverage marketing. See Teinowitz, Ira. "FTC Study: Dollars Spent on Marketing to Kids Much Lower Than Thought." *Advertising Age News RSS.* N.p., 29 July 2008. Web. 03 Feb. 2015. <http://adage.com/article/news/ftc-study-dollars-spent-marketing-kids-lower-thought/129974/>. The $15 billion estimate is from Schor, Juliet. *Born to buy: The commercialized child and the new consumer culture.* Simon and Schuster, 2004.

2. Matel and Hasbro are the largest toy manufacturers in the world, with their combined revenue being over $10 billion in 2010. China manufacturers 80% of the toys available globally, securing cheap labor from "Enterprise Processing Zones," in China, Thailand, or the Philippines, where young women work and live in crowded factories for low wages. See Seiter, E. *Sold separately: Children and parents in consumer culture.* Rutgers University Press, 1995. See also Schor, 2004, p. 13.

3. Kids see ads on television, on the internet and social media, in movies, on their phones, at school, and in many other private and public settings. See Buckingham, D. *After the death of childhood.* John Wiley & Sons, 2013. Schor, 2004. Schor, Juliet B. "When childhood gets commercialized, can children be protected?." *I U. Carlsson & C. von Feilitzen (red.), In the service of young people* (2006): 27-48.

4. For a complete list of references on this topic, see Shah, Anup. "Children as Consumers." *Global Issues.* N.p., 21 Nov. 10. Web. 13 Jan. 2015. <http://www.globalissues.org/article/237/children-as-consumers>.

5. Valkenburg, P. M. "Media and youth consumerism." *Journal of Adolescent Health* 27.2 (2000): 52-56.

6. Linn, Susan. "Consuming kids: The hostile takeover of childhood." (2004), p. 35.

7. McNeal, 1999.

8. The average purchase has three steps: 1) recognition of a need or want;

2) the product search; and 3) the decision about which brand of the product to buy. Children can potentially influence all of these stages. About 75% of parents get input from children on major purchases. Ibid.

9. Kunkel, D., et al. "Report of the APA task force on advertising and children." *Washington, DC: American Psychological Association* (2004).

10. See "Children and Advertising the European Dimension." *Peace Pledge Union.* N.p., n.d. Web. 04 Feb. 2015. <http://www.ppu.org.uk/chidren/advertising_toys_eu.html>.

11. Kunkel, et al., 2004.

12. For a review of these studies see: Ramsey, W. A. "Rethinking regulation of advertising aimed at children." *Fed. Comm. LJ* 58 (2006): 361.

13. For a review of these studies see: Kunkel, et al. 2004. School-based media literacy programs are intended to help children "defend" against advertisements, however research on the positive effects of media literacy programs is limited, and some studies indicate that it is difficult for children to apply the information they learn about media literacy when they actually view commercials.

14. McNeal, 1999.

15. John, 1999. A Harris survey of children's marketing experts revealed that on average, marketers think it is appropriate to begin marketing to kids at age 7, that kids have the capacity to critically view advertising around age 9, and are able to make 'intelligent choices as consumers' between the ages of 11 and 12. See Schor, 2004, p 107-108.

16. Kunkel, et al. 2004. Page 29 of the report states that "Long-standing public policy in the area of advertising holds that all commercial content must be clearly identifiable as such to its intended audience, in order to allow the consumer to consider the source of the message in evaluating its claims. Advertising that violates this standard is deemed unfair, and a violation of federal law. Given that young children inherently lack the cognitive capability to effectively recognize and defend against televised commercial persuasion in this manner, we recommend that policymakers pursue efforts to contstrain advertising specifically directed to this particular age group." School-based media literacy programs are intended to help children "defend" against advertisements, however research on the positive effects of media literacy programs is limited, and some studies indicate that it is difficult for children to apply the information they learn about media literacy when they actually view commercials.

17. Studies of CARU compliance indicate that most ads comply with their guidelines, however they note that the guidelines themselves are rather vague. See Kunkel et. al., 2004.

18. See Ramsey, 2006, p. 362-3. Host selling simply means that characters in a show are not allowed to be in commercials during that show. For example, it would be illegal for a commercial that used Spongebob Squarepants to air during a Spongebob Squarepants show.

19. In 1990, Congress passed the Children's Television Act (CTA), which instructed the FCC to enforce the policy that networks would air at least three hours of quality children's programming each week, and abide by the commercial limitations set in the 1970s.

20. Schor, 2004, p. 113.

21. For a discussion on this, see Schor, 2004, p.111.

22. Buckingham, 2013.

23. See Schor, 2006, p. 113-117.

24. McNeal, J. "From Savers to Spenders: How Children Became a Consumer Market." *Media and Values* (1990): 52-53.

25. Ibid.

26. Allowance amounts in my sample ranged from a few dollars a week for young children to $50 per week.

27. Madeline Levine describes materialism as: "a value system that emphasizes wealth, status, image, and material consumption. It is a measure of how much we value material things over other things in our lives, like friends, family, and work. It keeps us wedded to external measures of accomplishment for a sense of self—prestige, power, money for adults; grades, clothes, electronics for kids." Levine, M. *The price of privilege*. Harper Collins, 2009, p. 45.

28. Hays, 1996, p. 18.

29. Dittmar, H., et al. "The relationship between materialism and personal well-being: A meta-analysis." *Journal of personality and social psychology* 107.5 (2014): 879.

30. "Is the United States Materialistic? The Geography of Consumption." *Beyond The Purchase Blog*. N.p., n.d. Web. 02 Feb. 2015. <http://www.beyondthepurchase.org/blog/03/is-the-united-states-materialistic/>. The information in this blog is based on the following article: Zhang, J. W., R. T. Howell, and C. J. Howell. "Living in wealthy neighborhoods increases material desires and maladaptive consumption." *Journal of Consumer Culture* (2014): 1469540514521085.For a review of the literature, see Kasser, T. *The High Price of Materialism*. Cambridge, MA: The MIT Press, 2002.

31. Ibid., p. 914.

32. Ibid.

33. Schor, 2004, p. 13, and p. 111.

34. Schor notes that "surveys of children and teens suggest they are more materialistic than previous generations, that being rich is currently the most

popular aspiration of American youth and that youth have an unprecedented level of brand awareness and passion." Schor, 2004, p. 13, and p. 110.

35. Social comparison theories assert that most people compare themselves to other people within a self-defined referent group. In this way, media images can become the "generalized other" for those who identify with the group being portrayed by the media. See Milkie, M. A. "Social comparisons, reflected appraisals, and mass media: The impact of pervasive beauty images on Black and White girls' self-concepts." *Social Psychology Quarterly* (1999): 190-210, p. 203.

36. Research shows that individuals who live in neighborhoods with a higher socioeconomic status had "increased material desires," "more frequent impulsive buying," and "fewer savings behaviors," especially if they were young, and felt like they were less well-off than the other people in their neighborhood. People who actually had a high SES were less likely to be materialistic, however living in a wealthy neighborhood even made people with a high SES more likely to be materialistic. See Zhang, J. Wei, R. Howell, T. and C. J. Howell. "Living in wealthy neighborhoods increases material desires and maladaptive consumption." *Journal of Consumer Culture* (2014).

37. De Tocqueville, A. *Democracy in America*. Рипол Классик, 1972. See Bellah, E. R.N., et al. *Habits of the heart: Individualism and commitment in American life*. University of California Press, 1985:1.

38. Lieber, R. *The Opposite of Spoiled: Raising Kids who are Grounded, Generous, and Smart about Money*. Harper Collins, 2015, p. 8.

## NOTES FOR CHAPTER 10

1. Struggles can include addiction, eating disorders, trouble with the law, and a host of other things. See S. Elliott, R. Powell and J. Brenton, "Being a Good Mom: Low-Income, Black Single Mothers Negotiate Intensive Mothering," in *Journal of Family Issues* 36, no. 3 (2015): 351-370. M. Milkie and C. Warner, "Status Safeguarding: Mother's Work to Secure Children's Place in the Social Hierarchy," in *Intensive Mothering: The Cultural Contradictions of Modern Motherhood*, ed. L. Ennis (Bradford, ON: Demeter, 2014), 66-85. I. Singh, "Doing Their Jobs: Mothering with Ritalin in a Culture of Mother-Blame," in *Social Science and Medicine* 59 (2004): 1193-1205. Historically, we blamed working mothers for juvenile delinquency, African American mothers for welfare dependency, and we held mothers responsible if their adult children were homosexual, hippies, or serial killers. See discussion in M. Ladd-Taylor and L. Umansky, *"Bad" Mothers: The Politics of Blame in Twentieth-Century America* (New York: NYU Press, 1998).

2. Sharon Hays defines "intensive mothering" as a parenting model

that postulates that children are innocent and priceless and therefore calls for "child-rearing methods that are child-centered, expert-guided, emotionally absorbing, [and] labor intensive." S. Hays, *The Cultural Contradictions of Motherhood* (Yale University Press, 1998), 122.

3. Ibid., 1-2.

4. A. Lareau, *Unequal Childhoods: Class, Race, and Family Life* (University of California Press, 2011), 13.

5. Ibid., 83.

6. Milkie and Warner, "Status Safeguarding," 66.

7. Ibid., 76.

8. Ibid.

9. Ibid., 76-77.

10. Ibid., 66.

11. Lareau, *Unequal Childhoods*, 3.

12. C. Vincent and S. Ball, "Making Up the Middle-Class Child: Families, Activities and Class Dispositions," *Sociology* 41, no. 6 (2007): 1061-77.

13. Parents who use "hard" styles of individualism believe it is imperative for a child to develop a "thick skin," which they achieve through strict discipline, teasing, and teaching kids emotional control. Parents emphasize the importance of traits such as: "self-assertiveness, self-confidence, self-reliance, doggedness, and persistence" and viewed their children as being a person "against" the world. A. Kusserow, *American Individualisms: Child Rearing and Social Class in Three Neighborhoods.* New York: Palgrave Macmillan, 2004) 57, 26.

14. Milkie and Warner, "Status Safeguarding," 76.

15. See J. Brenner, "Overuse Injuries, Overtraining, and Burnout in Child and Adolescent Athletes," *Pediatrics* 119, no. 6 (2007): 1242-1245. Also see, J. DiFiori et al., "Overuse Injuries and Burnout in Youth Sports: A Position Statement from the American Medical Society for Sports Medicine," *British Journal of Sports Medicine* 48, no. 4 (2014): 287-288.

16. See M. Levine, *The Price of Privilege: How Parental Pressure and Material Advantage are Creating a Generation of Disconnected and Unhappy Kids* (New York: HarperCollins, 2006), 142.

17. T. Chin and M. Phillips, "Social Reproduction and Child-Rearing Practices: Social Class, Children's Agency, and the Summer Activity Gap," *Sociology of Education* 77, no. 3 (2004): 185-210.

18. Ibid, 185.

19. See N. Hill and D. Tyson, "Parental Involvement in Middle School: A Meta-Analytic Assessment of the Strategies that Promote Achievement," *Developmental Psychology* 45, no. 3 (2009): 740.

20. Ibid.

21. Ibid.

22. For a review of all the studies see Hill and Tyson, "Parental Involvement."

23. S. Catsambis, "Expanding Knowledge of Parental Involvement in Children's Secondary Education: Connections with High School Seniors' Academic Success," *Social Psychology of Education* 5, no. 2 (2001): 149-177.

24. Levine, *Price of Privilege*, 30. Also see the original study: S. Blatt, "The Destructiveness of Perfectionism: Implications for the Treatment of Depression," *American Psychologist* 50, no. 12 (1995): 1003.

25. See A. Lareau, *Unequal Childhoods: Class, Race, and Family Life* (University of California Press, 2011). Also see Urist's discussion of the "silent achievement gap." J. Urist, "Is College Really Harder To Get Into Than It Used to Be?" *The Atlantic*, April 4, 2014, <http://www.theatlantic.com/education/archive/2014/04/is-college-really-harder-to-get-into-than-it-used-to-be/360114/>.

26. J. Lythcott-Haims, *How to Raise an Adult: Break Free of the Over-Parenting Trap and Prepare Your Kid for Success* (Henry Holt & Co., 2015), 6.

27. Milkie and Warner, "Status Safeguarding", 66-85, 79.

28. Lythcott-Haims, *Raise an Adult*, chapters 13 through 20.

## Notes for Chapter 11

1. These were the top 13 traits women identified when I asked in surveys, interviews, and focus groups, "What traits do you hope to instill in your child?" More than one-third of the women replied that respect, honesty, kindness, and being polite were very important to them.

2. A. Kusserow, *American Individualisms: Child Rearing and Social Class in Three Neighborhoods.* New York: Palgrave Macmillan, 2004), 172.

3. "Minnesota Nice" is a term that for the last couple of decades has referred to "a vaguely defined set of cultural characteristics... [that ]...includes a polite friendliness, an aversion to confrontation, a tendency toward understatement, a disinclination to make a fuss or stand out, emotional restraint, and self deprecation." See A. Atkins, *Creating Minnesota: A History from the Inside Out* (Minnesota Historical Society, 2007), 242.

4. Economist Nancy Folbre observes, "no society oriented exclusively toward individual success—to the exclusion of care for the next generation—can reproduce itself." N. Folbre, *The Invisible Heart: Economics and Family Values* (Cambridge, MA: MIT Press, 2002), xx.

5. See R. Bellah et al. *Habits of the Heart: Individualism and Commitment in American Life* (University of California Press, 2007).

6. R. Fuller, *Spiritual, But Not Religious: Understanding Unchurched America* (Oxford University Press, 2001).

7. E. Durkheim, *The Elementary Forms of the Religious Life*, trans. Carol Cosman (Oxford University Press, 2008).

8. Charles Lippy notes that people "will remain part of the group while it functions to give some semblance of meaning, provides an experience of community, or offers opportunities for social contact. But they will not retain long-term loyalty once the group ceases to function in these ways." C. Lippy, *Being Religious, American Style: A History of Popular Religiosity in the United States* (Greenwood Publishing Group, 1994), 230.

9. Fuller notes that 55 percent of church-goers subscribe to some belief of the occult. Fuller, *Spiritual But Not Religious.*

10. Fuller, *Spiritual But Not Religious*, 210.

11. Ibid.

12. For a list of studies, see H. Schiffrin et al. "Helping or Hovering? The Effects of Helicopter Parenting on College Students' Well-Being," *Journal of Child and Family Studies* 23, no. 3 (2014): 548-557.

13. Ibid. The psychological literature refers to these kinds of parents as "autonomy supportive" parents, or as parents who have "positive parental engagement." Autonomy-Supportive" is used by Schiffrin, "Helping or Hovering." "Positive Parental Engagement" is used by P. Somers and J. Settle, "The Helicopter Parent: Research Toward a Typology," *College and University* 86, no. 1 (2010): 18.

14. Other western countries have criticized this style of parenting and use terms such as "curling" parents (parents who sweep away obstacles from their child's path) and "lawnmower" parents (parents who mow down obstacles in their child's path).

15. This is not the first time in American history mothers have been criticized for being over-involved in their child's life. Articles in popular women's magazines of the 1930s, 1940s, and 1950s, repeatedly painted mothers as "all-powerful influences on their children" while also "warning them against overindulgence and overprotection." See M. Patterson and R Smith-Fullerton, "Procrustean Motherhood: The Good Mother during Depression (1930s), War (1940s), and Prosperity (1950s)," *Canadian Journal of Media Studies*, August 2001, http://cjms.fims.uwo.ca/issues/08-01/patterson-smith.pdf.

16. The term "helicopter parent" is from J. Fay and C. Fay, *Love and Logic Magic for Early Childhood: Practical Parenting from Birth to Six* (Love and Logic Press, 2000).

17. Somers and J. Settle, "The Helicopter Parent," 19.

18. Ibid.

19. Ibid.

20. See Schiffrin, "Helping or Hovering." Also see, Somers and J. Settle, "The Helicopter Parent," 19.

21. A. Astin et al., "The American Freshman: National Norms for Fall 2006," *Higher Education Research Institute* (Los Angeles, 2007). See Somers and J. Settle, "The Helicopter Parent," for a summary of studies.

22. This study found that students with the most parental intervention had the lowest grades, which suggests that parents may be trying to "support a student who was having academic difficulties." Ibid.

23. S. Toepfer, "Flight Pattern of Helicopter Parents: Emotional Distance Regulation." (*Unpublished Manuscript, Kent State University* 2008). Reviewed in Somers and Settle, "The Helicopter Parent."

24. University employees described five different types of helicopter behavior. 1) The *consumer advocate* looked at college as a "consumer transaction," and wanted to "negotiate the best possible price" through tuition discounts and scholarships. 2) The *fairness advocate,* demands "fairness" for their child by wanting them to have the "best" dorm, major, internship, and so forth. 3) The *vicarious college student* parent wants to be involved in campus events, and attend every activity they can. 4) The *toxic parent* has psychological issues and are controlling and negative. The percentage of this type of parent is relatively small. 5) The *Safety Patrol Parents* are worried about campus safety, especially if there is a safety incident on campus, or a highly publicized safety event on another college campus. Consumer Advocate, Fairness Advocate, and Safety Patrol Parents are the types of "helicopter" parents most often encountered by university staff. See Somers and Settle, "The Helicopter Parent," 18.

## NOTES FOR CHAPTER 12

1. Throughout this book, I have argued that our expectations for mothers have increased in response to significant social changes over the last generation. Instead of responding to these social changes with public policies and revised workplace norms to offer institutional support for childrearing, our legislation has privileged the free market, emphasized individual responsibility, and reduced safety nets, which has given rise to "competitive individualism." Neoliberal policies have created an atmosphere characterized by deregulation, privatization, cutting funds for social services, the expansion of the free market, and "eliminating the concept of 'the public good', or 'community' and replacing it with 'individual responsibility.'" See E. Martinez and A. Garcia, "What is 'Neo-liberalism?' A Brief Definition for Activists,

*Corp Watch*, n.d., http://www.corpwatch.org/article.php?id=376. Anita Harris argues that this era of economic rationalism "has been accompanied by a shift to a new brand of competitive individualism, whereby people...must develop individual strategies and take personal responsibility for their success, happiness, and livelihood by making the right choices is an uncertain and changeable environment." See A. Harris, *Future Girl: Young Women in the Twenty-First Century* (New York: Routledge, 2004), 3-4.

2. For some mothers having joint custody was a source of parenting and/or financial support, while others had ongoing conflict with a child's father, which contributed to emotional and financial hardships. Some women had the sole responsibility of caring for and supporting their children because the children's father was deceased or was not involved in the child's life in any way.

3. C. Heath and D. Heath, *Switch: How to Change When Change is Hard* (Crowne Business, 2010).

4. J. Horowitz, et al.,"Nurse Home Visits Improve Maternal/Infant Interaction and Decrease Severity of Postpartum Depression," *Journal of Obstetric, Gynecologic, & Neonatal Nursing* 42, no. 3 (2013): 287-300.

5. B. Starr and J. Cleveland, "Early Childhood Family Education: Celebrating 40 Years of Learning for Minnesota's Parents and Children," Child Trends, November 5, 2014, http://www.childtrends.org/early-childhood-family-education-celebrating-40-years-of-learning-for-minnesotas-parents-and-children/.

6. V. Macintosh, M. Liss and H. Schiffrin, "Using a Quantitative Measure to Explore Intensive Mothering Ideology," in *Intensive Mothering: The Cultural Contradictions of Modern Motherhood*, ed. L. Ennis (Bradford, ON: Demeter, 2014), 142-159, 154.

7. L. Lapierre, et al., "Family-Supportive Organization Perceptions, Multiple Dimensions of Work–Family Conflict, and Employee Satisfaction: A Test of Model Across Five Samples," *Journal of Vocational Behavior* 73, no. 1 (2008): 92-106.

8. E. Kelly, P. Moen and E. Tranby, "Changing Workplaces to Reduce Work-Family Conflict Schedule Control in a White-Collar Organization," *American Sociological Review* 76, no. 2 (2011): 265-290.

9. Companies that have high employee ratings often "outperform the market as a whole by a stunning factor of 2 to 1." R. Friedman, *The Best Place to Work: The Art and Science of Creating an Extraordinary Workplace* (Penguin, 2014), see introduction.

10. See S. Douglas and M. Michaels, *The Mommy Myth: The Idealization of Motherhood and How it has Undermined All Women* (Simon and Schuster,

2005). Also see, C. Rivers, *Selling Anxiety: How the News Media Scare Women* (Upne, 2008).

11. D. Gardner, *The Science of Fear* (New York: Dutton, 2008).

12. J. Diamond, "That Daily Shower Can Be a Killer," *The New York Times*, January 28, 2013.

13. One such program is the Washington Nutrition and Physical Activity Plan, which included screen time reduction in their education outreach efforts. In a program called "Unplugged and Media Savvy," five schools in Washington, Oregon, and Idaho had their 4th and 5th grade classrooms participate in a plan that was designed to reduce children's screen time and minimize the affect of advertising. Teachers received a media education curriculum, students in each class experimented with a 30-day screen time break, and each family got informational kits about screen time throughout the year. Researchers who introduced the study are still analyzing the results to determine the impact of the intervention on screen time, food purchases of heavily advertised children's food, physical activity, and BMI. See N.A., "Unplugged and Media Savvy, A Collaborative Project of the University of Washington Center for Public Health Nutrition and The Northwest Center for Excellence in Media Literacy," http://depts.washington.edu/waaction/action/p2/c5.html.

See K. Marr, "Children Targets of 1.6 Bllion in Food Ads," *Washington Post*, July 30, 2008, http://www.washingtonpost.com/wp-dyn/content/article/2008/07/29/AR2008072902293.html.

14. J. Caifas, "Target to Remove Gender-Based Labeling," *USA Today*, August, 9, 2015, www.usatoday.com/story/news/nation-now/2015/08/09/target-remove-gender-based-labeling/31375863/.

15. K. Smith, "Summer Activities Arrive at the Doorstep for Low-Income Families," *StarTribune*, June 16, 2005, http://www.startribune.com/new-program-brings-summer-programs-to-low-income-immigrant-families-on-site-in-eden-prairie/307699091.

16. N.A., "Afterschool Programs in Minnesota" *Afterschool Alliance: Afterschool for All*, 2013, http://www.afterschoolalliance.org/policyStateFacts.cfm?state_abbr=MN.

17. Ibid.

18. D. Shernoff and D. Lowe Vandell, "Engagement in After-School Program Activities: Quality of Experience from the Perspective of Participants," *Journal of Youth and Adolescence* 36, no. 7 (2007): 891-903.

19. Minnesota Senator Amy Klobuchar remarked that "Quality afterschool programs connect children to caring adults and provide constructive activities during the peak hours of juvenile crime from 3 to 6 p.m. These

efforts are among the most powerful tools for preventing crime, and they save $3 for every $1 spent, without even counting the savings from crime reductions. See Afterschool Alliance: "Afterschool Programs in Minnesota."

## NOTES FOR APPENDIX I

1. For a detailed description of snowball sampling see Van Meter, K. M. "Methodological and design issues: techniques for assessing the representatives of snowball samples." *NIDA Research Monograph* 98, no. 51.40,1990: 31-43. Also see Vogt, W. P. *Dictionary of Statistics and Methodology: A Nontechnical Guide for the Social Sciences.* London: Sage, 1999.

2. For a detailed description of grounded theory methodology see Glaser, B., and A. Strauss. "The discovery grounded theory: strategies for qualitative inquiry." Aldin, Chicago, 1967. Corbin, J., and A. Strauss. *Basics of Qualitative Research: Techniques and Procedures for Developing Grounded Theory.* Sage publications, 2014.

3. Miles, M. B., and A. M. Huberman. *Qualitative Data Analysis: An Expanded Sourcebook.* Thousand Oaks: Sage Publications, 1994, p. 10, emphasis in the original.

# INDEX